THE UNSTOPPABLE WASP

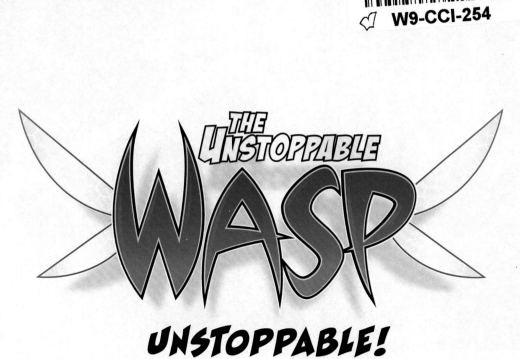

UNSTOPPABLE!

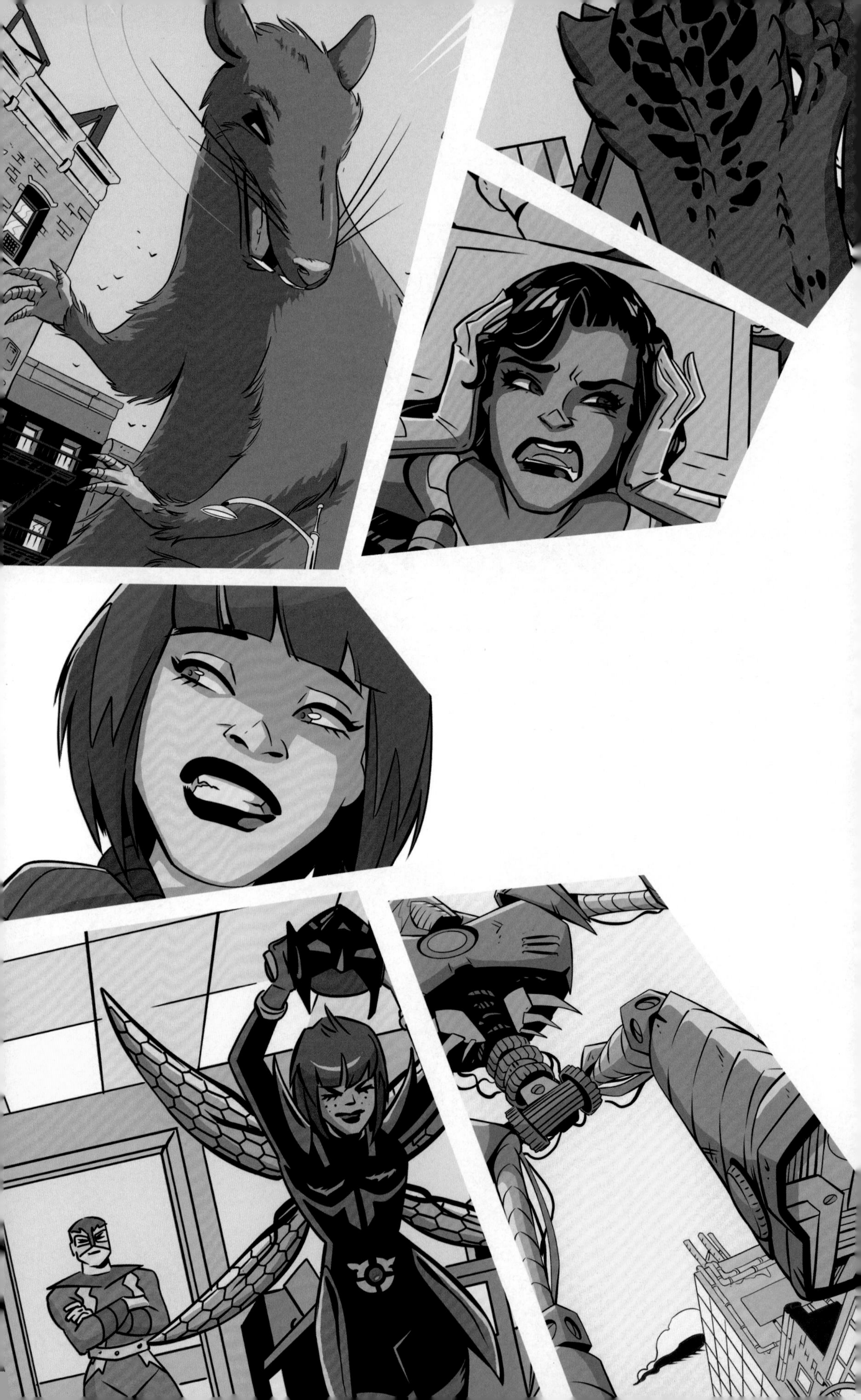

THE UNSTOPPABLE WASP

UNSTOPPABLE!

JEREMY WHITLEY
WRITER

ELSA CHARRETIER
ARTIST

MEGAN WILSON
COLOR ARTIST

VC'S JOE CARAMAGNA
LETTERER

ELSA CHARRETIER & NICOLAS BANNISTER
COVER ART

ALANNA SMITH & TOM BREVOORT
EDITORS

SPECIAL THANKS TO **PREETI CHHIBBER, MARK WAID & ALEX ROSS**

WASP CREATED BY **STAN LEE, ERNIE HART & JACK KIRBY**

COLLECTION EDITOR **JENNIFER GRÜNWALD** • ASSISTANT EDITOR **CAITLIN O'CONNELL**
ASSOCIATE MANAGING EDITOR **KATERI WOODY** • EDITOR, SPECIAL PROJECTS **MARK D. BEAZLEY**
VP PRODUCTION & SPECIAL PROJECTS **JEFF YOUNGQUIST** • SVP PRINT, SALES & MARKETING **DAVID GABRIEL**
BOOK DESIGNER **JAY BOWEN**

EDITOR IN CHIEF **AXEL ALONSO** • CHIEF CREATIVE OFFICER **JOE QUESADA**
PRESIDENT **DAN BUCKLEY** • EXECUTIVE PRODUCER **ALAN FINE**

THE UNSTOPPABLE WASP VOL. 1: UNSTOPPABLE!. Contains material originally published in magazine form as THE UNSTOPPABLE WASP #1-4 and ALL-NEW, ALL-DIFFERENT AVENGERS #14. First printing 2017. ISBN# 978-1-302-90646-7. Published by MARVEL WORLDWIDE, INC., a subsidiary of MARVEL ENTERTAINMENT, LLC. OFFICE OF PUBLICATION: 135 West 50th Street, New York, NY 10020. **Printed in Canada.** DAN BUCKLEY, President, Marvel Entertainment; JOE QUESADA, Chief Creative Officer; TOM BREVOORT, SVP of Publishing; DAVID BOGART, SVP of Business Affairs & Operations, Publishing & Partnership; C.B. CEBULSKI, VP of Brand Management & Development, Asia; DAVID GABRIEL, SVP of Sales & Marketing, Publishing; JEFF YOUNGQUIST, VP of Production & Special Projects; DAN CARR, Executive Director of Publishing Technology; ALEX MORALES, Director of Publishing Operations; SUSAN CRESPI, Production Manager; STAN LEE, Chairman Emeritus. For information regarding advertising in Marvel Comics or on Marvel.com, please contact Vit DeBellis, Integrated Sales Manager, at vdebellis@marvel.com. For Marvel subscription inquiries, please call 888-511-5480. **Manufactured between 7/7/2017 and 8/8/2017 by SOLISCO PRINTERS, SCOTT, QC, CANADA.**

10 9 8 7 6 5 4 3 2 1

1

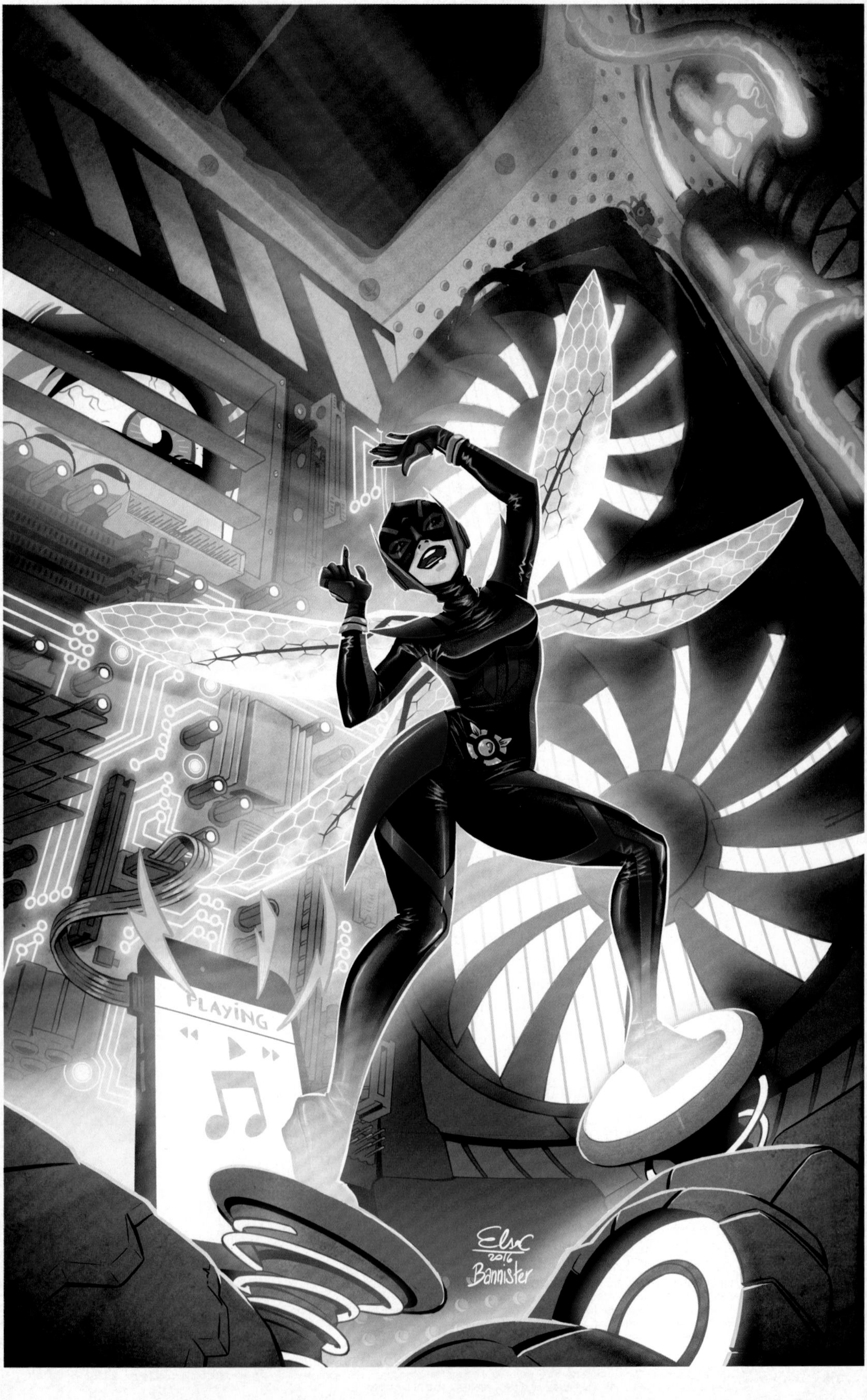
PLAYING
Bannister

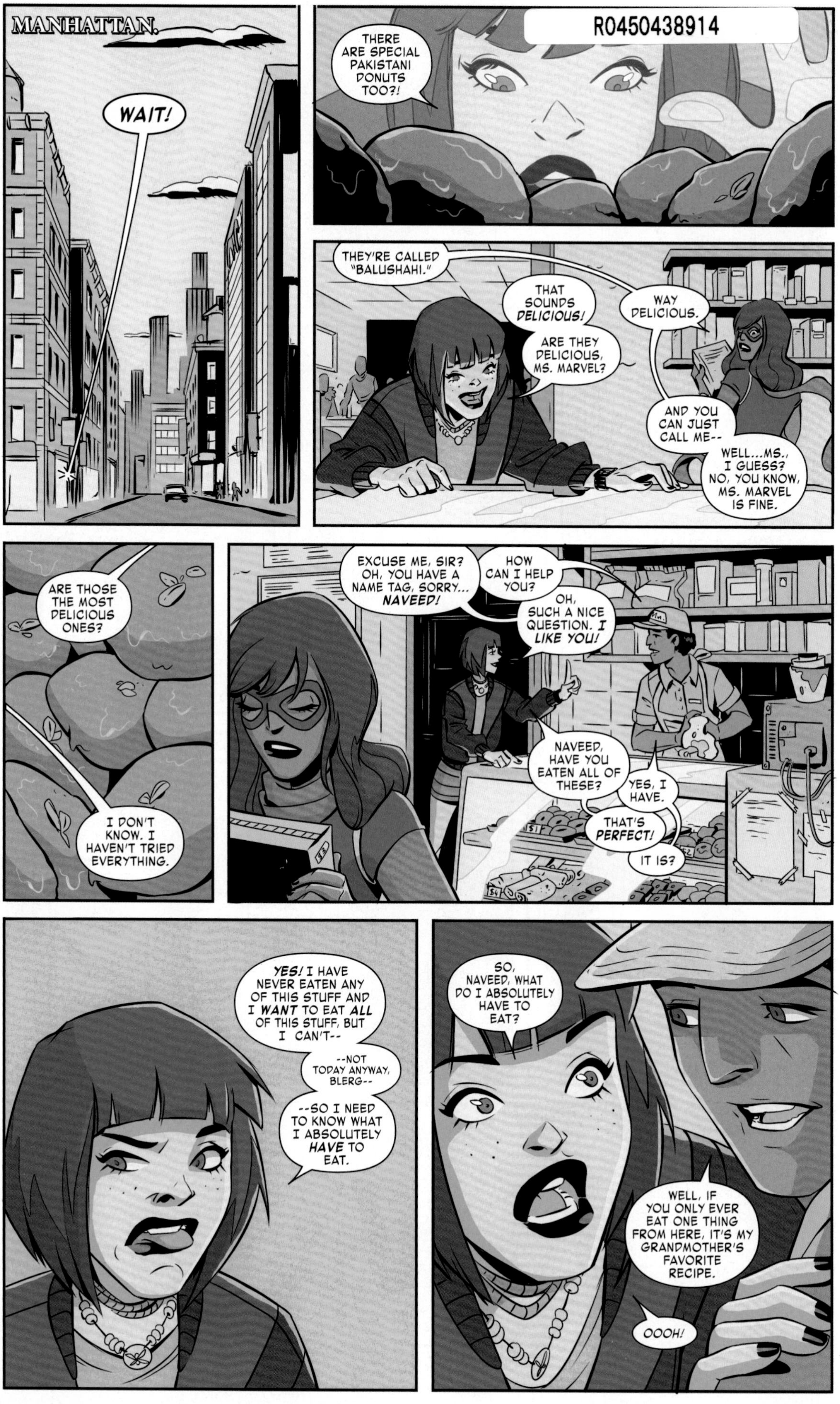
MANHATTAN.
WAIT!
THERE ARE SPECIAL PAKISTANI DONUTS TOO?!
THEY'RE CALLED "BALUSHAHI."
THAT SOUNDS DELICIOUS!
ARE THEY DELICIOUS, MS. MARVEL?
WAY DELICIOUS.
AND YOU CAN JUST CALL ME--
WELL...MS., I GUESS? NO, YOU KNOW, MS. MARVEL IS FINE.
ARE THOSE THE MOST DELICIOUS ONES?
I DON'T KNOW. I HAVEN'T TRIED EVERYTHING.
EXCUSE ME, SIR? OH, YOU HAVE A NAME TAG, SORRY... NAVEED!
HOW CAN I HELP YOU?
OH, SUCH A NICE QUESTION. I LIKE YOU!
NAVEED, HAVE YOU EATEN ALL OF THESE?
YES, I HAVE.
THAT'S PERFECT!
IT IS?
YES! I HAVE NEVER EATEN ANY OF THIS STUFF AND I WANT TO EAT ALL OF THIS STUFF, BUT I CAN'T--
--NOT TODAY ANYWAY, BLERG--
--SO I NEED TO KNOW WHAT I ABSOLUTELY HAVE TO EAT.
SO, NAVEED, WHAT DO I ABSOLUTELY HAVE TO EAT?
WELL, IF YOU ONLY EVER EAT ONE THING FROM HERE, IT'S MY GRANDMOTHER'S FAVORITE RECIPE.
OOOH!

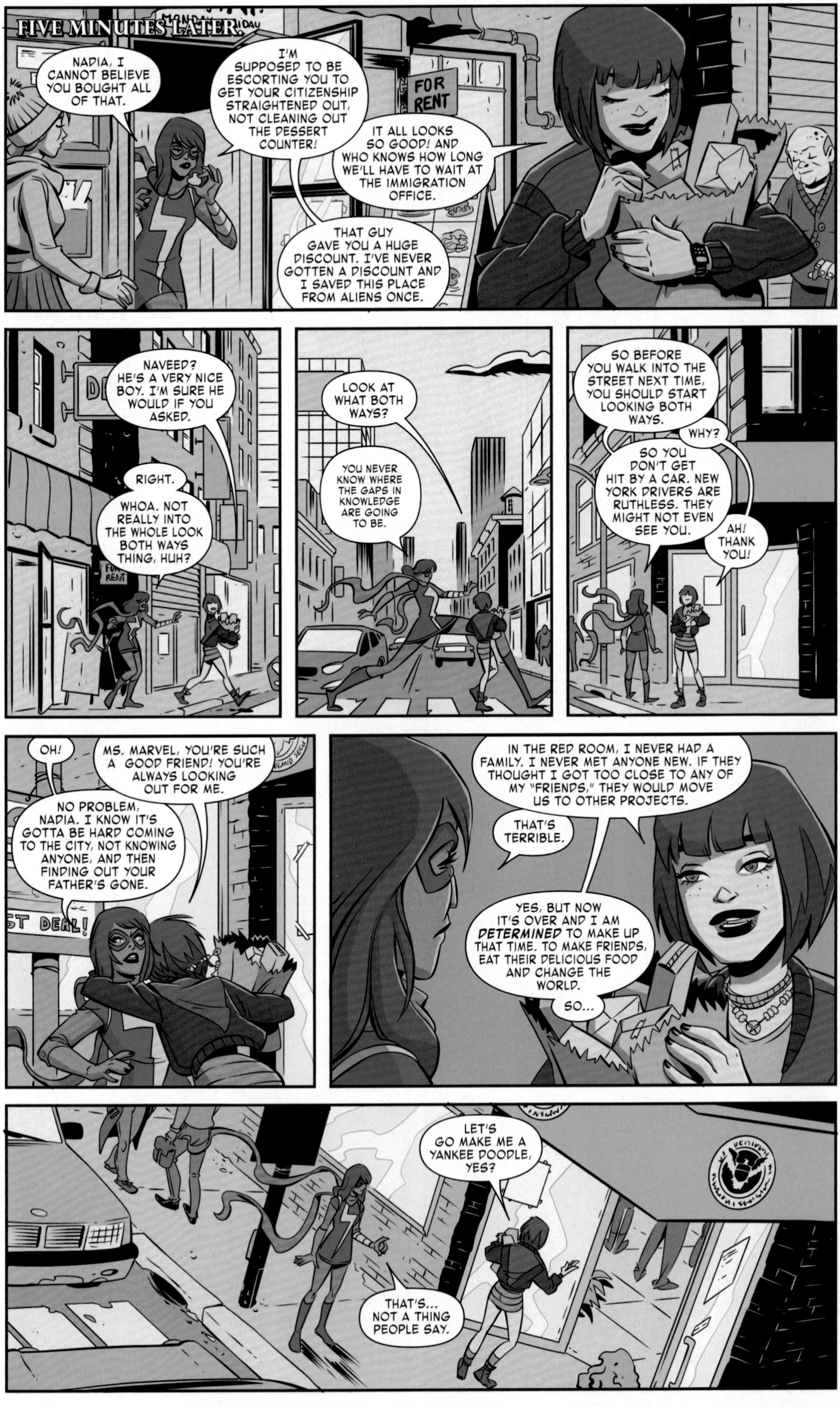

FIVE MINUTES LATER.
NADIA, I CANNOT BELIEVE YOU BOUGHT ALL OF THAT.
I'M SUPPOSED TO BE ESCORTING YOU TO GET YOUR CITIZENSHIP STRAIGHTENED OUT, NOT CLEANING OUT THE DESSERT COUNTER!
FOR RENT
IT ALL LOOKS SO GOOD! AND WHO KNOWS HOW LONG WE'LL HAVE TO WAIT AT THE IMMIGRATION OFFICE.
THAT GUY GAVE YOU A HUGE DISCOUNT. I'VE NEVER GOTTEN A DISCOUNT AND I SAVED THIS PLACE FROM ALIENS ONCE.
NAVEED? HE'S A VERY NICE BOY. I'M SURE HE WOULD IF YOU ASKED.
RIGHT.
WHOA. NOT REALLY INTO THE WHOLE LOOK BOTH WAYS THING, HUH?
FOR RENT
LOOK AT WHAT BOTH WAYS?
YOU NEVER KNOW WHERE THE GAPS IN KNOWLEDGE ARE GOING TO BE.
SO BEFORE YOU WALK INTO THE STREET NEXT TIME, YOU SHOULD START LOOKING BOTH WAYS.
WHY?
SO YOU DON'T GET HIT BY A CAR. NEW YORK DRIVERS ARE RUTHLESS. THEY MIGHT NOT EVEN SEE YOU.
AH! THANK YOU!
OH!
MS. MARVEL, YOU'RE SUCH A GOOD FRIEND! YOU'RE ALWAYS LOOKING OUT FOR ME.
NO PROBLEM, NADIA. I KNOW IT'S GOTTA BE HARD COMING TO THE CITY, NOT KNOWING ANYONE, AND THEN FINDING OUT YOUR FATHER'S GONE.
IN THE RED ROOM, I NEVER HAD A FAMILY. I NEVER MET ANYONE NEW. IF THEY THOUGHT I GOT TOO CLOSE TO ANY OF MY "FRIENDS," THEY WOULD MOVE US TO OTHER PROJECTS.
THAT'S TERRIBLE.
YES, BUT NOW IT'S OVER AND I AM *DETERMINED* TO MAKE UP THAT TIME. TO MAKE FRIENDS, EAT THEIR DELICIOUS FOOD AND CHANGE THE WORLD.
SO...
LET'S GO MAKE ME A YANKEE DOODLE, YES?
THAT'S... NOT A THING PEOPLE SAY.

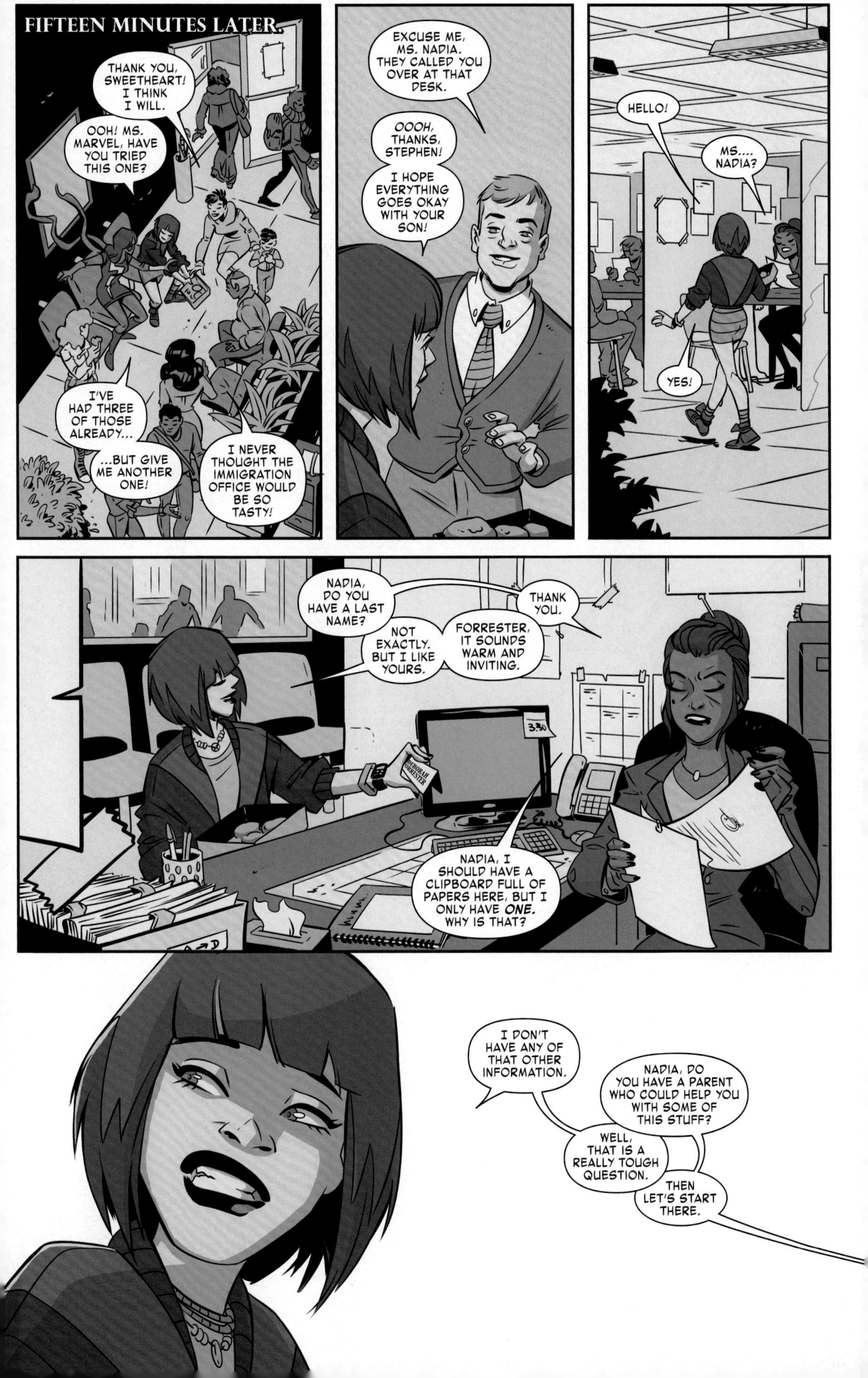
FIFTEEN MINUTES LATER.
THANK YOU, SWEETHEART! I THINK I WILL.
OOH! MS. MARVEL, HAVE YOU TRIED THIS ONE?
I'VE HAD THREE OF THOSE ALREADY...
...BUT GIVE ME ANOTHER ONE!
I NEVER THOUGHT THE IMMIGRATION OFFICE WOULD BE SO TASTY!
EXCUSE ME, MS. NADIA. THEY CALLED YOU OVER AT THAT DESK.
OOOH, THANKS, STEPHEN!
I HOPE EVERYTHING GOES OKAY WITH YOUR SON!
HELLO!
MS.... NADIA?
YES!
NADIA, DO YOU HAVE A LAST NAME?
NOT EXACTLY. BUT I LIKE YOURS.
FORRESTER. IT SOUNDS WARM AND INVITING.
THANK YOU.
DEBORAH FORRESTER
3:30
NADIA, I SHOULD HAVE A CLIPBOARD FULL OF PAPERS HERE, BUT I ONLY HAVE ONE. WHY IS THAT?
I DON'T HAVE ANY OF THAT OTHER INFORMATION.
NADIA, DO YOU HAVE A PARENT WHO COULD HELP YOU WITH SOME OF THIS STUFF?
WELL, THAT IS A REALLY TOUGH QUESTION.
THEN LET'S START THERE.

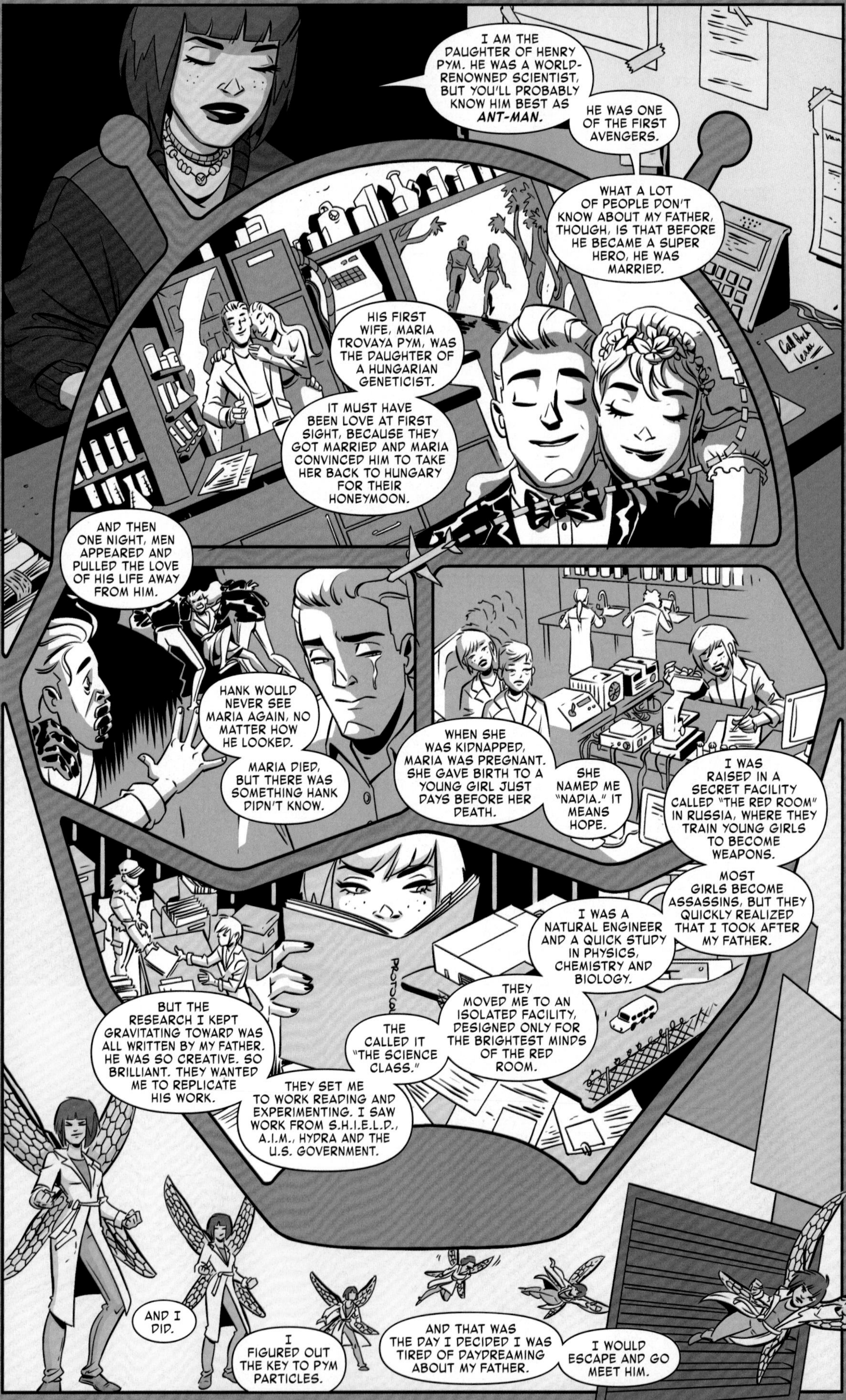
I AM THE DAUGHTER OF HENRY PYM. HE WAS A WORLD-RENOWNED SCIENTIST, BUT YOU'LL PROBABLY KNOW HIM BEST AS *ANT-MAN.*
HE WAS ONE OF THE FIRST AVENGERS.
WHAT A LOT OF PEOPLE DON'T KNOW ABOUT MY FATHER, THOUGH, IS THAT BEFORE HE BECAME A SUPER HERO, HE WAS MARRIED.
HIS FIRST WIFE, MARIA TROVAYA PYM, WAS THE DAUGHTER OF A HUNGARIAN GENETICIST.
IT MUST HAVE BEEN LOVE AT FIRST SIGHT, BECAUSE THEY GOT MARRIED AND MARIA CONVINCED HIM TO TAKE HER BACK TO HUNGARY FOR THEIR HONEYMOON.
AND THEN ONE NIGHT, MEN APPEARED AND PULLED THE LOVE OF HIS LIFE AWAY FROM HIM.
HANK WOULD NEVER SEE MARIA AGAIN, NO MATTER HOW HE LOOKED.
MARIA DIED, BUT THERE WAS SOMETHING HANK DIDN'T KNOW.
WHEN SHE WAS KIDNAPPED, MARIA WAS PREGNANT. SHE GAVE BIRTH TO A YOUNG GIRL JUST DAYS BEFORE HER DEATH.
SHE NAMED ME "NADIA." IT MEANS HOPE.
I WAS RAISED IN A SECRET FACILITY CALLED "THE RED ROOM" IN RUSSIA, WHERE THEY TRAIN YOUNG GIRLS TO BECOME WEAPONS.
MOST GIRLS BECOME ASSASSINS, BUT THEY QUICKLY REALIZED THAT I TOOK AFTER MY FATHER.
I WAS A NATURAL ENGINEER AND A QUICK STUDY IN PHYSICS, CHEMISTRY AND BIOLOGY.
THEY MOVED ME TO AN ISOLATED FACILITY, DESIGNED ONLY FOR THE BRIGHTEST MINDS OF THE RED ROOM.
THE CALLED IT "THE SCIENCE CLASS."
BUT THE RESEARCH I KEPT GRAVITATING TOWARD WAS ALL WRITTEN BY MY FATHER. HE WAS SO CREATIVE. SO BRILLIANT. THEY WANTED ME TO REPLICATE HIS WORK.
THEY SET ME TO WORK READING AND EXPERIMENTING. I SAW WORK FROM S.H.I.E.L.D., A.I.M., HYDRA AND THE U.S. GOVERNMENT.
AND I DID.
I FIGURED OUT THE KEY TO PYM PARTICLES.
AND THAT WAS THE DAY I DECIDED I WAS TIRED OF DAYDREAMING ABOUT MY FATHER.
I WOULD ESCAPE AND GO MEET HIM.

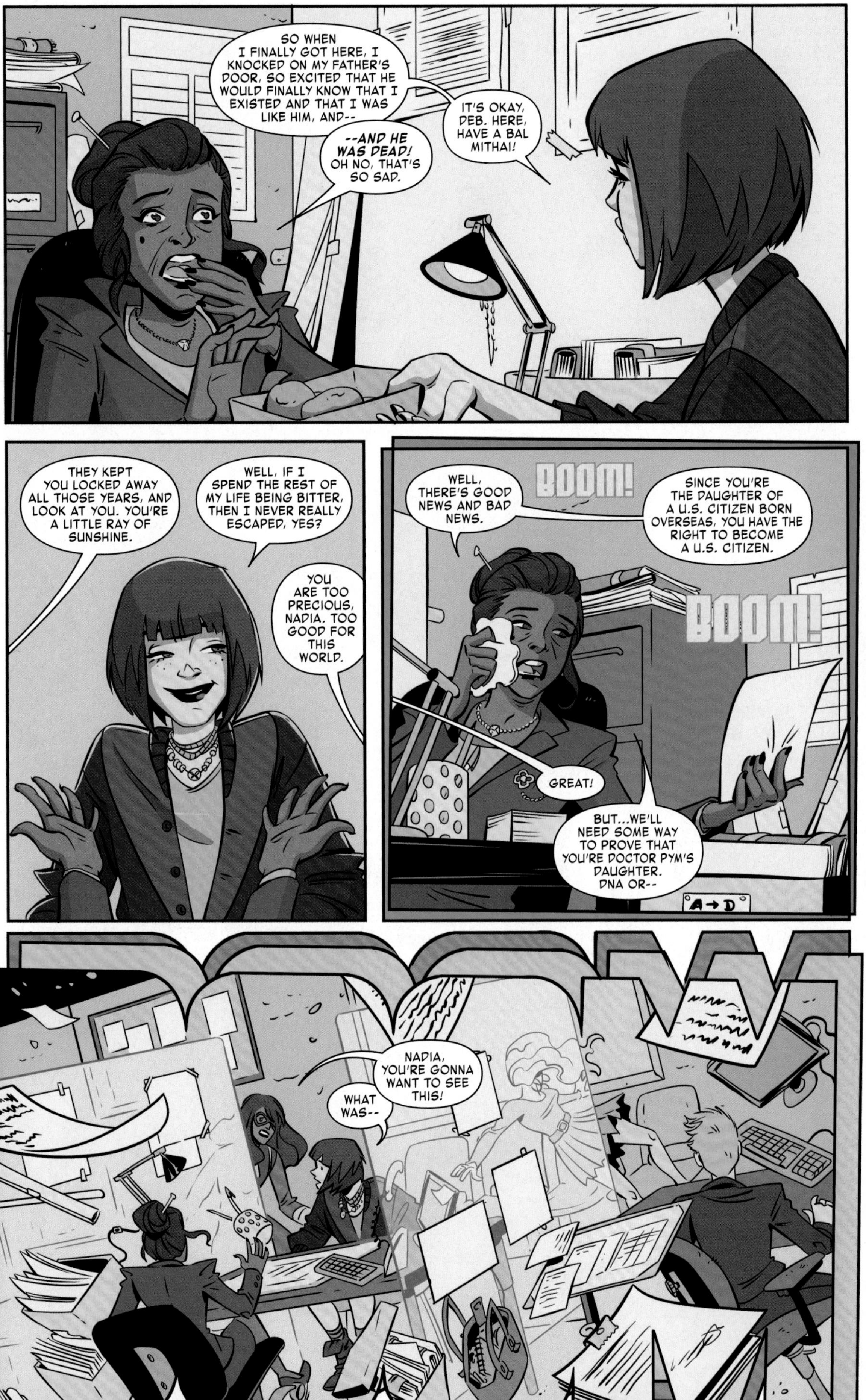
SO WHEN I FINALLY GOT HERE, I KNOCKED ON MY FATHER'S DOOR, SO EXCITED THAT HE WOULD FINALLY KNOW THAT I EXISTED AND THAT I WAS LIKE HIM, AND--
--AND HE WAS DEAD! OH NO, THAT'S SO SAD.
IT'S OKAY, DEB. HERE, HAVE A BAL MITHAI!
THEY KEPT YOU LOCKED AWAY ALL THOSE YEARS, AND LOOK AT YOU. YOU'RE A LITTLE RAY OF SUNSHINE.
WELL, IF I SPEND THE REST OF MY LIFE BEING BITTER, THEN I NEVER REALLY ESCAPED, YES?
YOU ARE TOO PRECIOUS, NADIA. TOO GOOD FOR THIS WORLD.
BOOM!
WELL, THERE'S GOOD NEWS AND BAD NEWS.
SINCE YOU'RE THE DAUGHTER OF A U.S. CITIZEN BORN OVERSEAS, YOU HAVE THE RIGHT TO BECOME A U.S. CITIZEN.
BOOM!
GREAT!
BUT...WE'LL NEED SOME WAY TO PROVE THAT YOU'RE DOCTOR PYM'S DAUGHTER. DNA OR--
A → D
NADIA, YOU'RE GONNA WANT TO SEE THIS!
WHAT WAS--

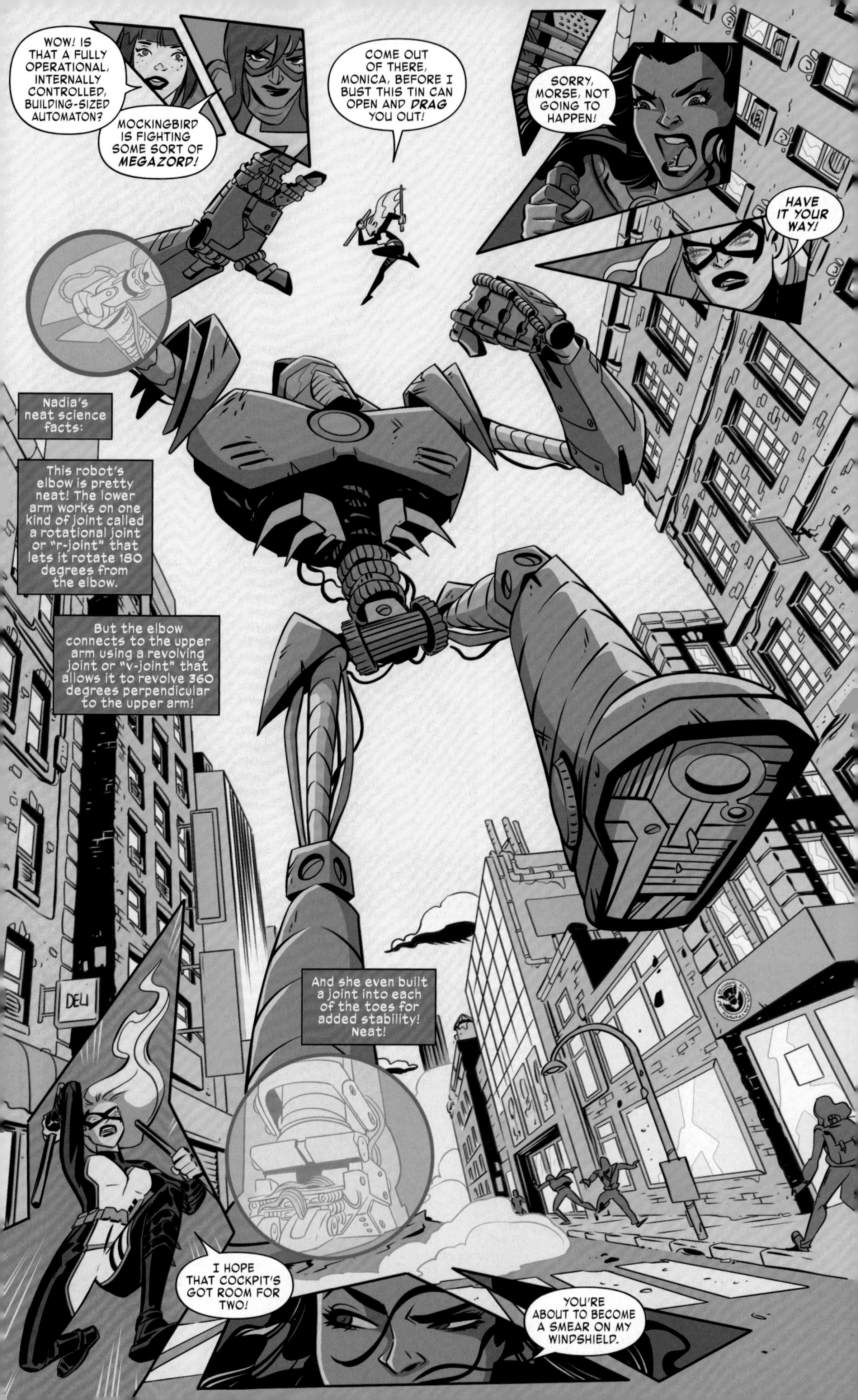
WOW! IS THAT A FULLY OPERATIONAL, INTERNALLY CONTROLLED, BUILDING-SIZED AUTOMATON?
MOCKINGBIRD IS FIGHTING SOME SORT OF MEGAZORD!
COME OUT OF THERE, MONICA, BEFORE I BUST THIS TIN CAN OPEN AND DRAG YOU OUT!
SORRY, MORSE, NOT GOING TO HAPPEN!
HAVE IT YOUR WAY!
Nadia's neat science facts:
This robot's elbow is pretty neat! The lower arm works on one kind of joint called a rotational joint or "r-joint" that lets it rotate 180 degrees from the elbow.
But the elbow connects to the upper arm using a revolving joint or "v-joint" that allows it to revolve 360 degrees perpendicular to the upper arm!
And she even built a joint into each of the toes for added stability! Neat!
DELI
I HOPE THAT COCKPIT'S GOT ROOM FOR TWO!
YOU'RE ABOUT TO BECOME A SMEAR ON MY WINDSHIELD.

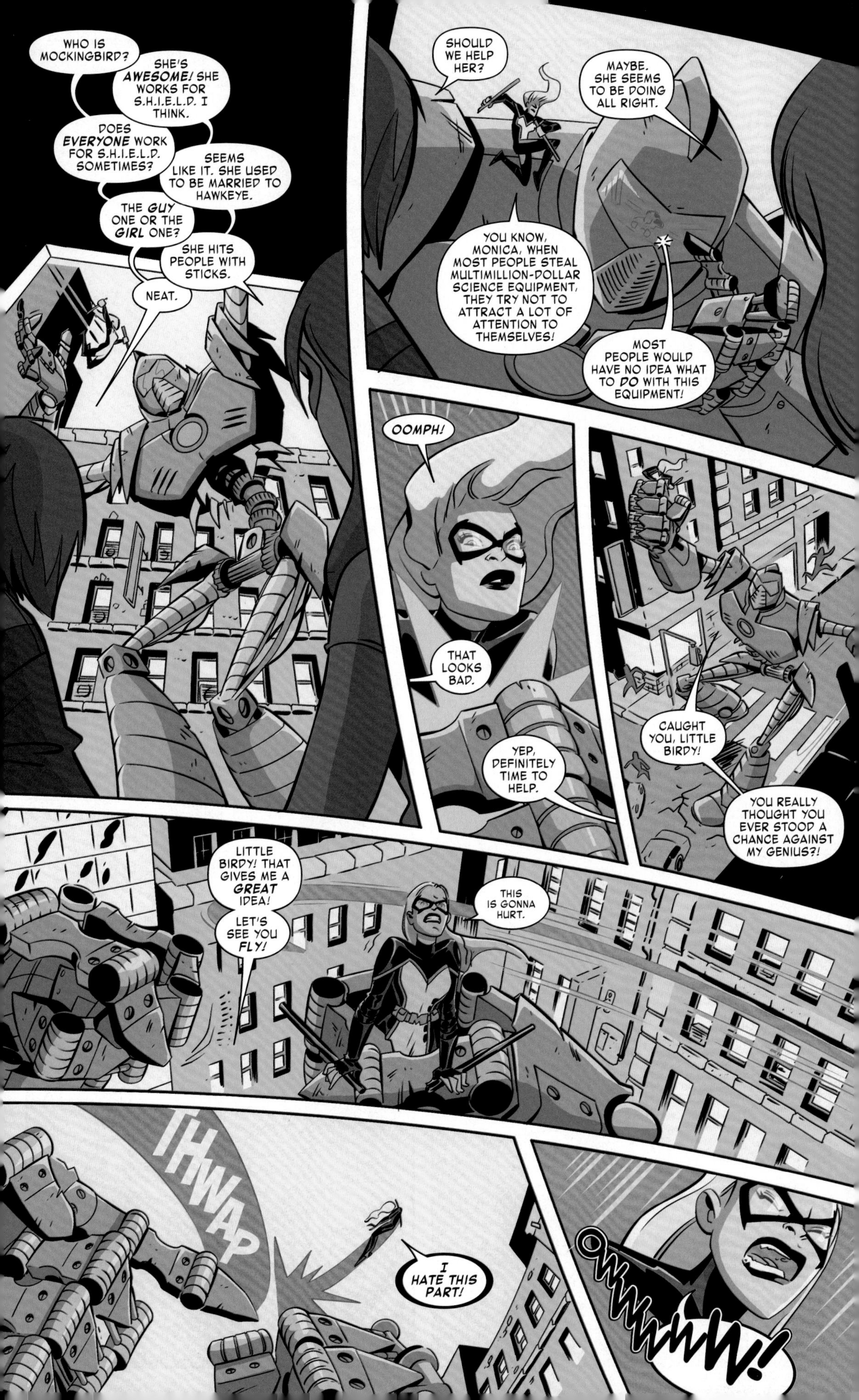
WHO IS MOCKINGBIRD?
SHE'S AWESOME! SHE WORKS FOR S.H.I.E.L.D. I THINK.
DOES EVERYONE WORK FOR S.H.I.E.L.D. SOMETIMES?
SEEMS LIKE IT. SHE USED TO BE MARRIED TO HAWKEYE.
THE GUY ONE OR THE GIRL ONE?
SHE HITS PEOPLE WITH STICKS.
NEAT.
SHOULD WE HELP HER?
MAYBE. SHE SEEMS TO BE DOING ALL RIGHT.
YOU KNOW, MONICA, WHEN MOST PEOPLE STEAL MULTIMILLION-DOLLAR SCIENCE EQUIPMENT, THEY TRY NOT TO ATTRACT A LOT OF ATTENTION TO THEMSELVES!
MOST PEOPLE WOULD HAVE NO IDEA WHAT TO DO WITH THIS EQUIPMENT!
OOMPH!
THAT LOOKS BAD.
YEP, DEFINITELY TIME TO HELP.
CAUGHT YOU, LITTLE BIRDY!
YOU REALLY THOUGHT YOU EVER STOOD A CHANCE AGAINST MY GENIUS?!
LITTLE BIRDY! THAT GIVES ME A GREAT IDEA!
LET'S SEE YOU FLY!
THIS IS GONNA HURT.
THWAP
I HATE THIS PART!
OWWWWW!

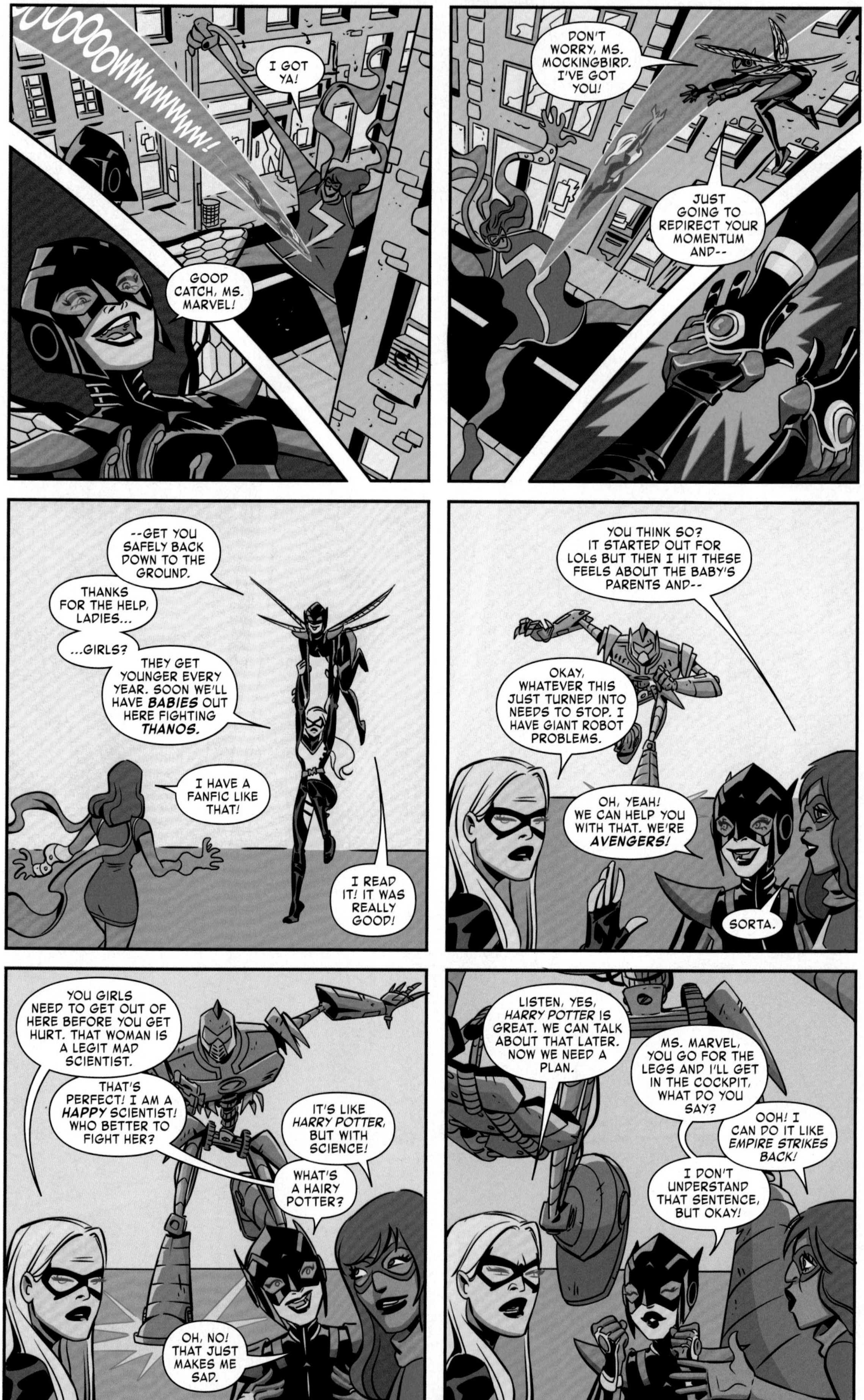
OOOOOOWWWWWWWW!
I GOT YA!
GOOD CATCH, MS. MARVEL!
DON'T WORRY, MS. MOCKINGBIRD. I'VE GOT YOU!
JUST GOING TO REDIRECT YOUR MOMENTUM AND--
--GET YOU SAFELY BACK DOWN TO THE GROUND.
THANKS FOR THE HELP, LADIES...
...GIRLS?
THEY GET YOUNGER EVERY YEAR. SOON WE'LL HAVE BABIES OUT HERE FIGHTING THANOS.
I HAVE A FANFIC LIKE THAT!
I READ IT! IT WAS REALLY GOOD!
YOU THINK SO? IT STARTED OUT FOR LOLs BUT THEN I HIT THESE FEELS ABOUT THE BABY'S PARENTS AND--
OKAY, WHATEVER THIS JUST TURNED INTO NEEDS TO STOP. I HAVE GIANT ROBOT PROBLEMS.
OH, YEAH! WE CAN HELP YOU WITH THAT. WE'RE AVENGERS!
SORTA.
YOU GIRLS NEED TO GET OUT OF HERE BEFORE YOU GET HURT. THAT WOMAN IS A LEGIT MAD SCIENTIST.
THAT'S PERFECT! I AM A HAPPY SCIENTIST! WHO BETTER TO FIGHT HER?
IT'S LIKE HARRY POTTER, BUT WITH SCIENCE!
WHAT'S A HAIRY POTTER?
OH, NO! THAT JUST MAKES ME SAD.
LISTEN, YES, HARRY POTTER IS GREAT. WE CAN TALK ABOUT THAT LATER. NOW WE NEED A PLAN.
MS. MARVEL, YOU GO FOR THE LEGS AND I'LL GET IN THE COCKPIT, WHAT DO YOU SAY?
OOH! I CAN DO IT LIKE EMPIRE STRIKES BACK!
I DON'T UNDERSTAND THAT SENTENCE, BUT OKAY!

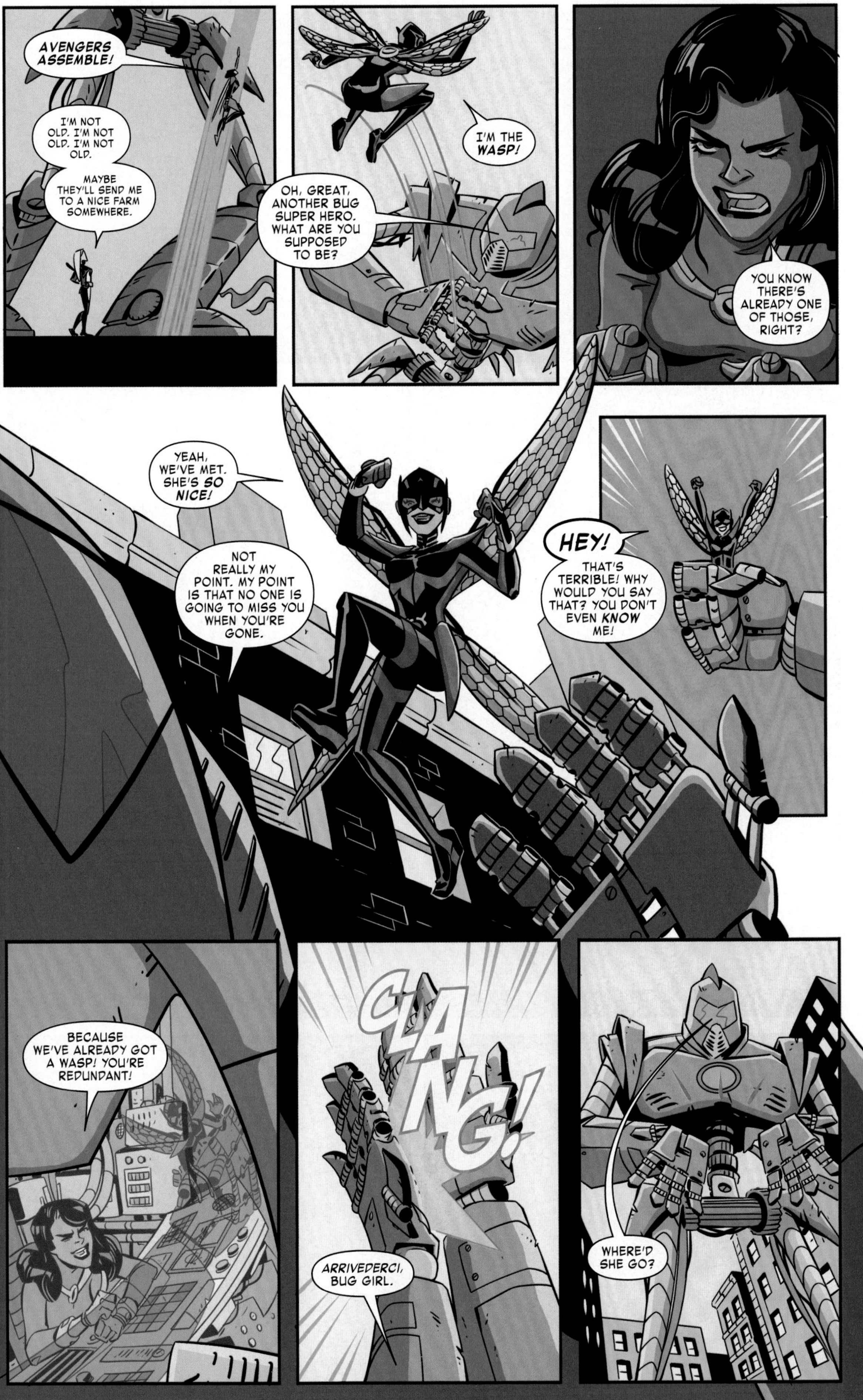
AVENGERS ASSEMBLE!
I'M NOT OLD. I'M NOT OLD. I'M NOT OLD.
MAYBE THEY'LL SEND ME TO A NICE FARM SOMEWHERE.
I'M THE WASP!
OH, GREAT, ANOTHER BUG SUPER HERO. WHAT ARE YOU SUPPOSED TO BE?
YOU KNOW THERE'S ALREADY ONE OF THOSE, RIGHT?
YEAH, WE'VE MET. SHE'S SO NICE!
NOT REALLY MY POINT. MY POINT IS THAT NO ONE IS GOING TO MISS YOU WHEN YOU'RE GONE.
HEY!
THAT'S TERRIBLE! WHY WOULD YOU SAY THAT? YOU DON'T EVEN KNOW ME!
BECAUSE WE'VE ALREADY GOT A WASP! YOU'RE REDUNDANT!
CLANG!
ARRIVEDERCI, BUG GIRL.
WHERE'D SHE GO?

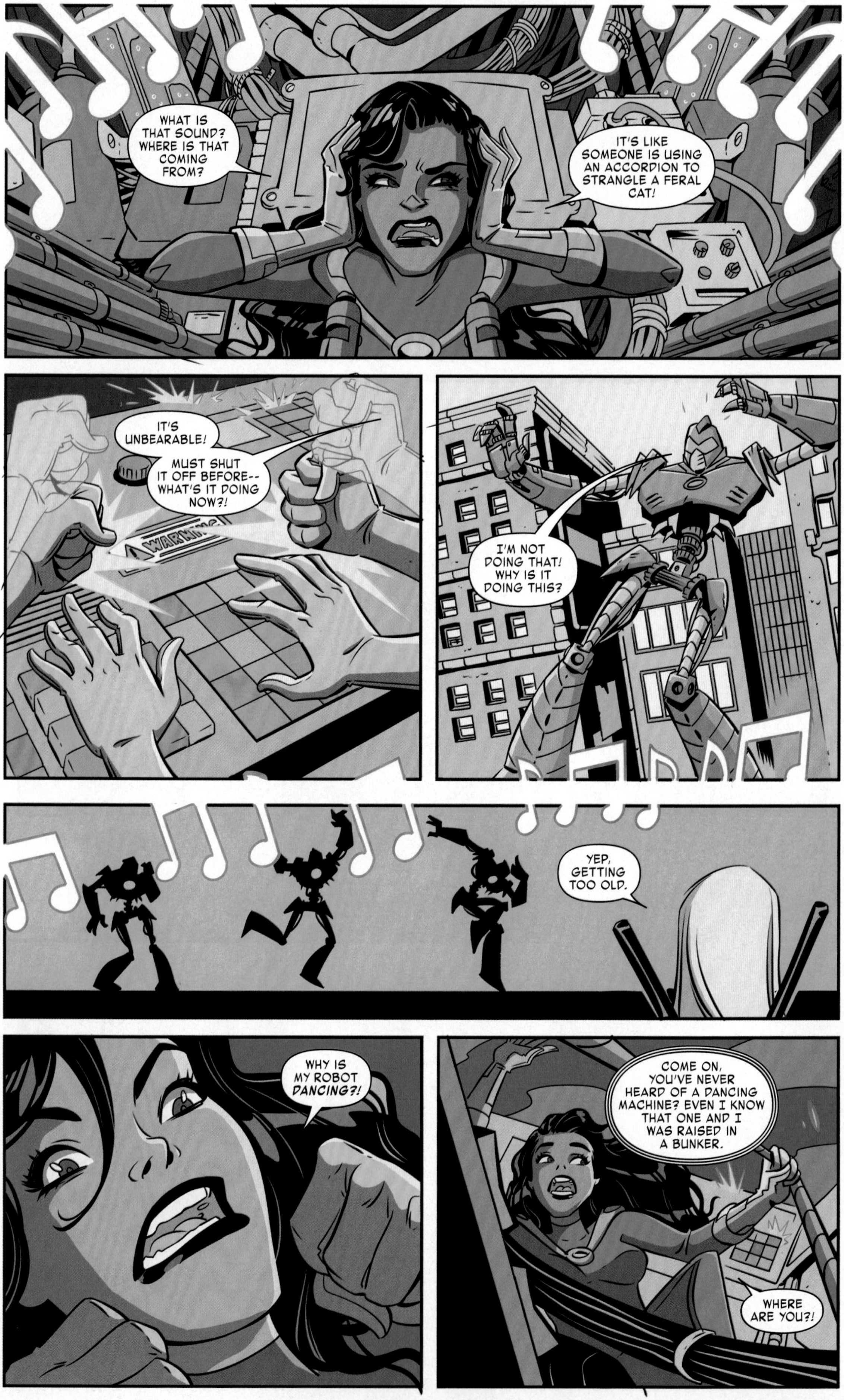
WHAT IS THAT SOUND? WHERE IS THAT COMING FROM?
IT'S LIKE SOMEONE IS USING AN ACCORDION TO STRANGLE A FERAL CAT!
IT'S UNBEARABLE!
MUST SHUT IT OFF BEFORE-- WHAT'S IT DOING NOW?!
WARNING
I'M NOT DOING THAT! WHY IS IT DOING THIS?
YEP, GETTING TOO OLD.
WHY IS MY ROBOT *DANCING?!*
COME ON, YOU'VE NEVER HEARD OF A DANCING MACHINE? EVEN I KNOW THAT ONE AND I WAS RAISED IN A BUNKER.
WHERE ARE YOU?!

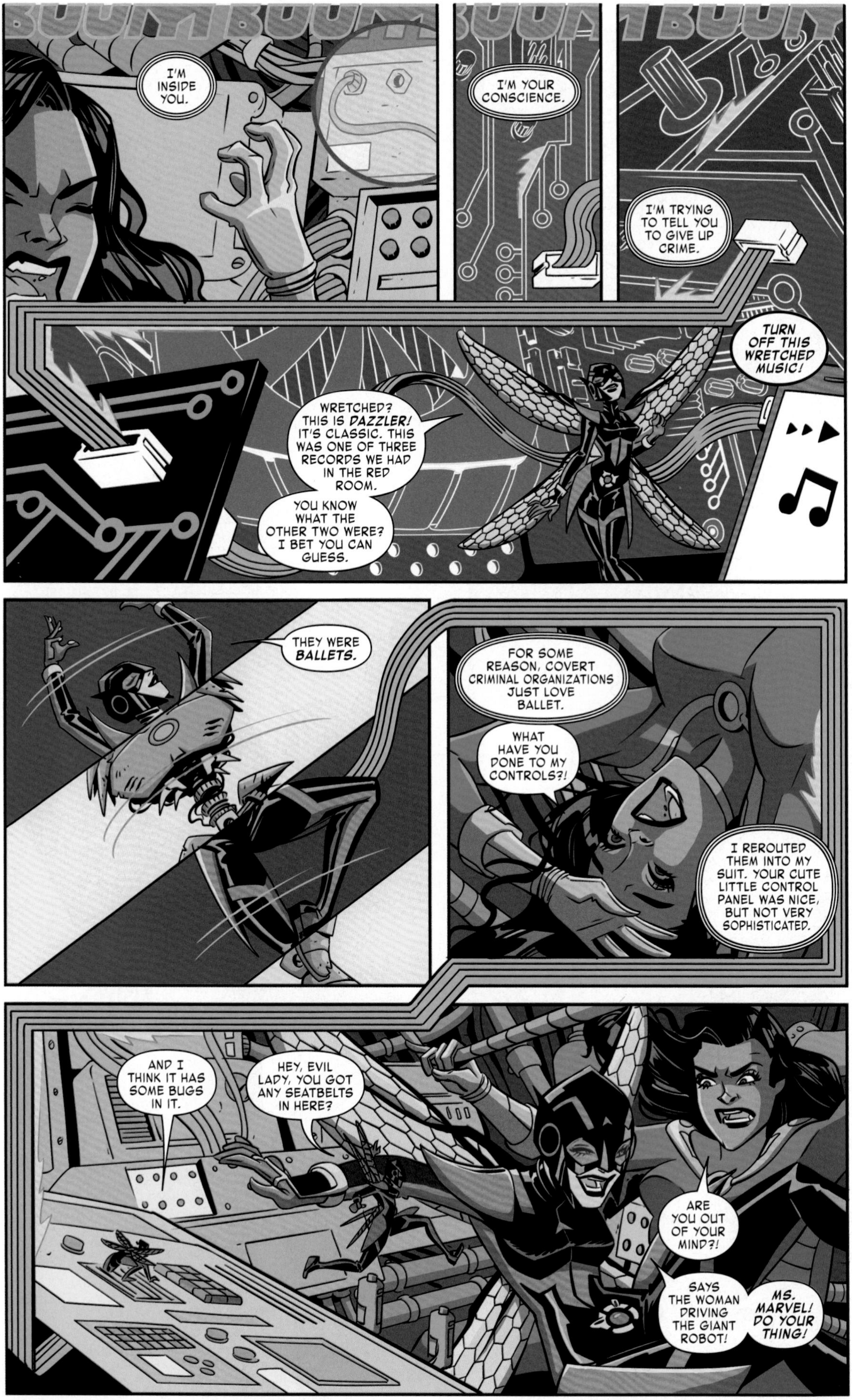
BOOM BOOM BOOM BOOM
I'M INSIDE YOU.
I'M YOUR CONSCIENCE.
I'M TRYING TO TELL YOU TO GIVE UP CRIME.
TURN OFF THIS WRETCHED MUSIC!
WRETCHED? THIS IS DAZZLER! IT'S CLASSIC. THIS WAS ONE OF THREE RECORDS WE HAD IN THE RED ROOM.
YOU KNOW WHAT THE OTHER TWO WERE? I BET YOU CAN GUESS.
THEY WERE BALLETS.
FOR SOME REASON, COVERT CRIMINAL ORGANIZATIONS JUST LOVE BALLET.
WHAT HAVE YOU DONE TO MY CONTROLS?!
I REROUTED THEM INTO MY SUIT. YOUR CUTE LITTLE CONTROL PANEL WAS NICE, BUT NOT VERY SOPHISTICATED.
AND I THINK IT HAS SOME BUGS IN IT.
HEY, EVIL LADY, YOU GOT ANY SEATBELTS IN HERE?
ARE YOU OUT OF YOUR MIND?!
SAYS THE WOMAN DRIVING THE GIANT ROBOT!
MS. MARVEL! DO YOUR THING!

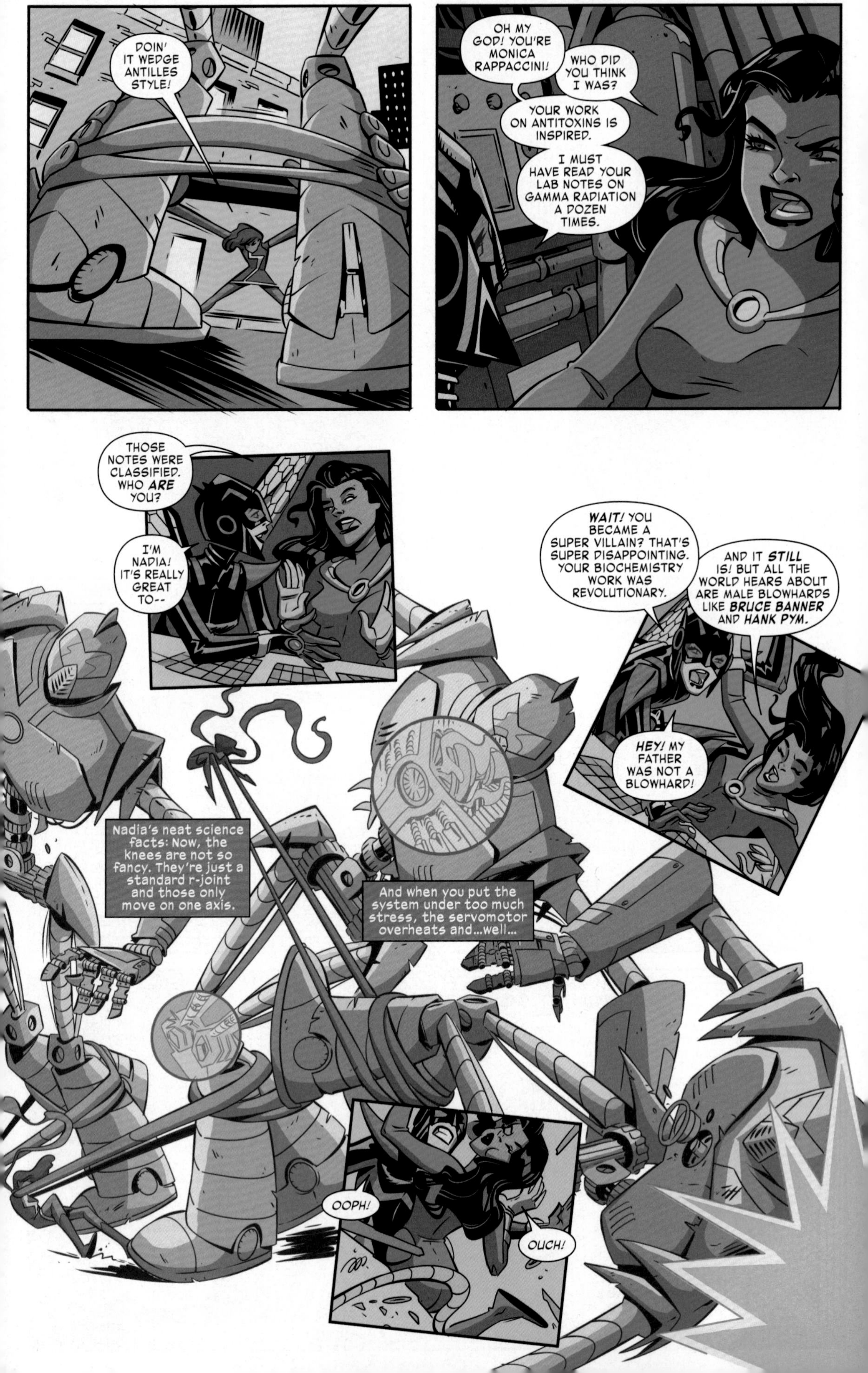
DOIN' IT WEDGE ANTILLES STYLE!
OH MY GOD! YOU'RE MONICA RAPPACCINI!
WHO DID YOU THINK I WAS?
YOUR WORK ON ANTITOXINS IS INSPIRED.
I MUST HAVE READ YOUR LAB NOTES ON GAMMA RADIATION A DOZEN TIMES.
THOSE NOTES WERE CLASSIFIED. WHO ARE YOU?
I'M NADIA! IT'S REALLY GREAT TO--
WAIT! YOU BECAME A SUPER VILLAIN? THAT'S SUPER DISAPPOINTING. YOUR BIOCHEMISTRY WORK WAS REVOLUTIONARY.
AND IT STILL IS! BUT ALL THE WORLD HEARS ABOUT ARE MALE BLOWHARDS LIKE BRUCE BANNER AND HANK PYM.
HEY! MY FATHER WAS NOT A BLOWHARD!
Nadia's neat science facts: Now, the knees are not so fancy. They're just a standard r-joint and those only move on one axis.
And when you put the system under too much stress, the servomotor overheats and...well...
OOPH!
OUCH!

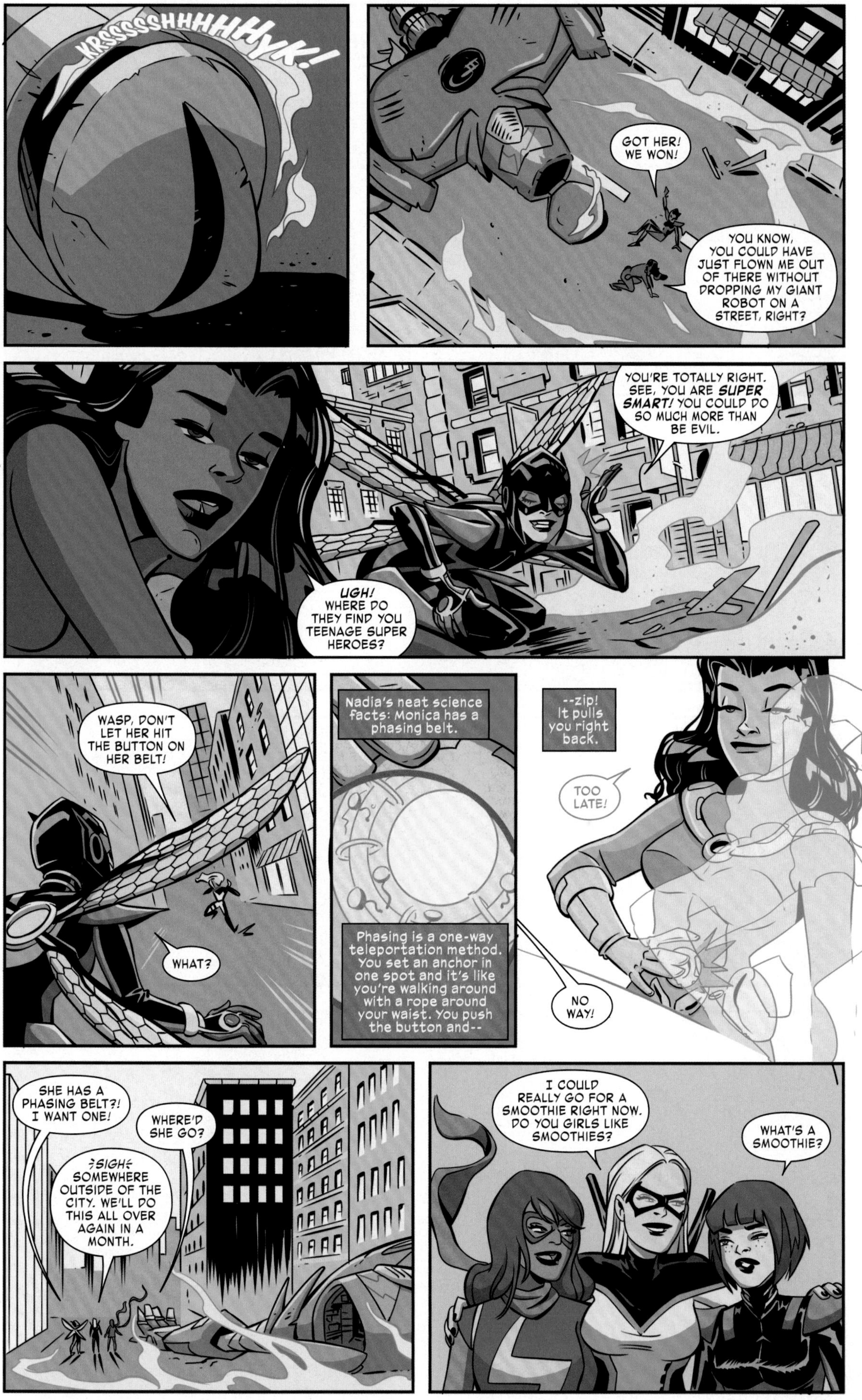
KRSSSSSHHHHHYK!
GOT HER! WE WON!
YOU KNOW, YOU COULD HAVE JUST FLOWN ME OUT OF THERE WITHOUT DROPPING MY GIANT ROBOT ON A STREET, RIGHT?
YOU'RE TOTALLY RIGHT. SEE, YOU ARE SUPER SMART! YOU COULD DO SO MUCH MORE THAN BE EVIL.
UGH! WHERE DO THEY FIND YOU TEENAGE SUPER HEROES?
WASP, DON'T LET HER HIT THE BUTTON ON HER BELT!
WHAT?
Nadia's neat science facts: Monica has a phasing belt.
Phasing is a one-way teleportation method. You set an anchor in one spot and it's like you're walking around with a rope around your waist. You push the button and--
--zip! It pulls you right back.
TOO LATE!
NO WAY!
SHE HAS A PHASING BELT?! I WANT ONE!
WHERE'D SHE GO?
SIGH SOMEWHERE OUTSIDE OF THE CITY. WE'LL DO THIS ALL OVER AGAIN IN A MONTH.
I COULD REALLY GO FOR A SMOOTHIE RIGHT NOW. DO YOU GIRLS LIKE SMOOTHIES?
WHAT'S A SMOOTHIE?

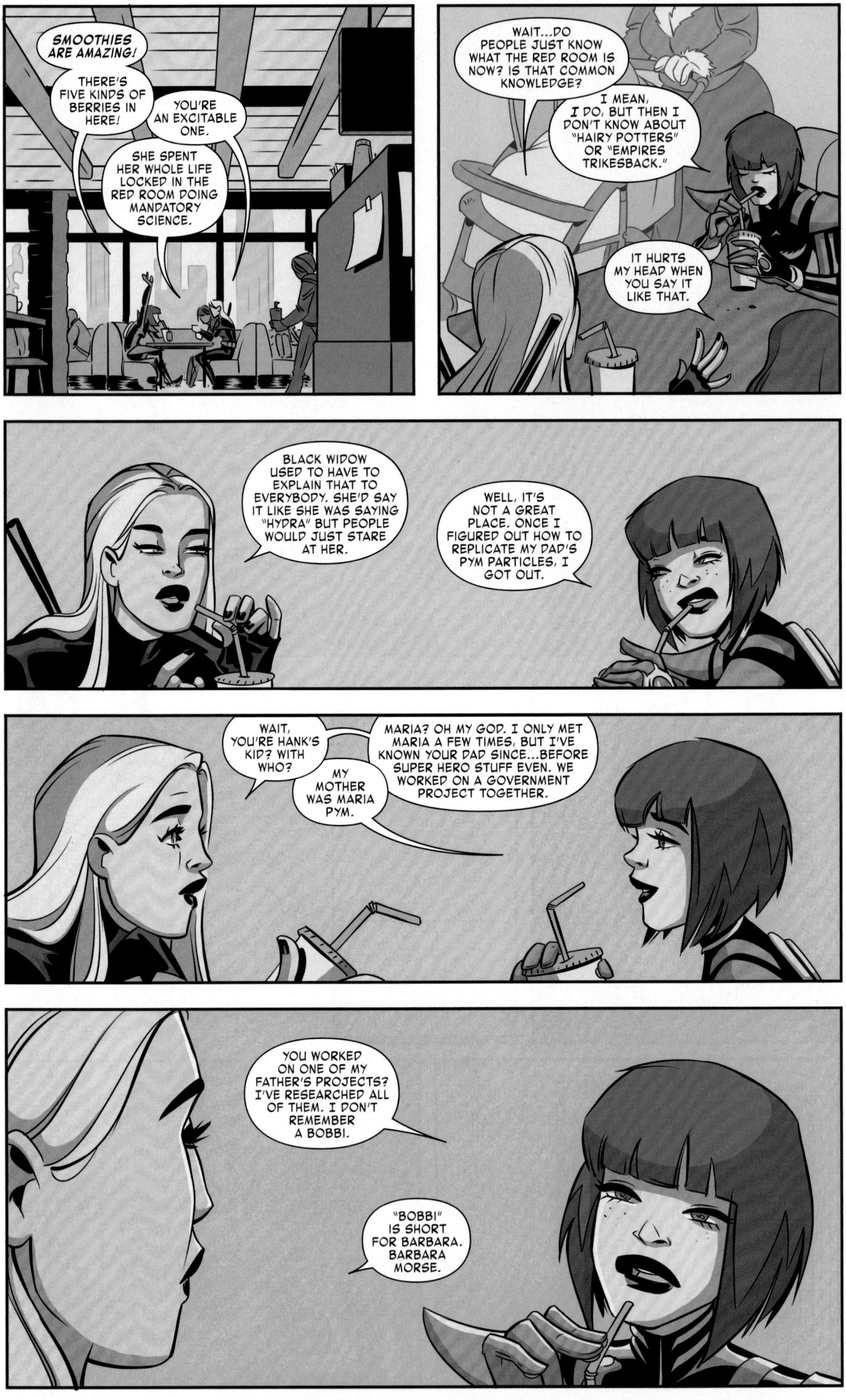
SMOOTHIES ARE AMAZING!
THERE'S FIVE KINDS OF BERRIES IN HERE!
YOU'RE AN EXCITABLE ONE.
SHE SPENT HER WHOLE LIFE LOCKED IN THE RED ROOM DOING MANDATORY SCIENCE.
WAIT...DO PEOPLE JUST KNOW WHAT THE RED ROOM IS NOW? IS THAT COMMON KNOWLEDGE?
I MEAN, I DO, BUT THEN I DON'T KNOW ABOUT "HAIRY POTTERS" OR "EMPIRES TRIKESBACK."
IT HURTS MY HEAD WHEN YOU SAY IT LIKE THAT.
BLACK WIDOW USED TO HAVE TO EXPLAIN THAT TO EVERYBODY. SHE'D SAY IT LIKE SHE WAS SAYING "HYDRA" BUT PEOPLE WOULD JUST STARE AT HER.
WELL, IT'S NOT A GREAT PLACE. ONCE I FIGURED OUT HOW TO REPLICATE MY DAD'S PYM PARTICLES, I GOT OUT.
WAIT, YOU'RE HANK'S KID? WITH WHO?
MY MOTHER WAS MARIA PYM.
MARIA? OH MY GOD. I ONLY MET MARIA A FEW TIMES, BUT I'VE KNOWN YOUR DAD SINCE...BEFORE SUPER HERO STUFF EVEN. WE WORKED ON A GOVERNMENT PROJECT TOGETHER.
YOU WORKED ON ONE OF MY FATHER'S PROJECTS? I'VE RESEARCHED ALL OF THEM. I DON'T REMEMBER A BOBBI.
"BOBBI" IS SHORT FOR BARBARA. BARBARA MORSE.

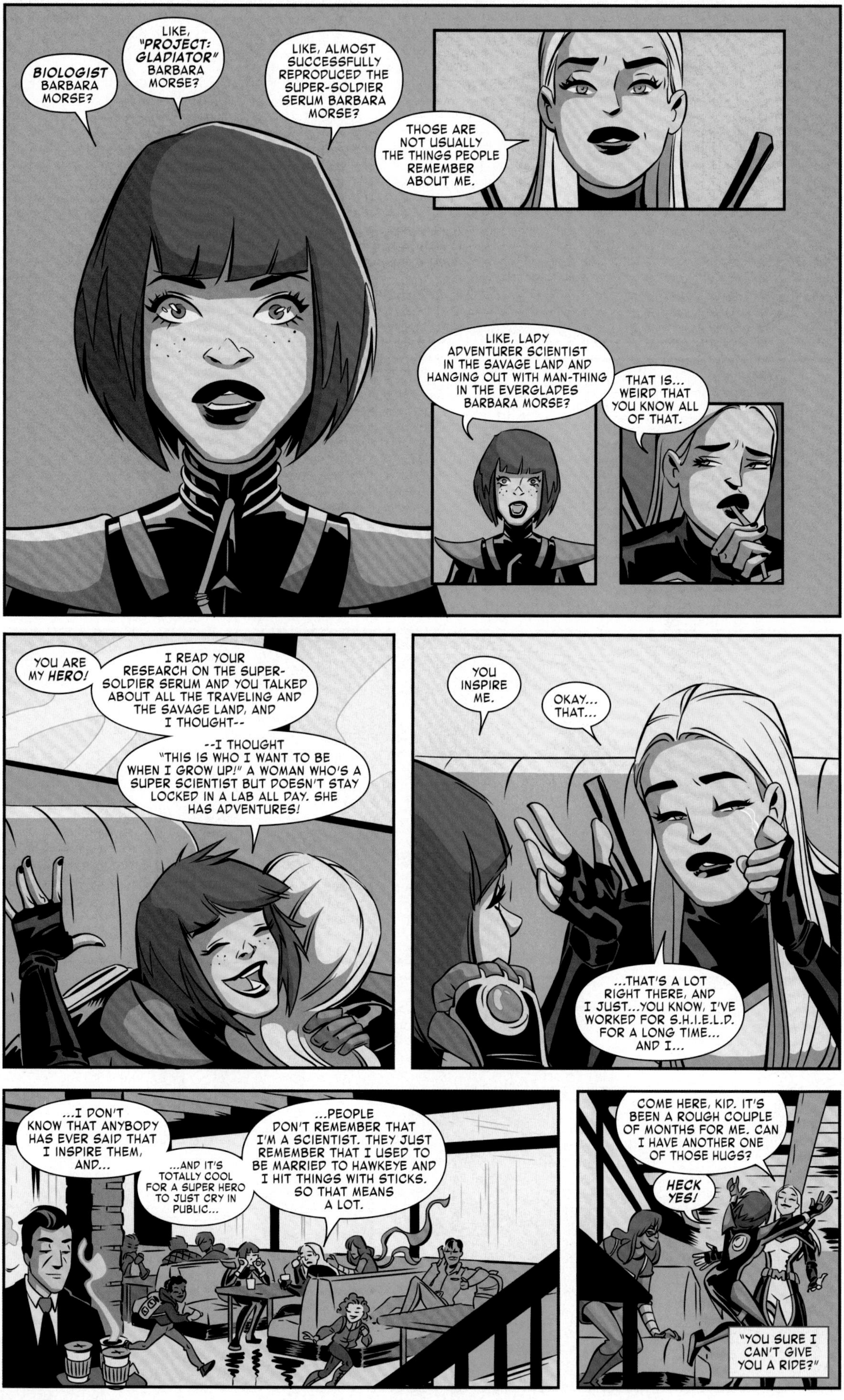

BIOLOGIST BARBARA MORSE?
LIKE, "PROJECT: GLADIATOR" BARBARA MORSE?
LIKE, ALMOST SUCCESSFULLY REPRODUCED THE SUPER-SOLDIER SERUM BARBARA MORSE?
THOSE ARE NOT USUALLY THE THINGS PEOPLE REMEMBER ABOUT ME.
LIKE, LADY ADVENTURER SCIENTIST IN THE SAVAGE LAND AND HANGING OUT WITH MAN-THING IN THE EVERGLADES BARBARA MORSE?
THAT IS... WEIRD THAT YOU KNOW ALL OF THAT.
YOU ARE MY HERO!
I READ YOUR RESEARCH ON THE SUPER-SOLDIER SERUM AND YOU TALKED ABOUT ALL THE TRAVELING AND THE SAVAGE LAND, AND I THOUGHT--
--I THOUGHT "THIS IS WHO I WANT TO BE WHEN I GROW UP!" A WOMAN WHO'S A SUPER SCIENTIST BUT DOESN'T STAY LOCKED IN A LAB ALL DAY. SHE HAS ADVENTURES!
YOU INSPIRE ME.
OKAY... THAT...
...THAT'S A LOT RIGHT THERE, AND I JUST...YOU KNOW, I'VE WORKED FOR S.H.I.E.L.D. FOR A LONG TIME... AND I...
...I DON'T KNOW THAT ANYBODY HAS EVER SAID THAT I INSPIRE THEM, AND...
...AND IT'S TOTALLY COOL FOR A SUPER HERO TO JUST CRY IN PUBLIC...
...PEOPLE DON'T REMEMBER THAT I'M A SCIENTIST. THEY JUST REMEMBER THAT I USED TO BE MARRIED TO HAWKEYE AND I HIT THINGS WITH STICKS. SO THAT MEANS A LOT.
COME HERE, KID. IT'S BEEN A ROUGH COUPLE OF MONTHS FOR ME. CAN I HAVE ANOTHER ONE OF THOSE HUGS?
HECK YES!
"YOU SURE I CAN'T GIVE YOU A RIDE?"

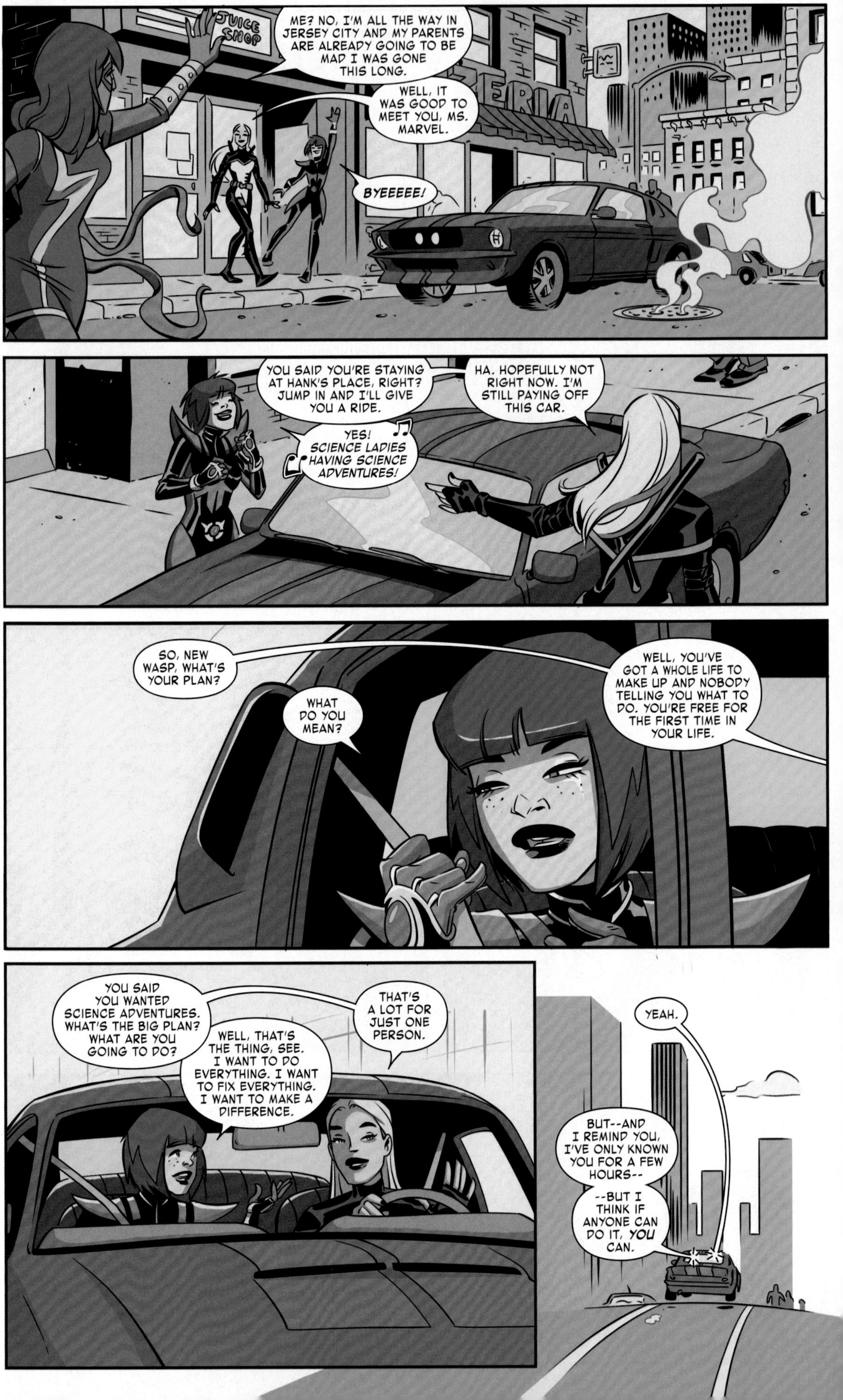
JUICE SHOP
ME? NO, I'M ALL THE WAY IN JERSEY CITY AND MY PARENTS ARE ALREADY GOING TO BE MAD I WAS GONE THIS LONG.
WELL, IT WAS GOOD TO MEET YOU, MS. MARVEL.
BYEEEEE!
YOU SAID YOU'RE STAYING AT HANK'S PLACE, RIGHT? JUMP IN AND I'LL GIVE YOU A RIDE.
HA. HOPEFULLY NOT RIGHT NOW. I'M STILL PAYING OFF THIS CAR.
YES! SCIENCE LADIES HAVING SCIENCE ADVENTURES!
SO, NEW WASP, WHAT'S YOUR PLAN?
WHAT DO YOU MEAN?
WELL, YOU'VE GOT A WHOLE LIFE TO MAKE UP AND NOBODY TELLING YOU WHAT TO DO. YOU'RE FREE FOR THE FIRST TIME IN YOUR LIFE.
YOU SAID YOU WANTED SCIENCE ADVENTURES. WHAT'S THE BIG PLAN? WHAT ARE YOU GOING TO DO?
WELL, THAT'S THE THING, SEE. I WANT TO DO EVERYTHING. I WANT TO FIX EVERYTHING. I WANT TO MAKE A DIFFERENCE.
THAT'S A LOT FOR JUST ONE PERSON.
YEAH.
BUT--AND I REMIND YOU, I'VE ONLY KNOWN YOU FOR A FEW HOURS--
--BUT I THINK IF ANYONE CAN DO IT, YOU CAN.

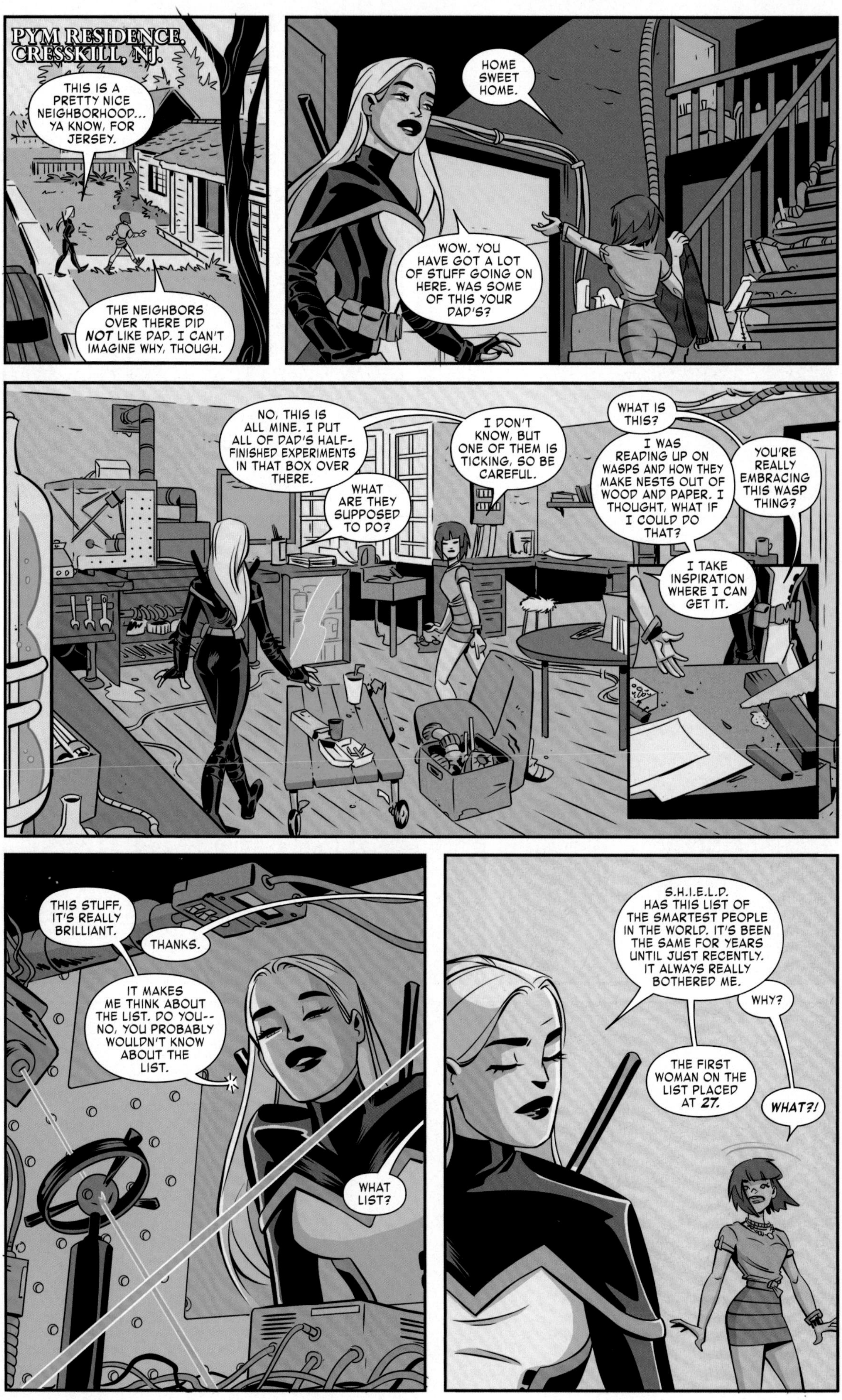
PYM RESIDENCE. CRESSKILL, NJ.
THIS IS A PRETTY NICE NEIGHBORHOOD... YA KNOW, FOR JERSEY.
THE NEIGHBORS OVER THERE DID NOT LIKE DAD. I CAN'T IMAGINE WHY, THOUGH.
HOME SWEET HOME.
WOW. YOU HAVE GOT A LOT OF STUFF GOING ON HERE. WAS SOME OF THIS YOUR DAD'S?
NO, THIS IS ALL MINE. I PUT ALL OF DAD'S HALF-FINISHED EXPERIMENTS IN THAT BOX OVER THERE.
WHAT ARE THEY SUPPOSED TO DO?
I DON'T KNOW, BUT ONE OF THEM IS TICKING, SO BE CAREFUL.
WHAT IS THIS?
I WAS READING UP ON WASPS AND HOW THEY MAKE NESTS OUT OF WOOD AND PAPER. I THOUGHT, WHAT IF I COULD DO THAT?
YOU'RE REALLY EMBRACING THIS WASP THING?
I TAKE INSPIRATION WHERE I CAN GET IT.
THIS STUFF, IT'S REALLY BRILLIANT.
THANKS.
IT MAKES ME THINK ABOUT THE LIST. DO YOU--NO, YOU PROBABLY WOULDN'T KNOW ABOUT THE LIST.
WHAT LIST?
S.H.I.E.L.D. HAS THIS LIST OF THE SMARTEST PEOPLE IN THE WORLD. IT'S BEEN THE SAME FOR YEARS UNTIL JUST RECENTLY. IT ALWAYS REALLY BOTHERED ME.
WHY?
THE FIRST WOMAN ON THE LIST PLACED AT 27.
WHAT?!

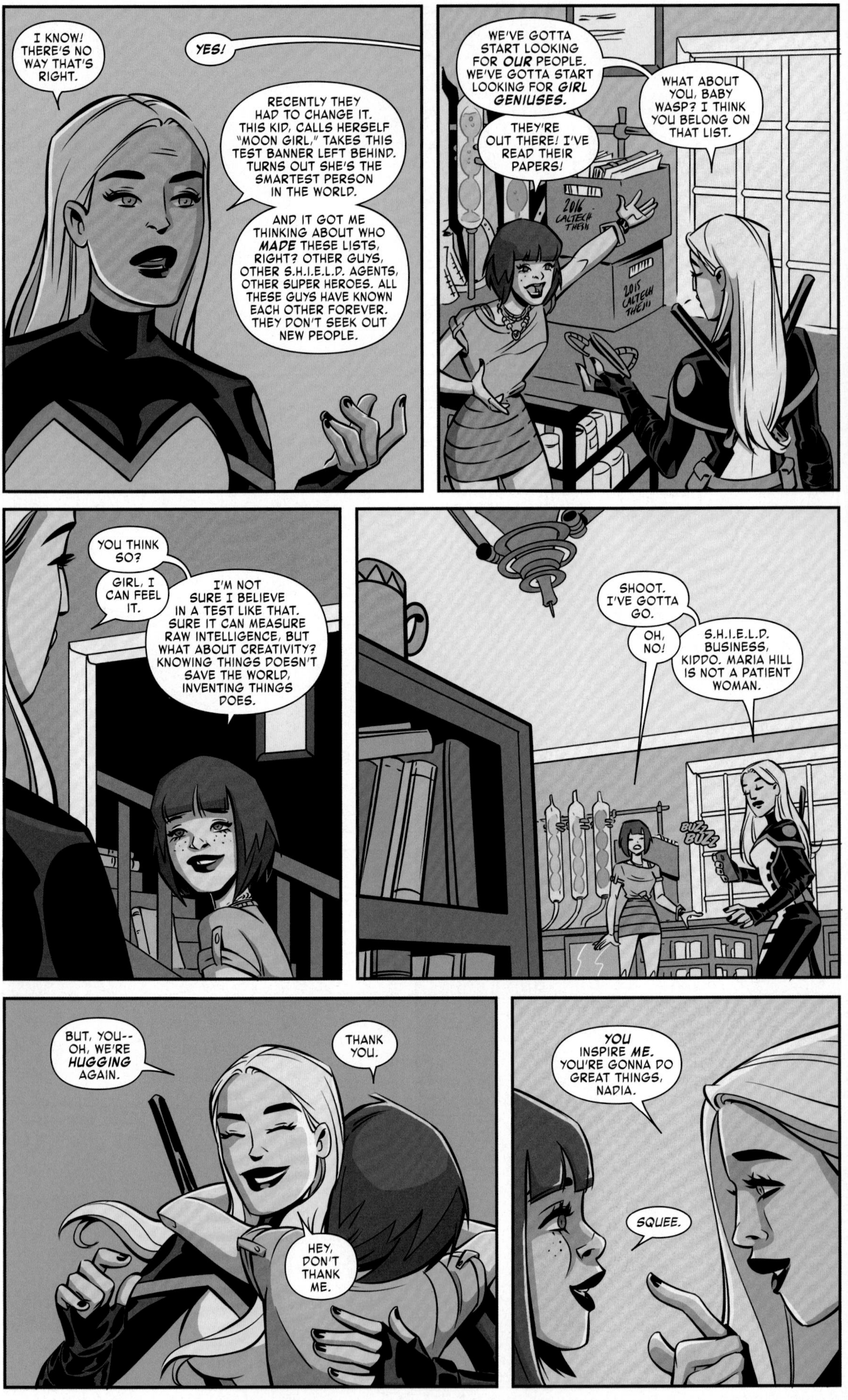

I KNOW! THERE'S NO WAY THAT'S RIGHT.
YES!
RECENTLY THEY HAD TO CHANGE IT. THIS KID, CALLS HERSELF "MOON GIRL," TAKES THIS TEST BANNER LEFT BEHIND. TURNS OUT SHE'S THE SMARTEST PERSON IN THE WORLD.
AND IT GOT ME THINKING ABOUT WHO MADE THESE LISTS, RIGHT? OTHER GUYS, OTHER S.H.I.E.L.D. AGENTS, OTHER SUPER HEROES. ALL THESE GUYS HAVE KNOWN EACH OTHER FOREVER. THEY DON'T SEEK OUT NEW PEOPLE.
WE'VE GOTTA START LOOKING FOR OUR PEOPLE. WE'VE GOTTA START LOOKING FOR GIRL GENIUSES.
THEY'RE OUT THERE! I'VE READ THEIR PAPERS!
WHAT ABOUT YOU, BABY WASP? I THINK YOU BELONG ON THAT LIST.
2016 CALTECH THESIS
2015 CALTECH THESIS
YOU THINK SO?
GIRL, I CAN FEEL IT.
I'M NOT SURE I BELIEVE IN A TEST LIKE THAT. SURE IT CAN MEASURE RAW INTELLIGENCE, BUT WHAT ABOUT CREATIVITY? KNOWING THINGS DOESN'T SAVE THE WORLD, INVENTING THINGS DOES.
SHOOT. I'VE GOTTA GO.
OH, NO!
S.H.I.E.L.D. BUSINESS, KIDDO. MARIA HILL IS NOT A PATIENT WOMAN.
BUZZ BUZZ
BUT, YOU-- OH, WE'RE HUGGING AGAIN.
THANK YOU.
HEY, DON'T THANK ME.
YOU INSPIRE ME. YOU'RE GONNA DO GREAT THINGS, NADIA.
SQUEE.

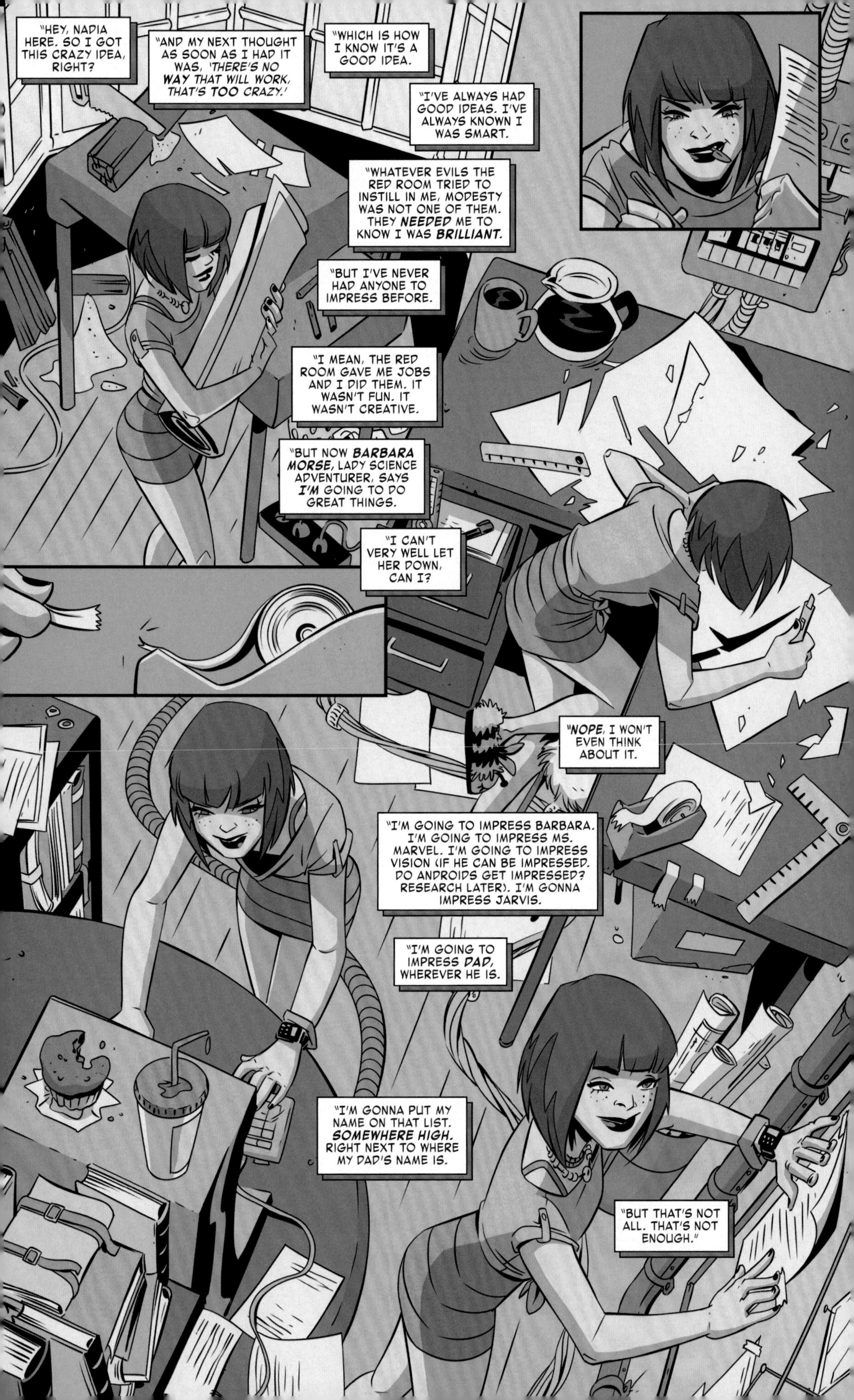
"HEY, NADIA HERE. SO I GOT THIS CRAZY IDEA, RIGHT?
"AND MY NEXT THOUGHT AS SOON AS I HAD IT WAS, 'THERE'S NO WAY THAT WILL WORK, THAT'S TOO CRAZY.'
"WHICH IS HOW I KNOW IT'S A GOOD IDEA.
"I'VE ALWAYS HAD GOOD IDEAS. I'VE ALWAYS KNOWN I WAS SMART.
"WHATEVER EVILS THE RED ROOM TRIED TO INSTILL IN ME, MODESTY WAS NOT ONE OF THEM. THEY NEEDED ME TO KNOW I WAS BRILLIANT.
"BUT I'VE NEVER HAD ANYONE TO IMPRESS BEFORE.
"I MEAN, THE RED ROOM GAVE ME JOBS AND I DID THEM. IT WASN'T FUN. IT WASN'T CREATIVE.
"BUT NOW BARBARA MORSE, LADY SCIENCE ADVENTURER, SAYS I'M GOING TO DO GREAT THINGS.
"I CAN'T VERY WELL LET HER DOWN, CAN I?
"NOPE, I WON'T EVEN THINK ABOUT IT.
"I'M GOING TO IMPRESS BARBARA. I'M GOING TO IMPRESS MS. MARVEL. I'M GOING TO IMPRESS VISION (IF HE CAN BE IMPRESSED. DO ANDROIDS GET IMPRESSED? RESEARCH LATER). I'M GONNA IMPRESS JARVIS.
"I'M GOING TO IMPRESS DAD, WHEREVER HE IS.
"I'M GONNA PUT MY NAME ON THAT LIST. SOMEWHERE HIGH. RIGHT NEXT TO WHERE MY DAD'S NAME IS.
"BUT THAT'S NOT ALL. THAT'S NOT ENOUGH."

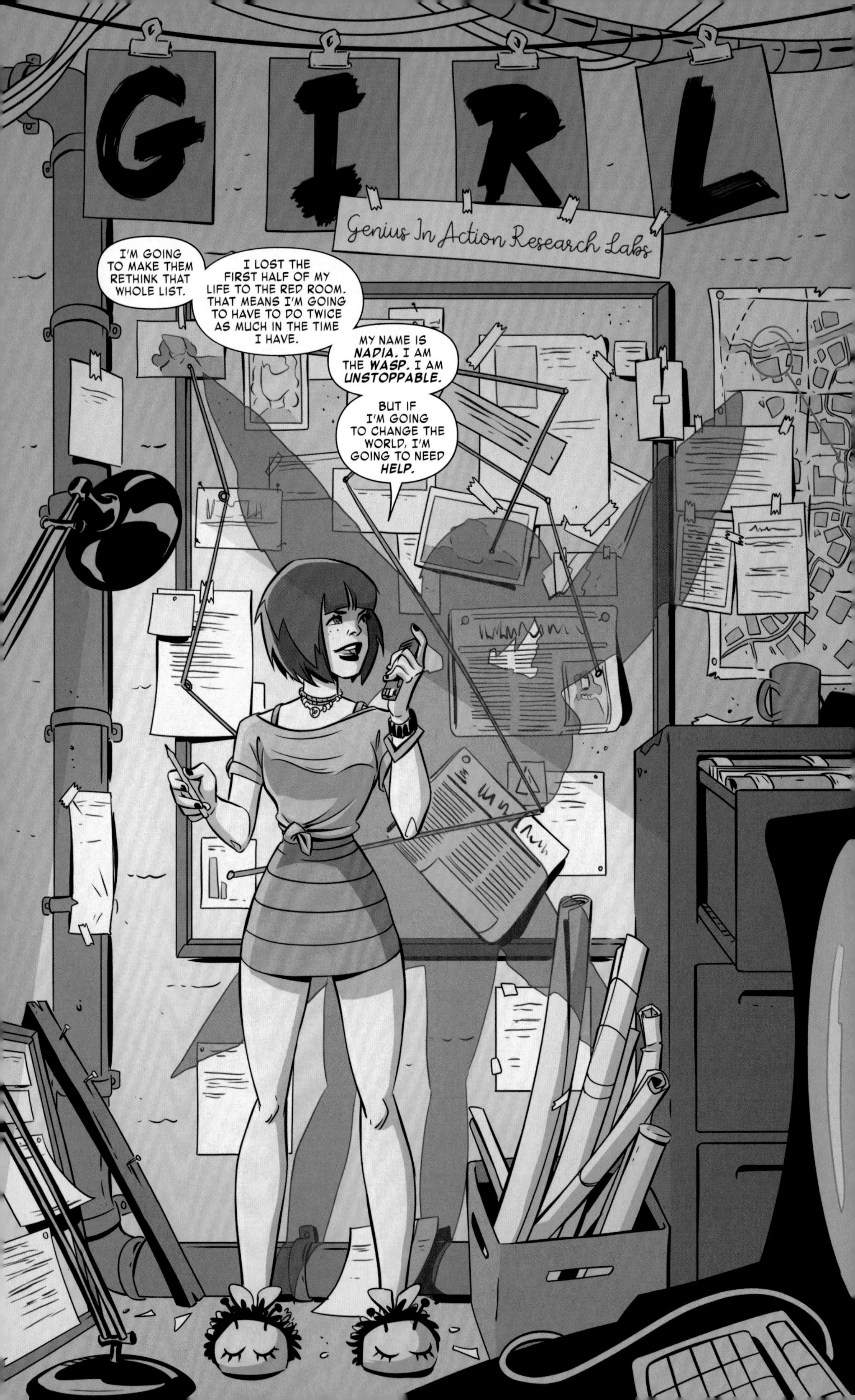

GIRL
Genius In Action Research Labs
I'M GOING TO MAKE THEM RETHINK THAT WHOLE LIST.
I LOST THE FIRST HALF OF MY LIFE TO THE RED ROOM. THAT MEANS I'M GOING TO HAVE TO DO TWICE AS MUCH IN THE TIME I HAVE.
MY NAME IS NADIA. I AM THE WASP. I AM UNSTOPPABLE.
BUT IF I'M GOING TO CHANGE THE WORLD, I'M GOING TO NEED HELP.

2

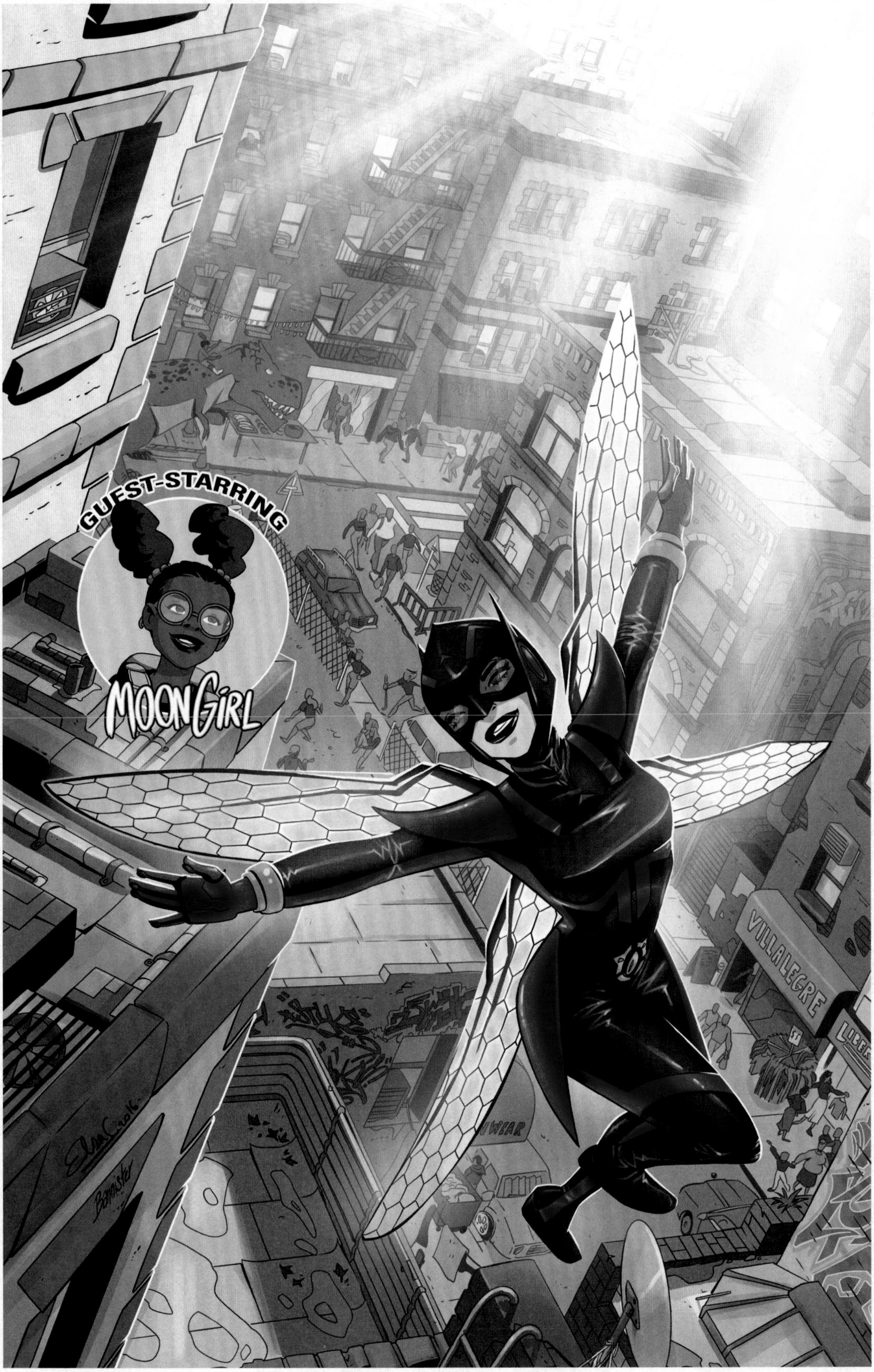
GUEST-STARRING
MOON GIRL
VILLALEGRE

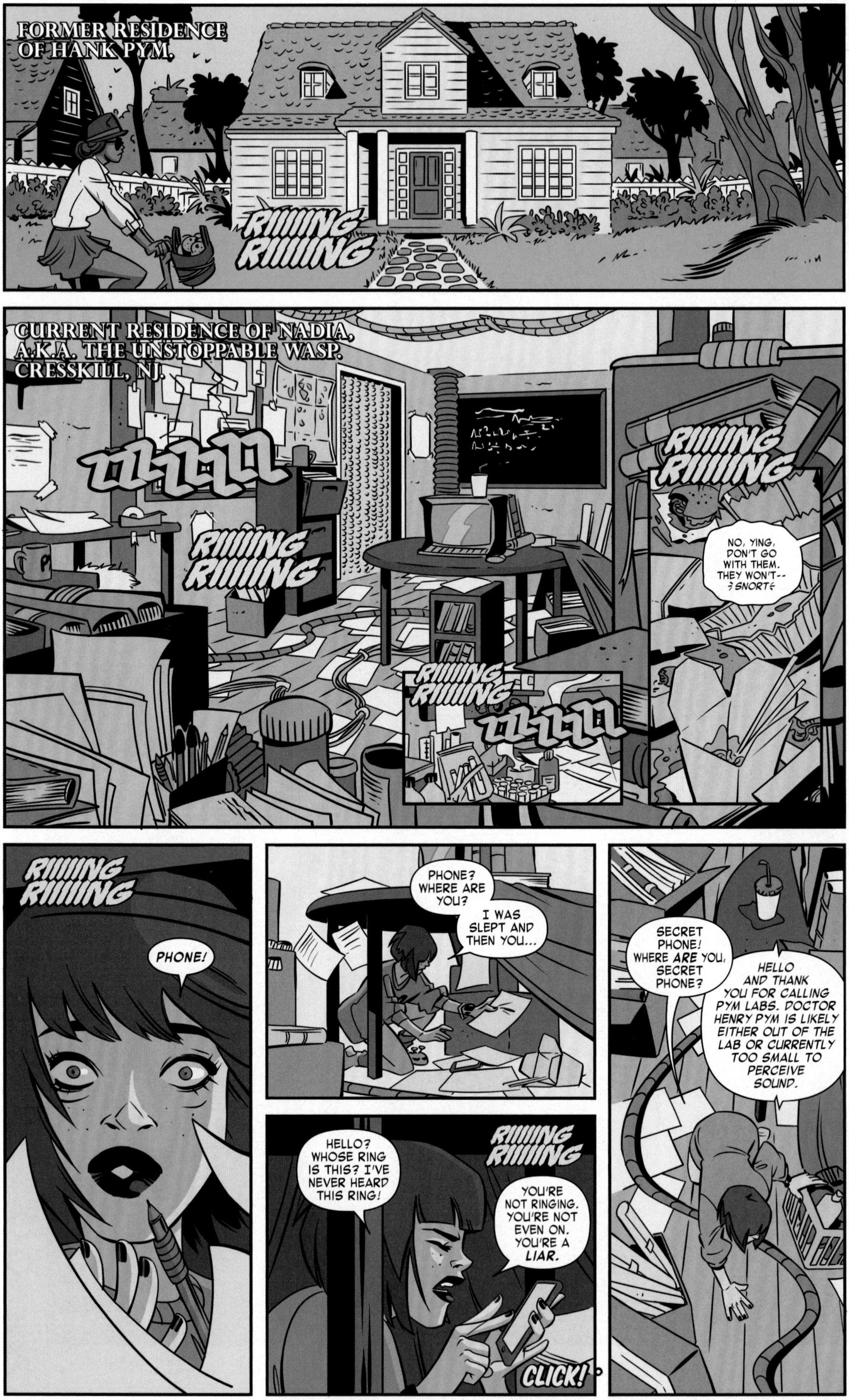
FORMER RESIDENCE OF HANK PYM.
RIIIIING RIIIIING
CURRENT RESIDENCE OF NADIA, A.K.A. THE UNSTOPPABLE WASP. CRESSKILL, NJ.
ZZZZZ
RIIIIING RIIIIING
RIIIIING RIIIIING
NO, YING, DON'T GO WITH THEM. THEY WON'T-- SNORT
RIIIIING RIIIIING
ZZZZZ
RIIIIING RIIIIING
PHONE!
PHONE? WHERE ARE YOU?
I WAS SLEPT AND THEN YOU...
HELLO? WHOSE RING IS THIS? I'VE NEVER HEARD THIS RING!
RIIIIING RIIIIING
YOU'RE NOT RINGING. YOU'RE NOT EVEN ON. YOU'RE A LIAR.
CLICK!
SECRET PHONE! WHERE ARE YOU, SECRET PHONE?
HELLO AND THANK YOU FOR CALLING PYM LABS. DOCTOR HENRY PYM IS LIKELY EITHER OUT OF THE LAB OR CURRENTLY TOO SMALL TO PERCEIVE SOUND.

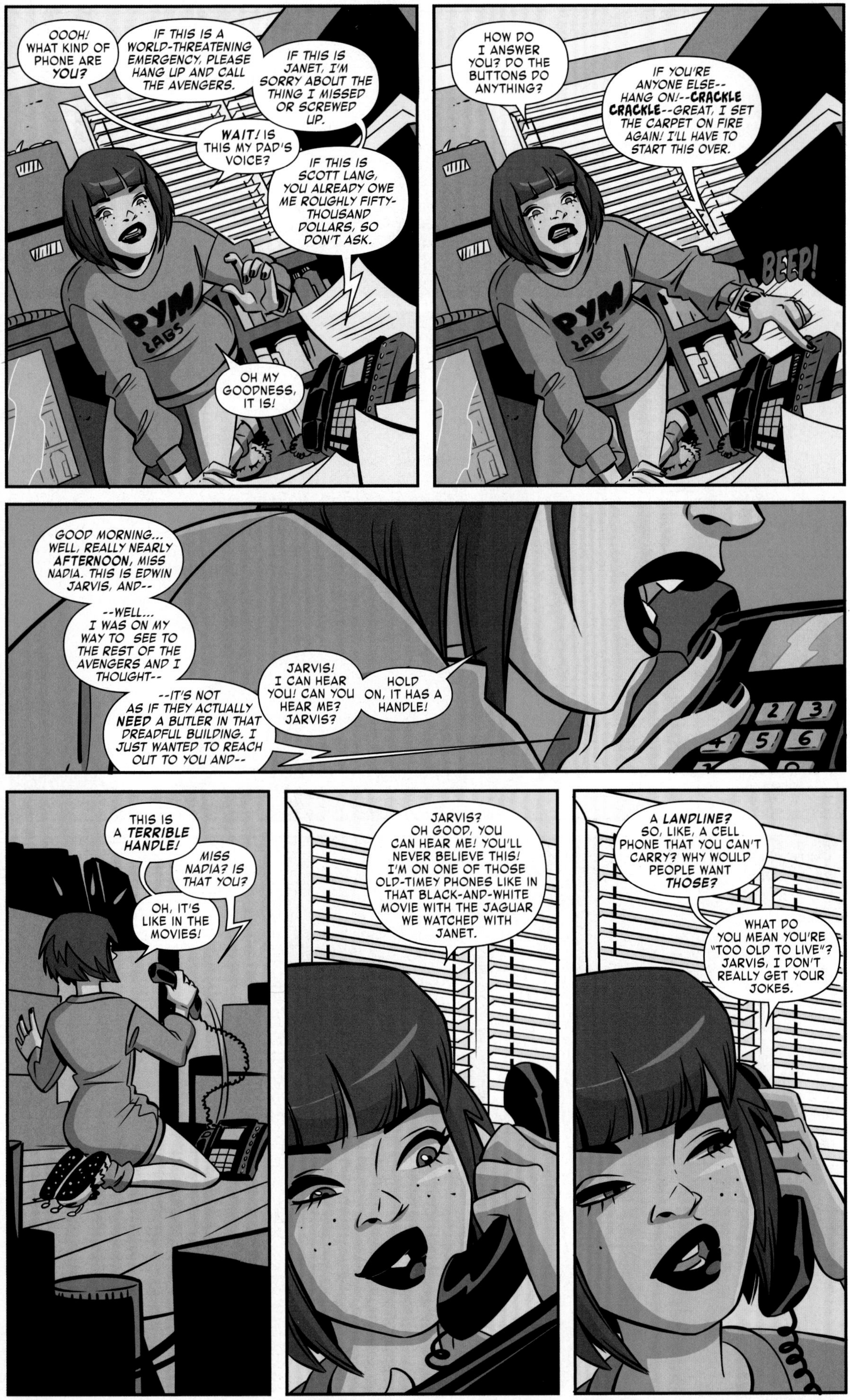
OOOH! WHAT KIND OF PHONE ARE YOU?
IF THIS IS A WORLD-THREATENING EMERGENCY, PLEASE HANG UP AND CALL THE AVENGERS.
IF THIS IS JANET, I'M SORRY ABOUT THE THING I MISSED OR SCREWED UP.
WAIT! IS THIS MY DAD'S VOICE?
IF THIS IS SCOTT LANG, YOU ALREADY OWE ME ROUGHLY FIFTY-THOUSAND DOLLARS, SO DON'T ASK.
OH MY GOODNESS, IT IS!
PYM LABS
HOW DO I ANSWER YOU? DO THE BUTTONS DO ANYTHING?
IF YOU'RE ANYONE ELSE--HANG ON!--CRACKLE CRACKLE--GREAT, I SET THE CARPET ON FIRE AGAIN! I'LL HAVE TO START THIS OVER.
BEEP!
PYM LABS
GOOD MORNING... WELL, REALLY NEARLY AFTERNOON, MISS NADIA. THIS IS EDWIN JARVIS, AND--
--WELL... I WAS ON MY WAY TO SEE TO THE REST OF THE AVENGERS AND I THOUGHT--
--IT'S NOT AS IF THEY ACTUALLY NEED A BUTLER IN THAT DREADFUL BUILDING. I JUST WANTED TO REACH OUT TO YOU AND--
JARVIS! I CAN HEAR YOU! CAN YOU HEAR ME? JARVIS?
HOLD ON, IT HAS A HANDLE!
THIS IS A TERRIBLE HANDLE!
MISS NADIA? IS THAT YOU?
OH, IT'S LIKE IN THE MOVIES!
JARVIS? OH GOOD, YOU CAN HEAR ME! YOU'LL NEVER BELIEVE THIS! I'M ON ONE OF THOSE OLD-TIMEY PHONES LIKE IN THAT BLACK-AND-WHITE MOVIE WITH THE JAGUAR WE WATCHED WITH JANET.
A LANDLINE? SO, LIKE, A CELL PHONE THAT YOU CAN'T CARRY? WHY WOULD PEOPLE WANT THOSE?
WHAT DO YOU MEAN YOU'RE "TOO OLD TO LIVE"? JARVIS, I DON'T REALLY GET YOUR JOKES.

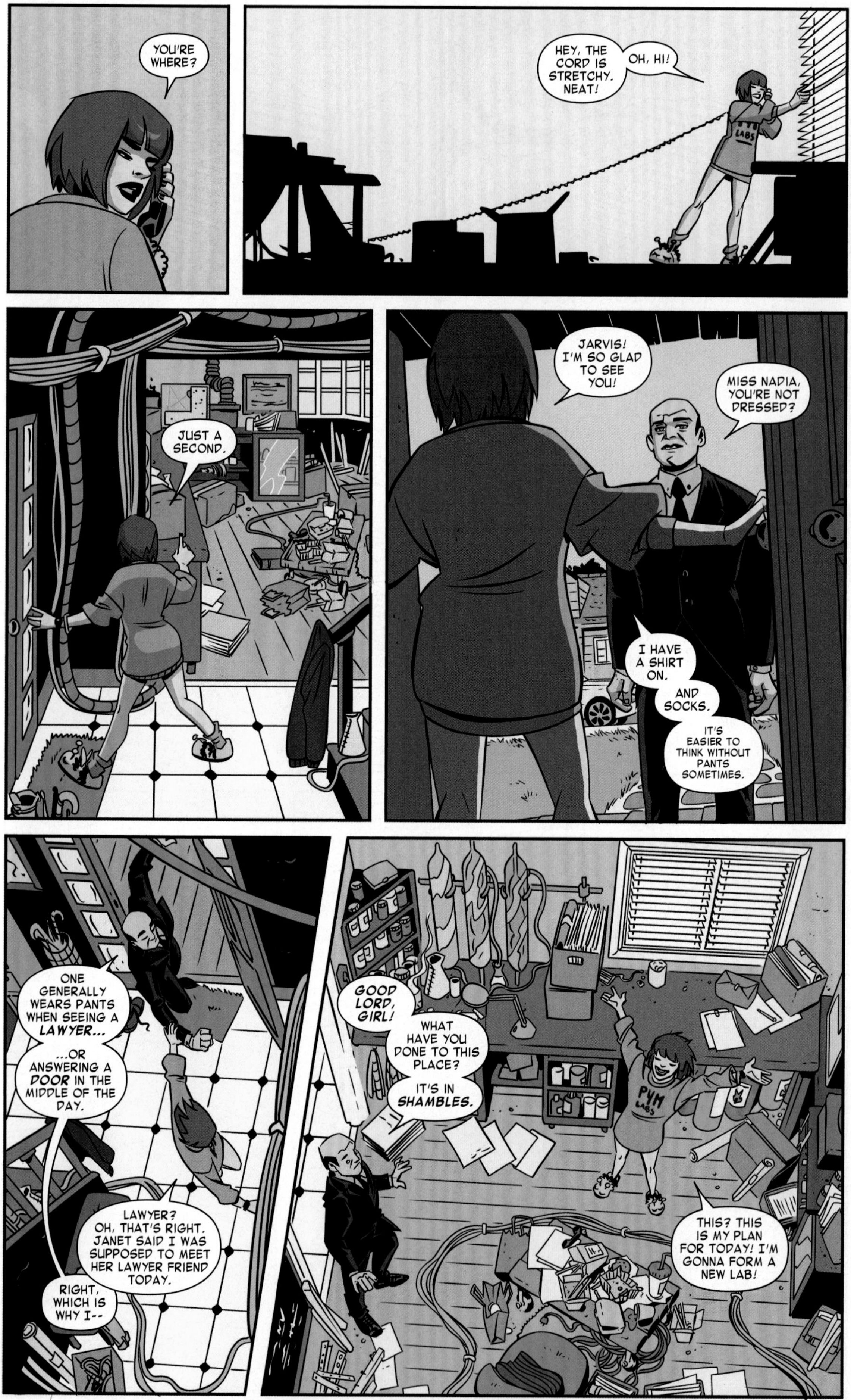

YOU'RE WHERE?
HEY, THE CORD IS STRETCHY. NEAT!
OH, HI!
LABS
JUST A SECOND.
JARVIS! I'M SO GLAD TO SEE YOU!
MISS NADIA, YOU'RE NOT DRESSED?
I HAVE A SHIRT ON.
AND SOCKS.
IT'S EASIER TO THINK WITHOUT PANTS SOMETIMES.
ONE GENERALLY WEARS PANTS WHEN SEEING A LAWYER...
...OR ANSWERING A DOOR IN THE MIDDLE OF THE DAY.
LAWYER? OH, THAT'S RIGHT. JANET SAID I WAS SUPPOSED TO MEET HER LAWYER FRIEND TODAY.
RIGHT, WHICH IS WHY I--
GOOD LORD, GIRL!
WHAT HAVE YOU DONE TO THIS PLACE?
IT'S IN SHAMBLES.
PYM LABS
THIS? THIS IS MY PLAN FOR TODAY! I'M GONNA FORM A NEW LAB!

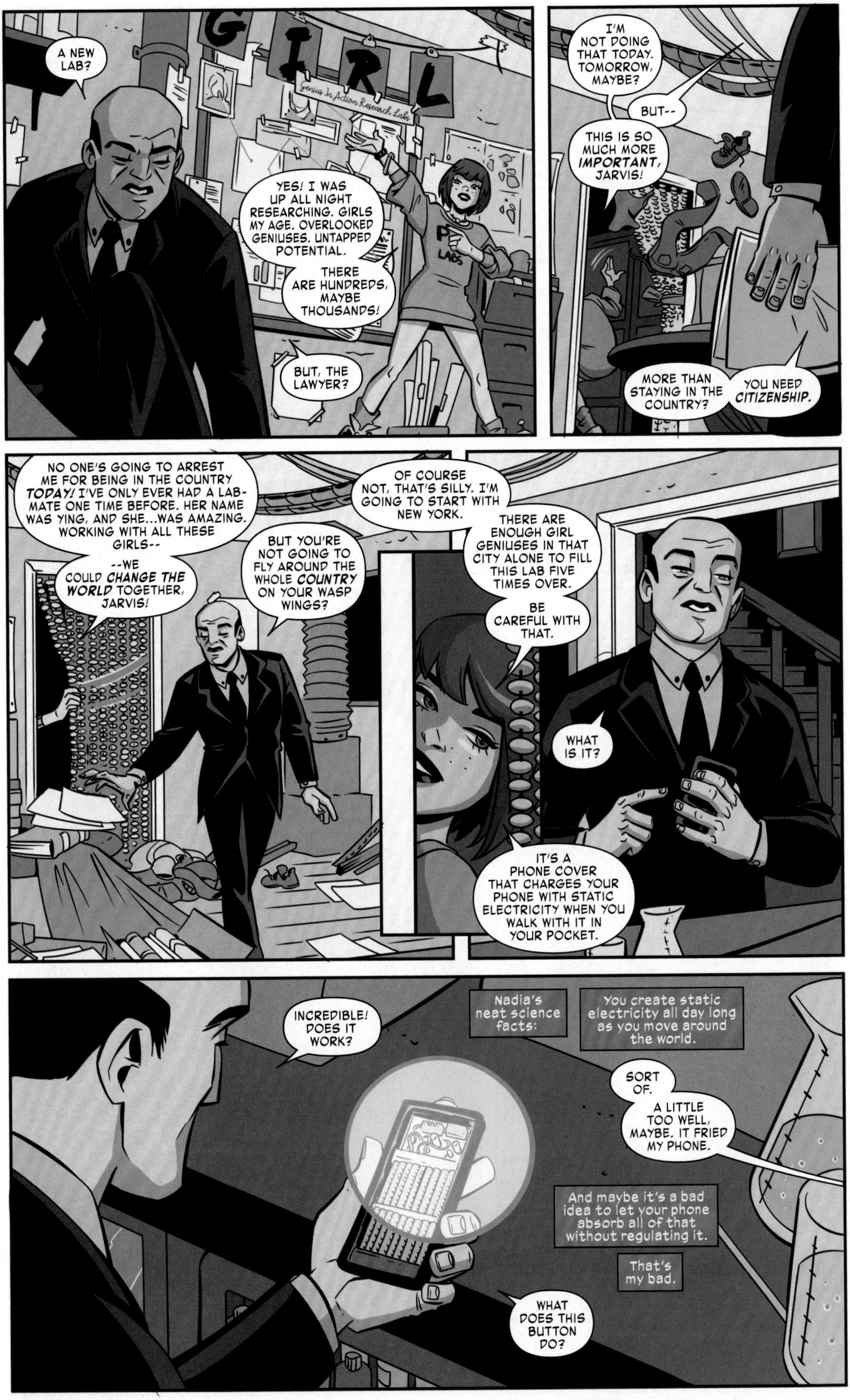
GIRL
Genius In Action Research Labs
A NEW LAB?
YES! I WAS UP ALL NIGHT RESEARCHING. GIRLS MY AGE. OVERLOOKED GENIUSES. UNTAPPED POTENTIAL.
THERE ARE HUNDREDS, MAYBE THOUSANDS!
BUT, THE LAWYER?
I'M NOT DOING THAT TODAY. TOMORROW, MAYBE?
BUT--
THIS IS SO MUCH MORE IMPORTANT, JARVIS!
MORE THAN STAYING IN THE COUNTRY?
YOU NEED CITIZENSHIP.
NO ONE'S GOING TO ARREST ME FOR BEING IN THE COUNTRY TODAY! I'VE ONLY EVER HAD A LAB-MATE ONE TIME BEFORE. HER NAME WAS YING, AND SHE...WAS AMAZING. WORKING WITH ALL THESE GIRLS--
--WE COULD CHANGE THE WORLD TOGETHER, JARVIS!
BUT YOU'RE NOT GOING TO FLY AROUND THE WHOLE COUNTRY ON YOUR WASP WINGS?
OF COURSE NOT, THAT'S SILLY. I'M GOING TO START WITH NEW YORK.
THERE ARE ENOUGH GIRL GENIUSES IN THAT CITY ALONE TO FILL THIS LAB FIVE TIMES OVER.
BE CAREFUL WITH THAT.
WHAT IS IT?
IT'S A PHONE COVER THAT CHARGES YOUR PHONE WITH STATIC ELECTRICITY WHEN YOU WALK WITH IT IN YOUR POCKET.
INCREDIBLE! DOES IT WORK?
Nadia's neat science facts:
You create static electricity all day long as you move around the world.
SORT OF.
A LITTLE TOO WELL, MAYBE. IT FRIED MY PHONE.
And maybe it's a bad idea to let your phone absorb all of that without regulating it.
That's my bad.
WHAT DOES THIS BUTTON DO?

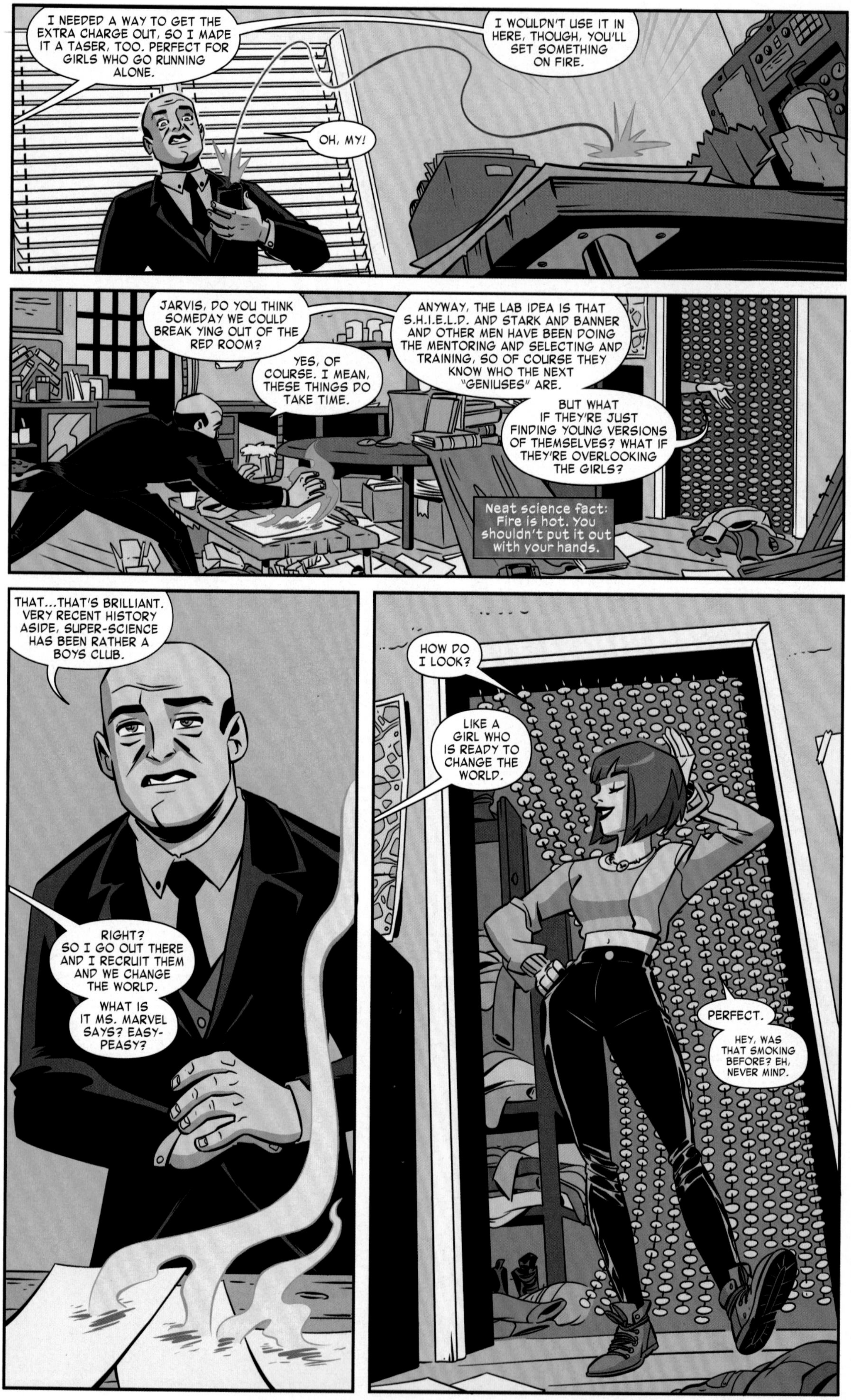
I NEEDED A WAY TO GET THE EXTRA CHARGE OUT, SO I MADE IT A TASER, TOO. PERFECT FOR GIRLS WHO GO RUNNING ALONE.
I WOULDN'T USE IT IN HERE, THOUGH, YOU'LL SET SOMETHING ON FIRE.
OH, MY!
JARVIS, DO YOU THINK SOMEDAY WE COULD BREAK YING OUT OF THE RED ROOM?
YES, OF COURSE. I MEAN, THESE THINGS DO TAKE TIME.
ANYWAY, THE LAB IDEA IS THAT S.H.I.E.L.D. AND STARK AND BANNER AND OTHER MEN HAVE BEEN DOING THE MENTORING AND SELECTING AND TRAINING, SO OF COURSE THEY KNOW WHO THE NEXT "GENIUSES" ARE.
BUT WHAT IF THEY'RE JUST FINDING YOUNG VERSIONS OF THEMSELVES? WHAT IF THEY'RE OVERLOOKING THE GIRLS?
Neat science fact: Fire is hot. You shouldn't put it out with your hands.
THAT...THAT'S BRILLIANT. VERY RECENT HISTORY ASIDE, SUPER-SCIENCE HAS BEEN RATHER A BOYS CLUB.
RIGHT? SO I GO OUT THERE AND I RECRUIT THEM AND WE CHANGE THE WORLD.
WHAT IS IT MS. MARVEL SAYS? EASY-PEASY?
HOW DO I LOOK?
LIKE A GIRL WHO IS READY TO CHANGE THE WORLD.
PERFECT.
HEY, WAS THAT SMOKING BEFORE? EH, NEVER MIND.

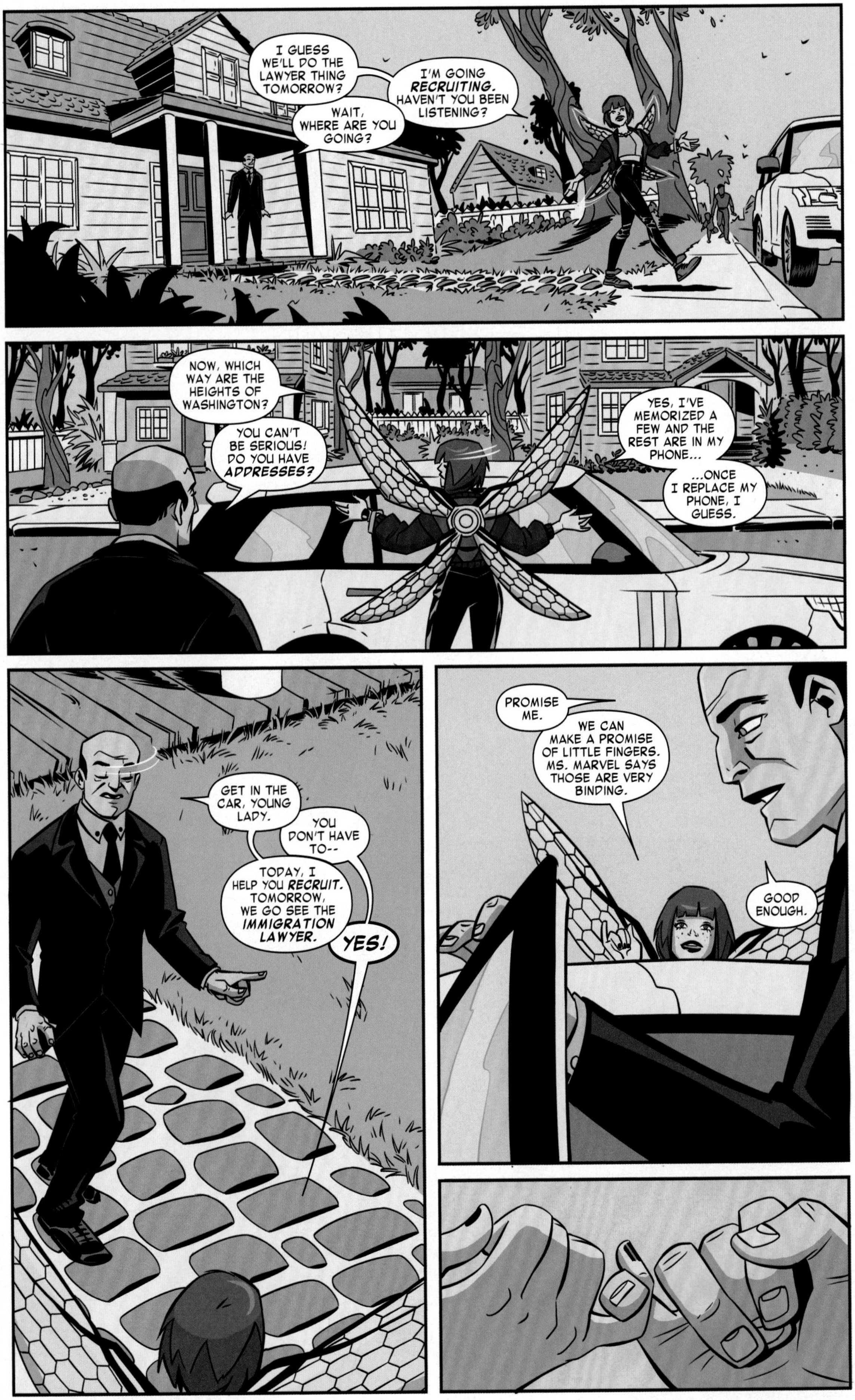

I GUESS WE'LL DO THE LAWYER THING TOMORROW?
WAIT, WHERE ARE YOU GOING?
I'M GOING RECRUITING. HAVEN'T YOU BEEN LISTENING?
NOW, WHICH WAY ARE THE HEIGHTS OF WASHINGTON?
YOU CAN'T BE SERIOUS! DO YOU HAVE ADDRESSES?
YES, I'VE MEMORIZED A FEW AND THE REST ARE IN MY PHONE...
...ONCE I REPLACE MY PHONE, I GUESS.
GET IN THE CAR, YOUNG LADY.
YOU DON'T HAVE TO--
TODAY, I HELP YOU RECRUIT. TOMORROW, WE GO SEE THE IMMIGRATION LAWYER.
YES!
PROMISE ME.
WE CAN MAKE A PROMISE OF LITTLE FINGERS. MS. MARVEL SAYS THOSE ARE VERY BINDING.
GOOD ENOUGH.

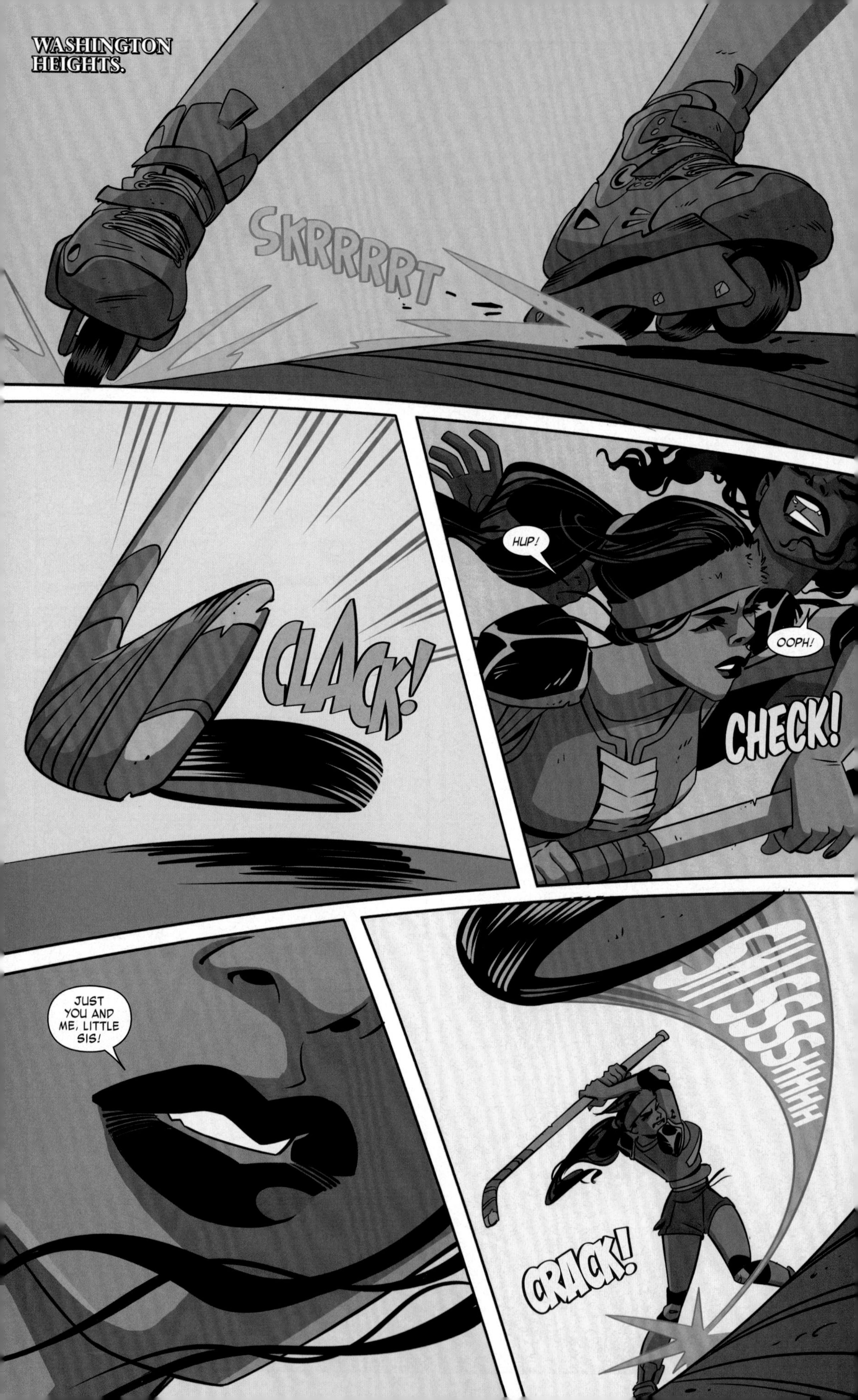
WASHINGTON HEIGHTS.
SKRRRRT
CLACK!
HUP!
OOPH!
CHECK!
JUST YOU AND ME, LITTLE SIS!
SHSSSSHHHH
CRACK!

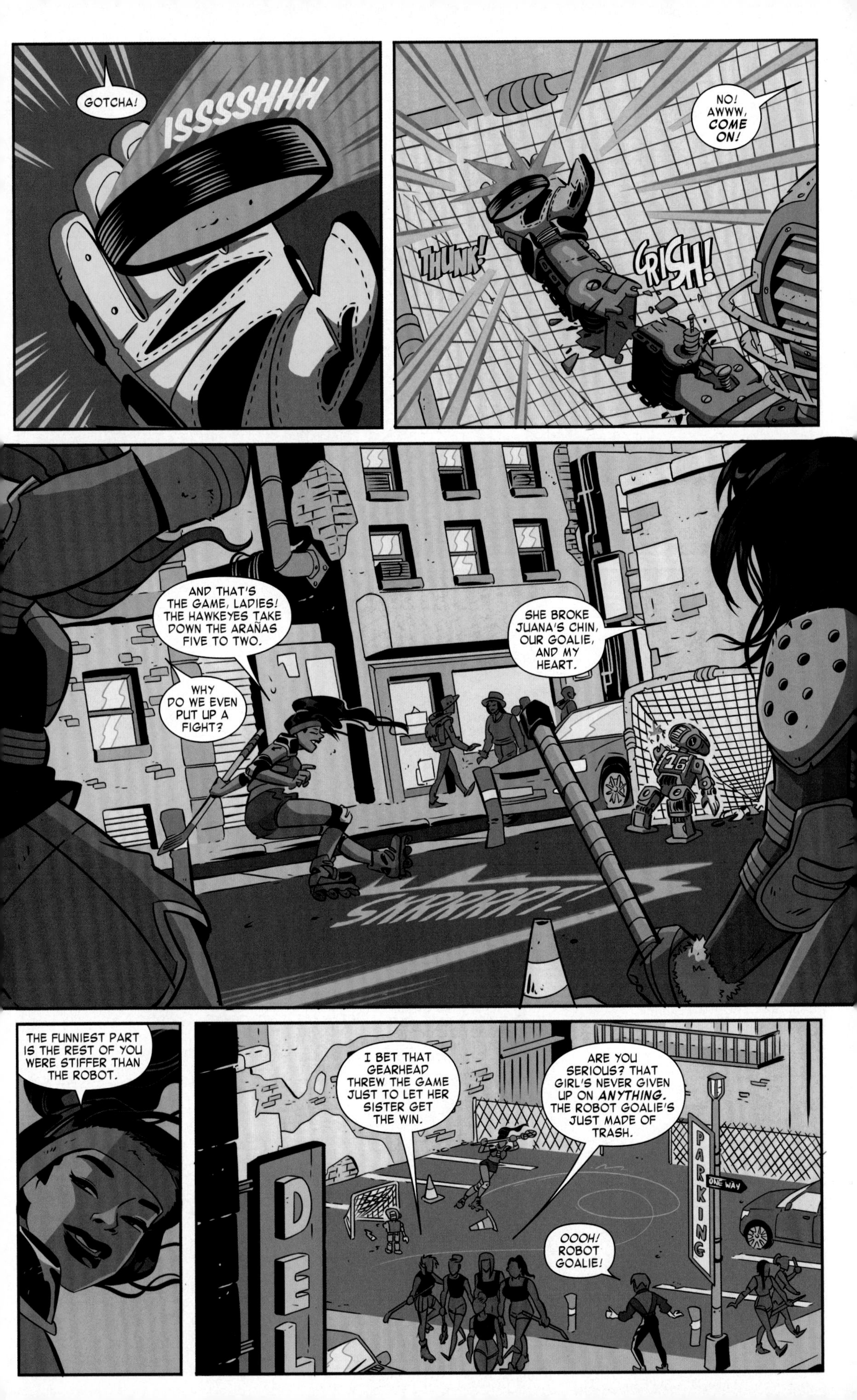
GOTCHA!
ISSSSHHH
NO! AWWW, COME ON!
THUNK!
CRISH!
AND THAT'S THE GAME, LADIES! THE HAWKEYES TAKE DOWN THE ARAÑAS FIVE TO TWO.
WHY DO WE EVEN PUT UP A FIGHT?
SHE BROKE JUANA'S CHIN, OUR GOALIE, AND MY HEART.
16
SKRRRRT!
THE FUNNIEST PART IS THE REST OF YOU WERE STIFFER THAN THE ROBOT.
I BET THAT GEARHEAD THREW THE GAME JUST TO LET HER SISTER GET THE WIN.
ARE YOU SERIOUS? THAT GIRL'S NEVER GIVEN UP ON ANYTHING. THE ROBOT GOALIE'S JUST MADE OF TRASH.
OOOH! ROBOT GOALIE!
PARKING
ONE WAY
DEL

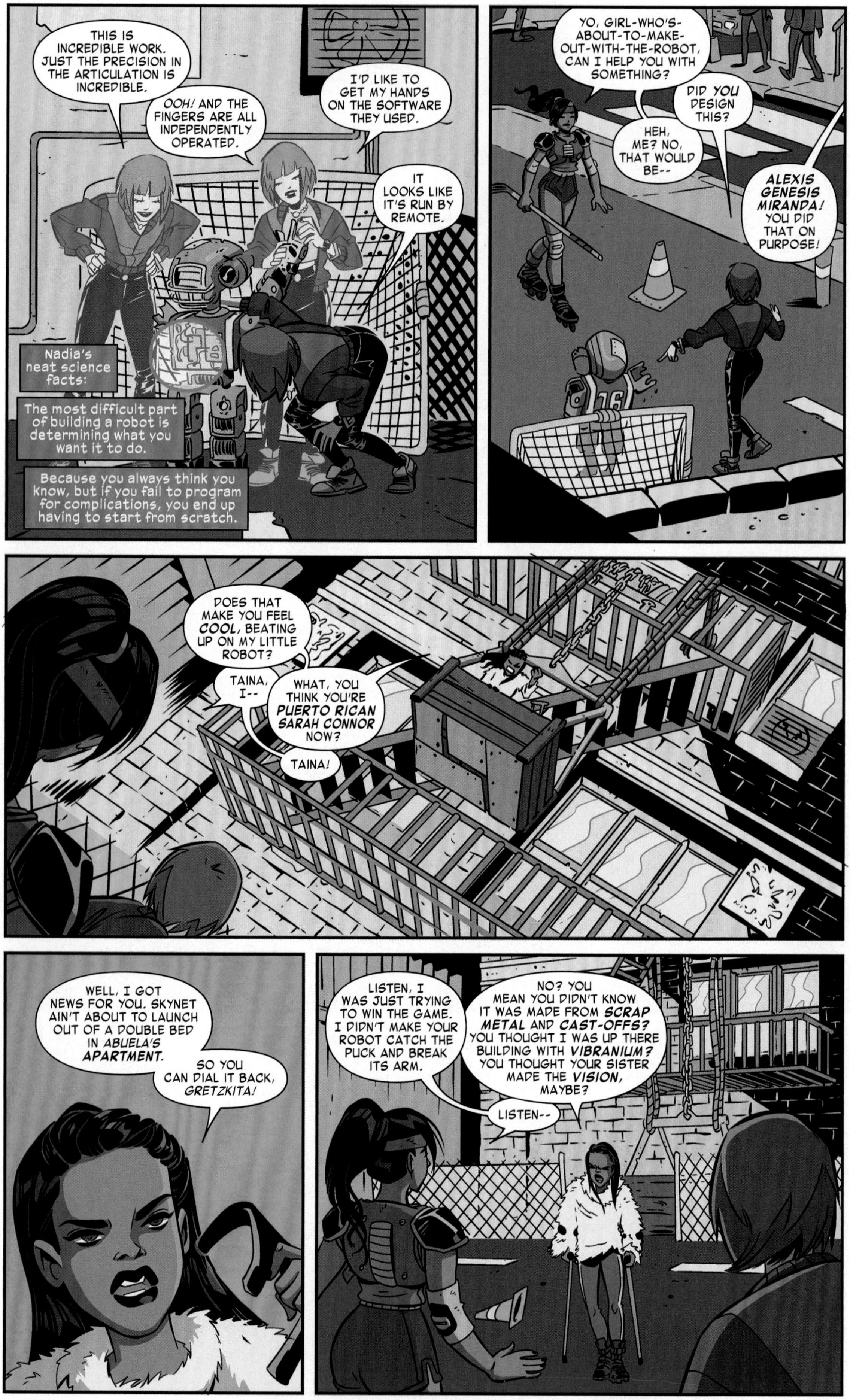
THIS IS INCREDIBLE WORK. JUST THE PRECISION IN THE ARTICULATION IS INCREDIBLE.
OOH! AND THE FINGERS ARE ALL INDEPENDENTLY OPERATED.
I'D LIKE TO GET MY HANDS ON THE SOFTWARE THEY USED.
IT LOOKS LIKE IT'S RUN BY REMOTE.
Nadia's neat science facts:
The most difficult part of building a robot is determining what you want it to do.
Because you always think you know, but if you fail to program for complications, you end up having to start from scratch.
YO, GIRL-WHO'S-ABOUT-TO-MAKE-OUT-WITH-THE-ROBOT, CAN I HELP YOU WITH SOMETHING?
DID YOU DESIGN THIS?
HEH, ME? NO, THAT WOULD BE--
ALEXIS GENESIS MIRANDA! YOU DID THAT ON PURPOSE!
DOES THAT MAKE YOU FEEL COOL, BEATING UP ON MY LITTLE ROBOT?
TAINA, I--
WHAT, YOU THINK YOU'RE PUERTO RICAN SARAH CONNOR NOW?
TAINA!
WELL, I GOT NEWS FOR YOU. SKYNET AIN'T ABOUT TO LAUNCH OUT OF A DOUBLE BED IN ABUELA'S APARTMENT.
SO YOU CAN DIAL IT BACK, GRETZKITA!
LISTEN, I WAS JUST TRYING TO WIN THE GAME. I DIDN'T MAKE YOUR ROBOT CATCH THE PUCK AND BREAK ITS ARM.
NO? YOU MEAN YOU DIDN'T KNOW IT WAS MADE FROM SCRAP METAL AND CAST-OFFS? YOU THOUGHT I WAS UP THERE BUILDING WITH VIBRANIUM? YOU THOUGHT YOUR SISTER MADE THE VISION, MAYBE?
LISTEN--

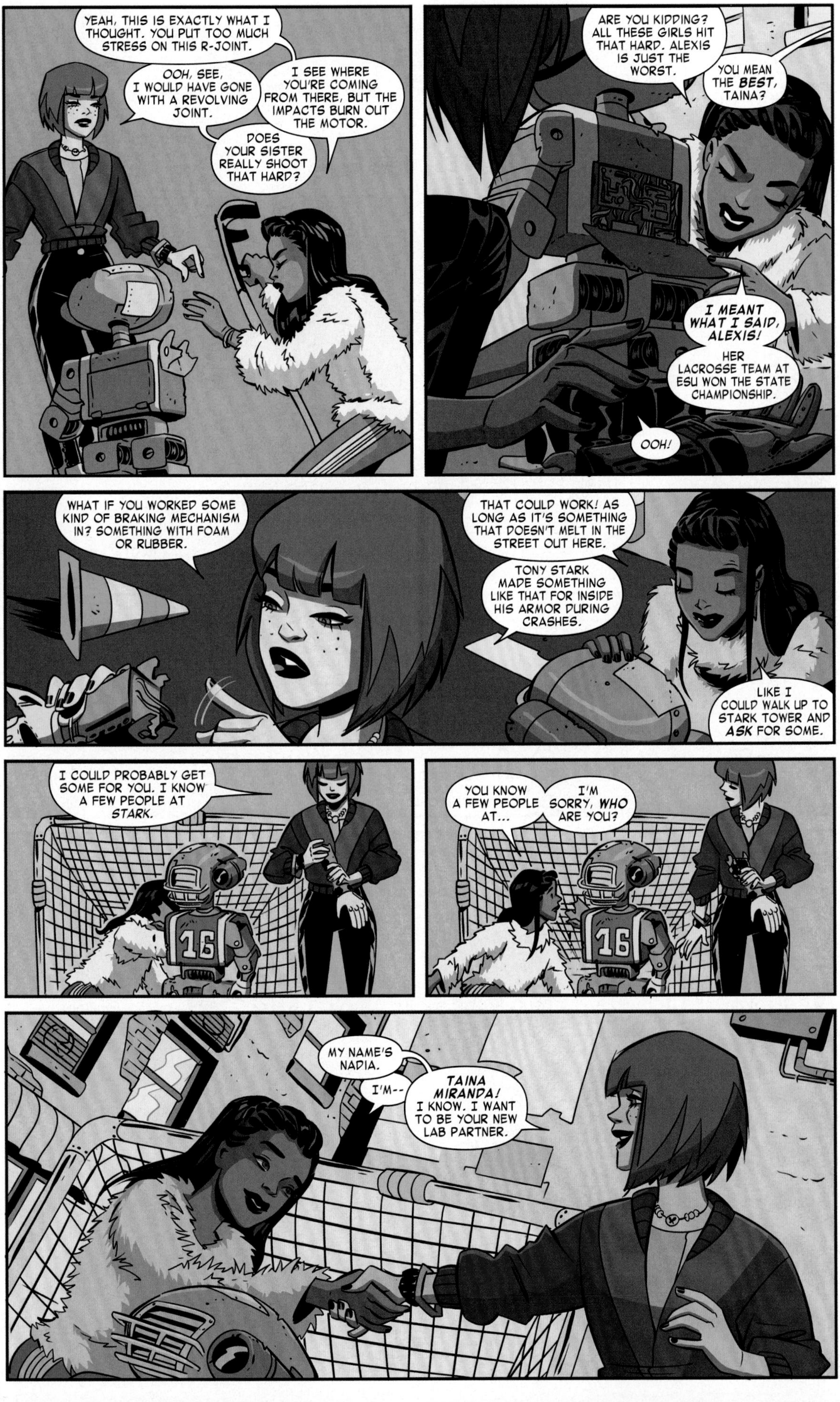

YEAH, THIS IS EXACTLY WHAT I THOUGHT. YOU PUT TOO MUCH STRESS ON THIS R-JOINT.
OOH, SEE, I WOULD HAVE GONE WITH A REVOLVING JOINT.
I SEE WHERE YOU'RE COMING FROM THERE, BUT THE IMPACTS BURN OUT THE MOTOR.
DOES YOUR SISTER REALLY SHOOT THAT HARD?
ARE YOU KIDDING? ALL THESE GIRLS HIT THAT HARD. ALEXIS IS JUST THE WORST.
YOU MEAN THE *BEST*, TAINA?
I MEANT WHAT I SAID, ALEXIS!
HER LACROSSE TEAM AT ESU WON THE STATE CHAMPIONSHIP.
OOH!
WHAT IF YOU WORKED SOME KIND OF BRAKING MECHANISM IN? SOMETHING WITH FOAM OR RUBBER.
THAT COULD WORK! AS LONG AS IT'S SOMETHING THAT DOESN'T MELT IN THE STREET OUT HERE.
TONY STARK MADE SOMETHING LIKE THAT FOR INSIDE HIS ARMOR DURING CRASHES.
LIKE I COULD WALK UP TO STARK TOWER AND *ASK* FOR SOME.
I COULD PROBABLY GET SOME FOR YOU. I KNOW A FEW PEOPLE AT *STARK.*
YOU KNOW A FEW PEOPLE AT...
I'M SORRY, *WHO* ARE YOU?
MY NAME'S NADIA.
I'M--
TAINA MIRANDA! I KNOW. I WANT TO BE YOUR NEW LAB PARTNER.

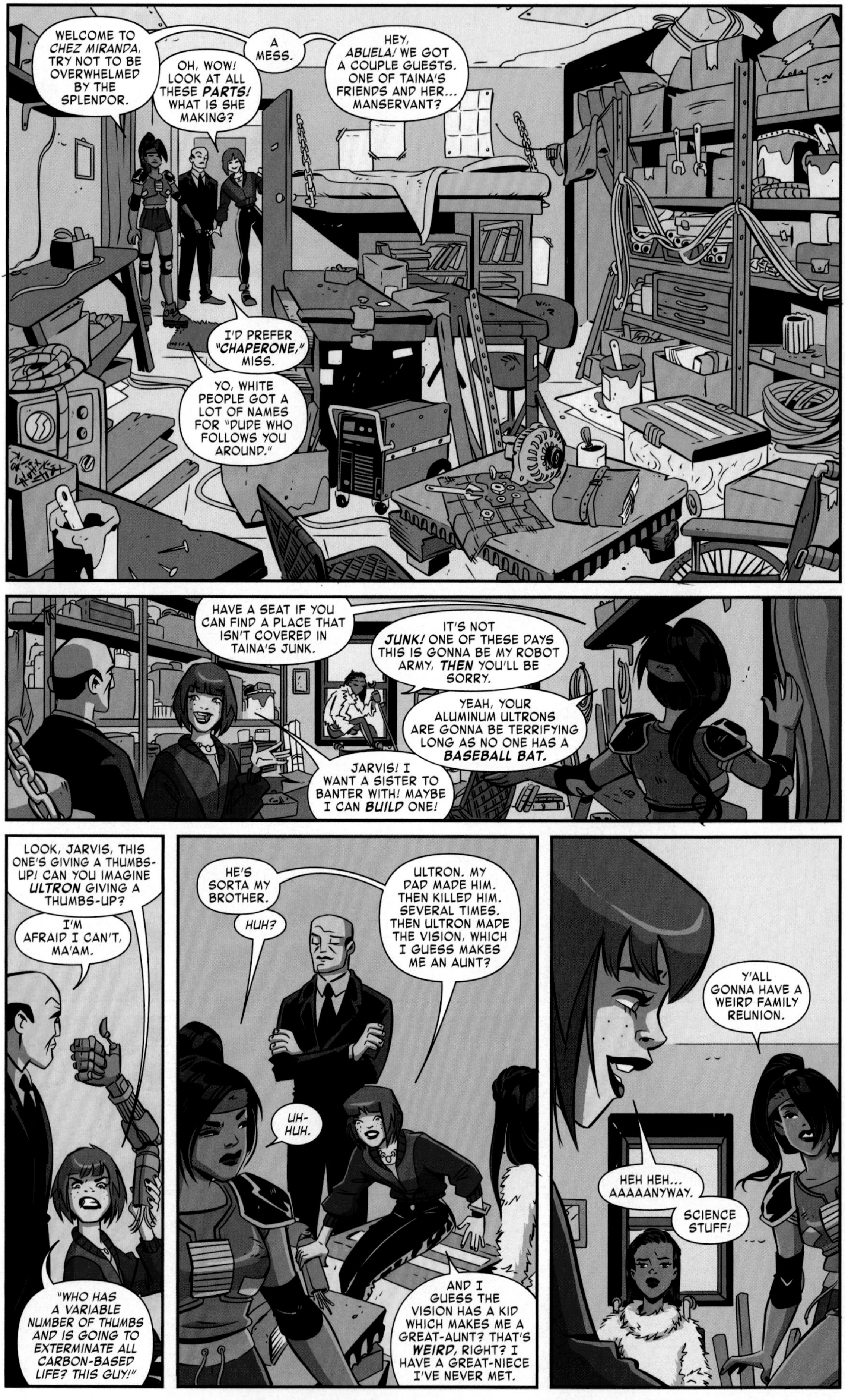
WELCOME TO CHEZ MIRANDA. TRY NOT TO BE OVERWHELMED BY THE SPLENDOR.
A MESS.
OH, WOW! LOOK AT ALL THESE PARTS! WHAT IS SHE MAKING?
HEY, ABUELA! WE GOT A COUPLE GUESTS. ONE OF TAINA'S FRIENDS AND HER... MANSERVANT?
I'D PREFER "CHAPERONE," MISS.
YO, WHITE PEOPLE GOT A LOT OF NAMES FOR "DUDE WHO FOLLOWS YOU AROUND."
HAVE A SEAT IF YOU CAN FIND A PLACE THAT ISN'T COVERED IN TAINA'S JUNK.
IT'S NOT JUNK! ONE OF THESE DAYS THIS IS GONNA BE MY ROBOT ARMY. THEN YOU'LL BE SORRY.
YEAH, YOUR ALUMINUM ULTRONS ARE GONNA BE TERRIFYING LONG AS NO ONE HAS A BASEBALL BAT.
JARVIS! I WANT A SISTER TO BANTER WITH! MAYBE I CAN BUILD ONE!
LOOK, JARVIS, THIS ONE'S GIVING A THUMBS-UP! CAN YOU IMAGINE ULTRON GIVING A THUMBS-UP?
I'M AFRAID I CAN'T, MA'AM.
"WHO HAS A VARIABLE NUMBER OF THUMBS AND IS GOING TO EXTERMINATE ALL CARBON-BASED LIFE? THIS GUY!"
HE'S SORTA MY BROTHER.
HUH?
ULTRON. MY DAD MADE HIM. THEN KILLED HIM. SEVERAL TIMES. THEN ULTRON MADE THE VISION, WHICH I GUESS MAKES ME AN AUNT?
UH-HUH.
AND I GUESS THE VISION HAS A KID WHICH MAKES ME A GREAT-AUNT? THAT'S WEIRD, RIGHT? I HAVE A GREAT-NIECE I'VE NEVER MET.
Y'ALL GONNA HAVE A WEIRD FAMILY REUNION.
HEH HEH... AAAAANYWAY.
SCIENCE STUFF!

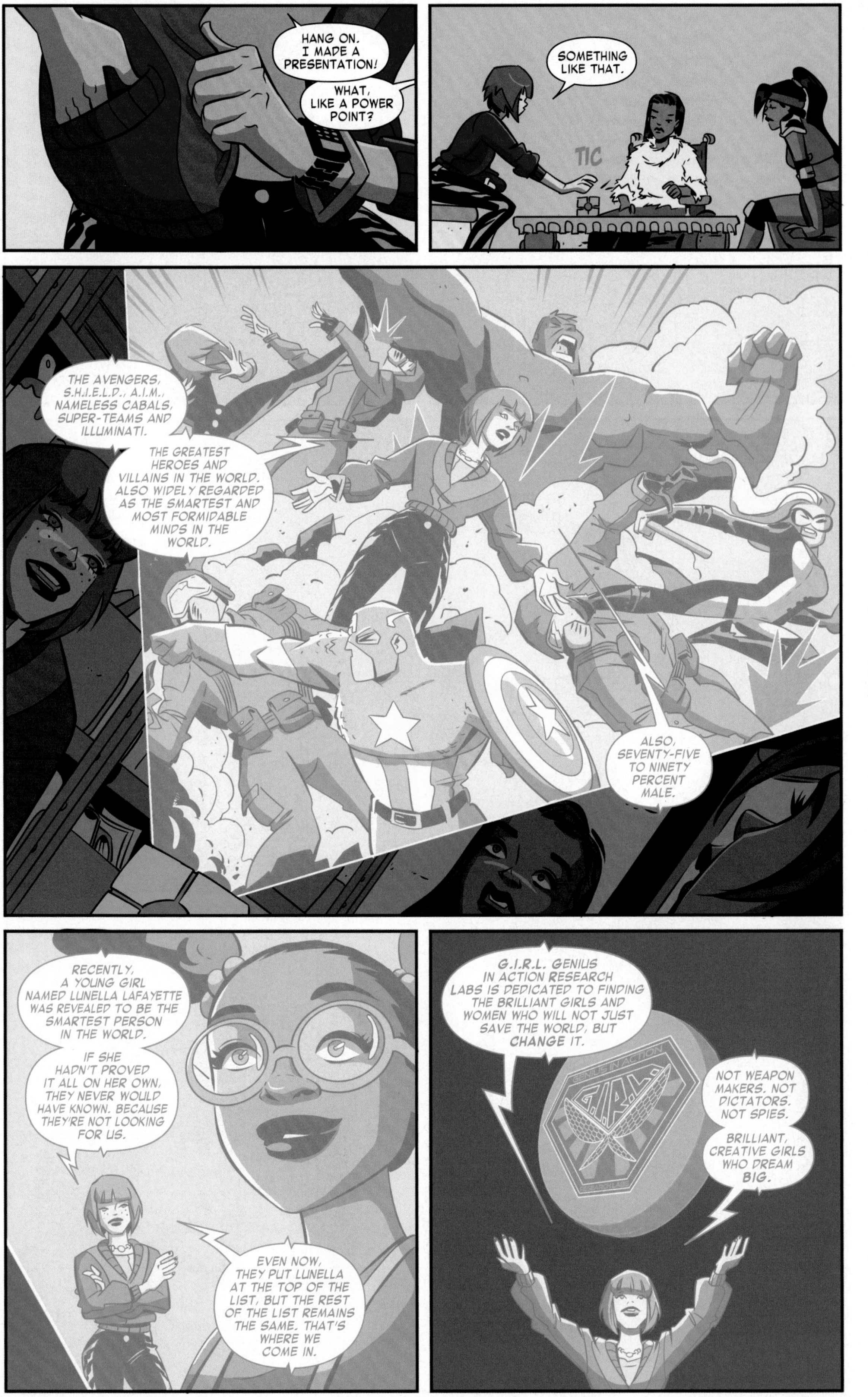
HANG ON. I MADE A PRESENTATION!
WHAT, LIKE A POWER POINT?
SOMETHING LIKE THAT.
TIC
THE AVENGERS, S.H.I.E.L.D., A.I.M., NAMELESS CABALS, SUPER-TEAMS AND ILLUMINATI.
THE GREATEST HEROES AND VILLAINS IN THE WORLD. ALSO WIDELY REGARDED AS THE SMARTEST AND MOST FORMIDABLE MINDS IN THE WORLD.
ALSO, SEVENTY-FIVE TO NINETY PERCENT MALE.
RECENTLY, A YOUNG GIRL NAMED LUNELLA LAFAYETTE WAS REVEALED TO BE THE SMARTEST PERSON IN THE WORLD.
IF SHE HADN'T PROVED IT ALL ON HER OWN, THEY NEVER WOULD HAVE KNOWN. BECAUSE THEY'RE NOT LOOKING FOR US.
EVEN NOW, THEY PUT LUNELLA AT THE TOP OF THE LIST, BUT THE REST OF THE LIST REMAINS THE SAME. THAT'S WHERE WE COME IN.
G.I.R.L. GENIUS IN ACTION RESEARCH LABS IS DEDICATED TO FINDING THE BRILLIANT GIRLS AND WOMEN WHO WILL NOT JUST SAVE THE WORLD, BUT CHANGE IT.
GENIUS IN ACTION
G.I.R.L.
NOT WEAPON MAKERS. NOT DICTATORS. NOT SPIES.
BRILLIANT, CREATIVE GIRLS WHO DREAM BIG.

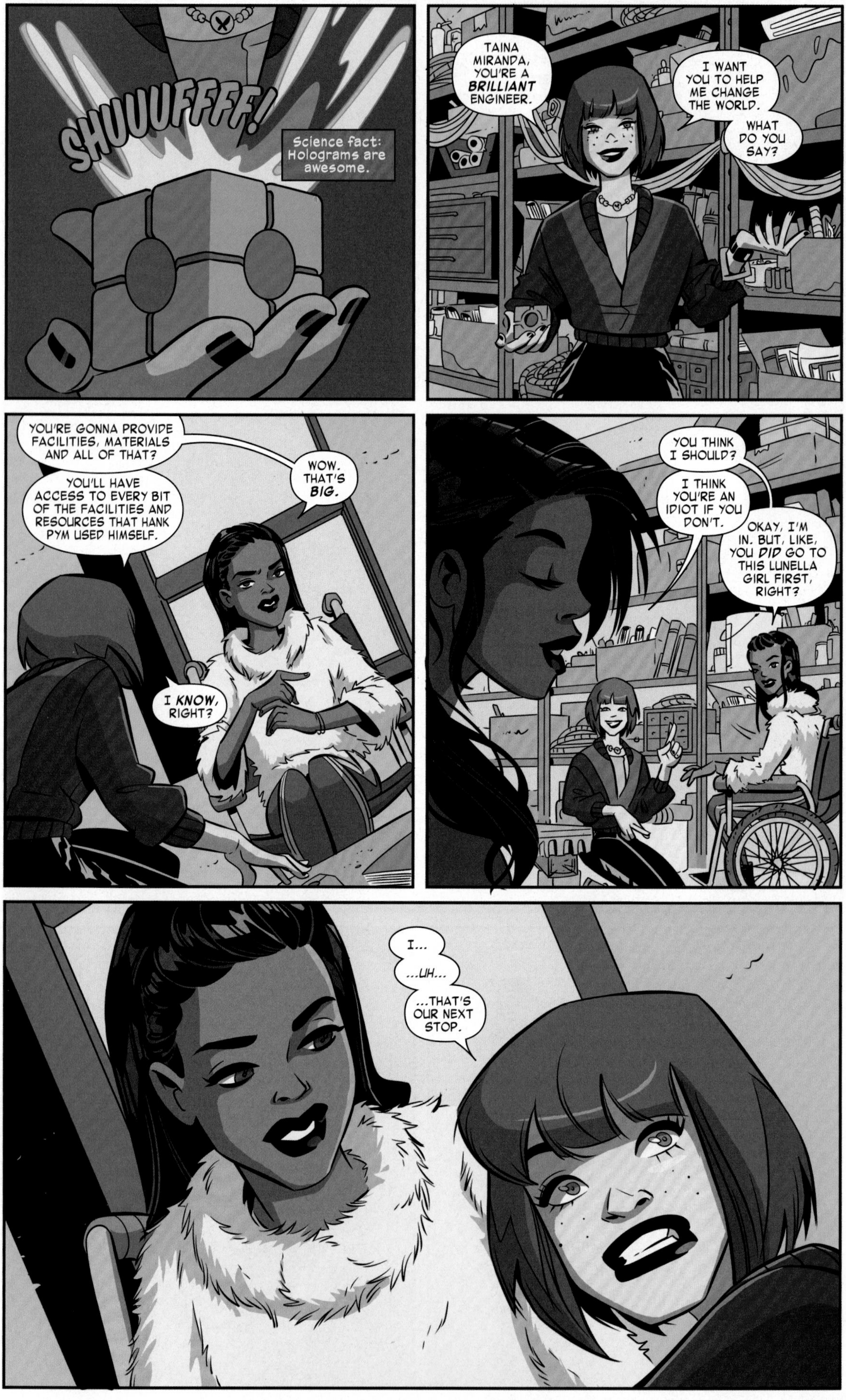
SHUUUFFFF!
Science fact: Holograms are awesome.
TAINA MIRANDA, YOU'RE A BRILLIANT ENGINEER.
I WANT YOU TO HELP ME CHANGE THE WORLD.
WHAT DO YOU SAY?
YOU'RE GONNA PROVIDE FACILITIES, MATERIALS AND ALL OF THAT?
YOU'LL HAVE ACCESS TO EVERY BIT OF THE FACILITIES AND RESOURCES THAT HANK PYM USED HIMSELF.
WOW. THAT'S BIG.
I KNOW, RIGHT?
YOU THINK I SHOULD?
I THINK YOU'RE AN IDIOT IF YOU DON'T.
OKAY, I'M IN. BUT, LIKE, YOU DID GO TO THIS LUNELLA GIRL FIRST, RIGHT?
I...
...UH...
...THAT'S OUR NEXT STOP.

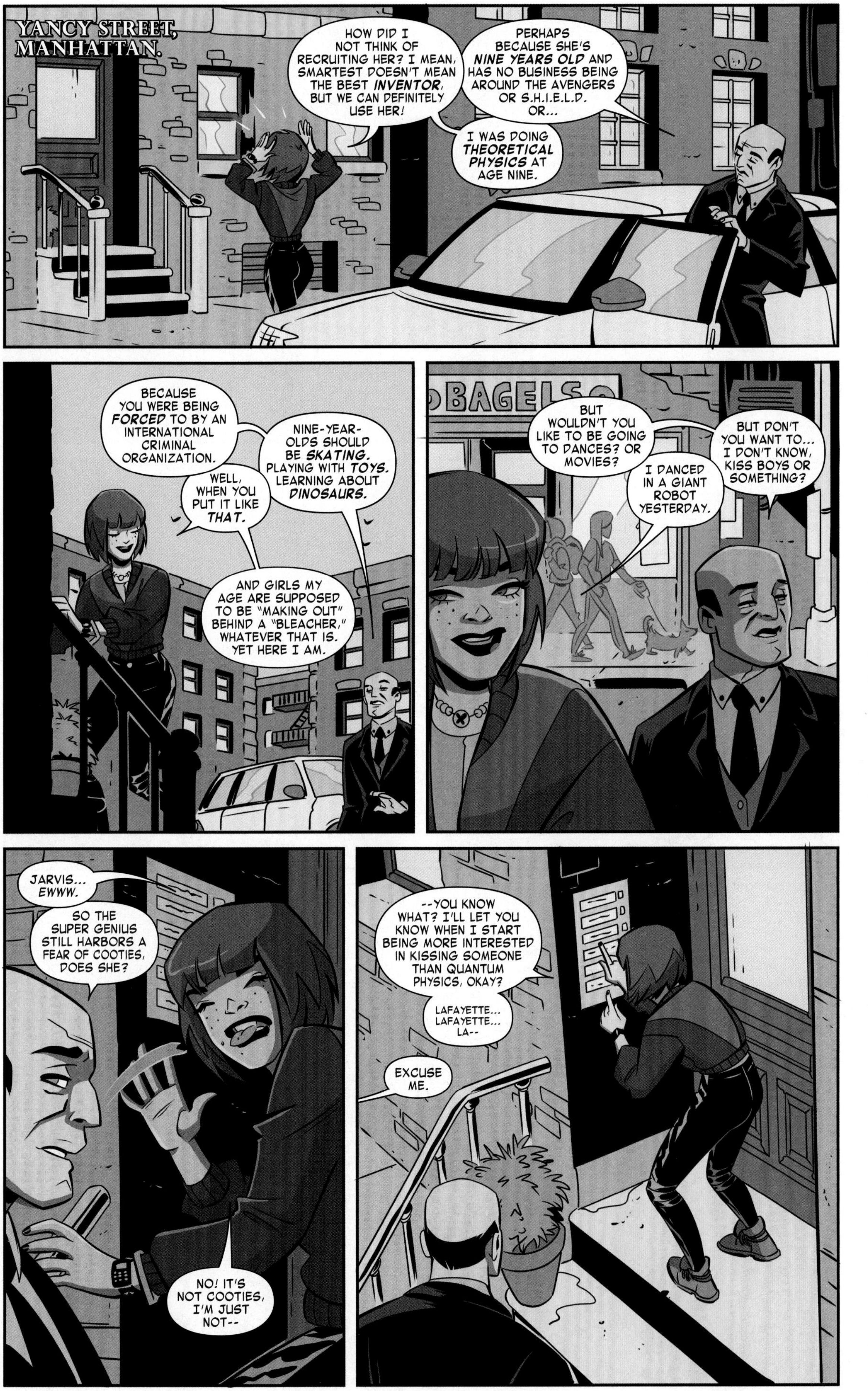

YANCY STREET, MANHATTAN.
HOW DID I NOT THINK OF RECRUITING HER? I MEAN, SMARTEST DOESN'T MEAN THE BEST INVENTOR, BUT WE CAN DEFINITELY USE HER!
PERHAPS BECAUSE SHE'S NINE YEARS OLD AND HAS NO BUSINESS BEING AROUND THE AVENGERS OR S.H.I.E.L.D. OR...
I WAS DOING THEORETICAL PHYSICS AT AGE NINE.
BECAUSE YOU WERE BEING FORCED TO BY AN INTERNATIONAL CRIMINAL ORGANIZATION.
NINE-YEAR-OLDS SHOULD BE SKATING. PLAYING WITH TOYS. LEARNING ABOUT DINOSAURS.
WELL, WHEN YOU PUT IT LIKE THAT.
AND GIRLS MY AGE ARE SUPPOSED TO BE "MAKING OUT" BEHIND A "BLEACHER," WHATEVER THAT IS. YET HERE I AM.
BAGELS
BUT WOULDN'T YOU LIKE TO BE GOING TO DANCES? OR MOVIES?
I DANCED IN A GIANT ROBOT YESTERDAY.
BUT DON'T YOU WANT TO... I DON'T KNOW, KISS BOYS OR SOMETHING?
JARVIS... EWWW.
SO THE SUPER GENIUS STILL HARBORS A FEAR OF COOTIES, DOES SHE?
NO! IT'S NOT COOTIES, I'M JUST NOT--
--YOU KNOW WHAT? I'LL LET YOU KNOW WHEN I START BEING MORE INTERESTED IN KISSING SOMEONE THAN QUANTUM PHYSICS, OKAY?
LAFAYETTE... LAFAYETTE... LA--
EXCUSE ME.

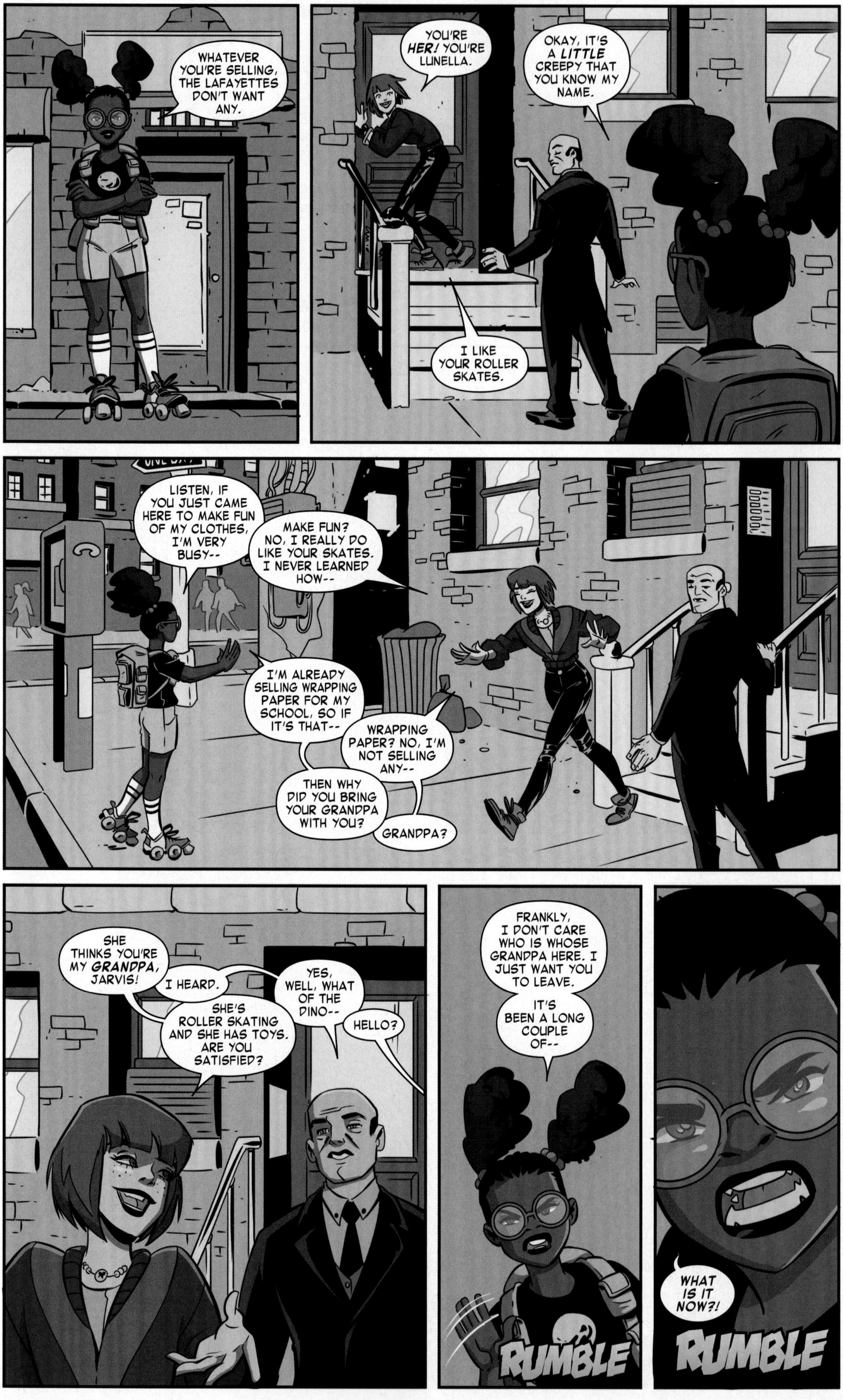
WHATEVER YOU'RE SELLING, THE LAFAYETTES DON'T WANT ANY.
YOU'RE HER! YOU'RE LUNELLA.
OKAY, IT'S A LITTLE CREEPY THAT YOU KNOW MY NAME.
I LIKE YOUR ROLLER SKATES.
LISTEN, IF YOU JUST CAME HERE TO MAKE FUN OF MY CLOTHES, I'M VERY BUSY--
MAKE FUN? NO, I REALLY DO LIKE YOUR SKATES. I NEVER LEARNED HOW--
I'M ALREADY SELLING WRAPPING PAPER FOR MY SCHOOL, SO IF IT'S THAT--
WRAPPING PAPER? NO, I'M NOT SELLING ANY--
THEN WHY DID YOU BRING YOUR GRANDPA WITH YOU?
GRANDPA?
SHE THINKS YOU'RE MY GRANDPA, JARVIS!
I HEARD.
SHE'S ROLLER SKATING AND SHE HAS TOYS. ARE YOU SATISFIED?
YES, WELL, WHAT OF THE DINO--
HELLO?
FRANKLY, I DON'T CARE WHO IS WHOSE GRANDPA HERE. I JUST WANT YOU TO LEAVE.
IT'S BEEN A LONG COUPLE OF--
RUMBLE
WHAT IS IT NOW?!
RUMBLE

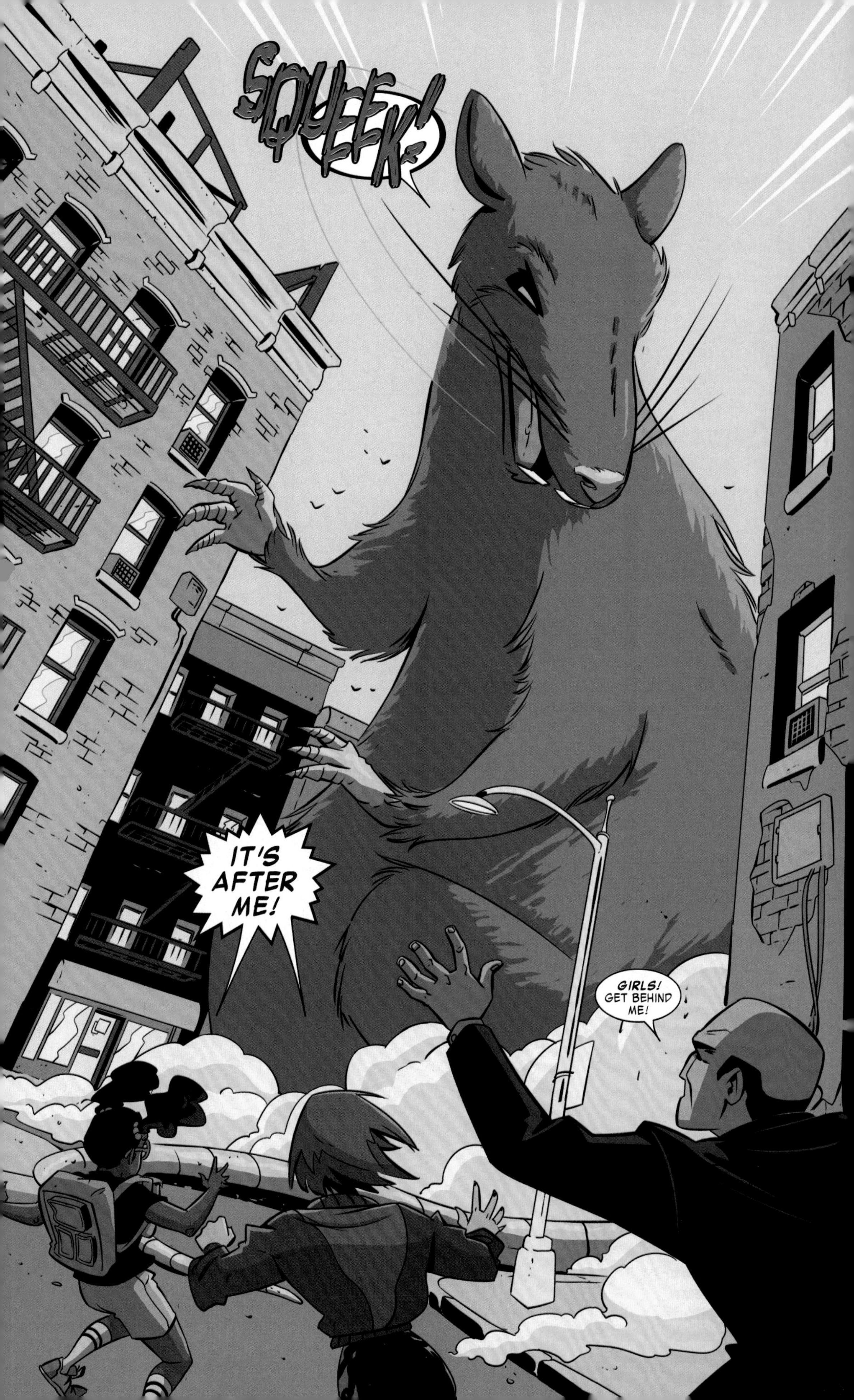
SQUEEK!
IT'S AFTER ME!
GIRLS! GET BEHIND ME!

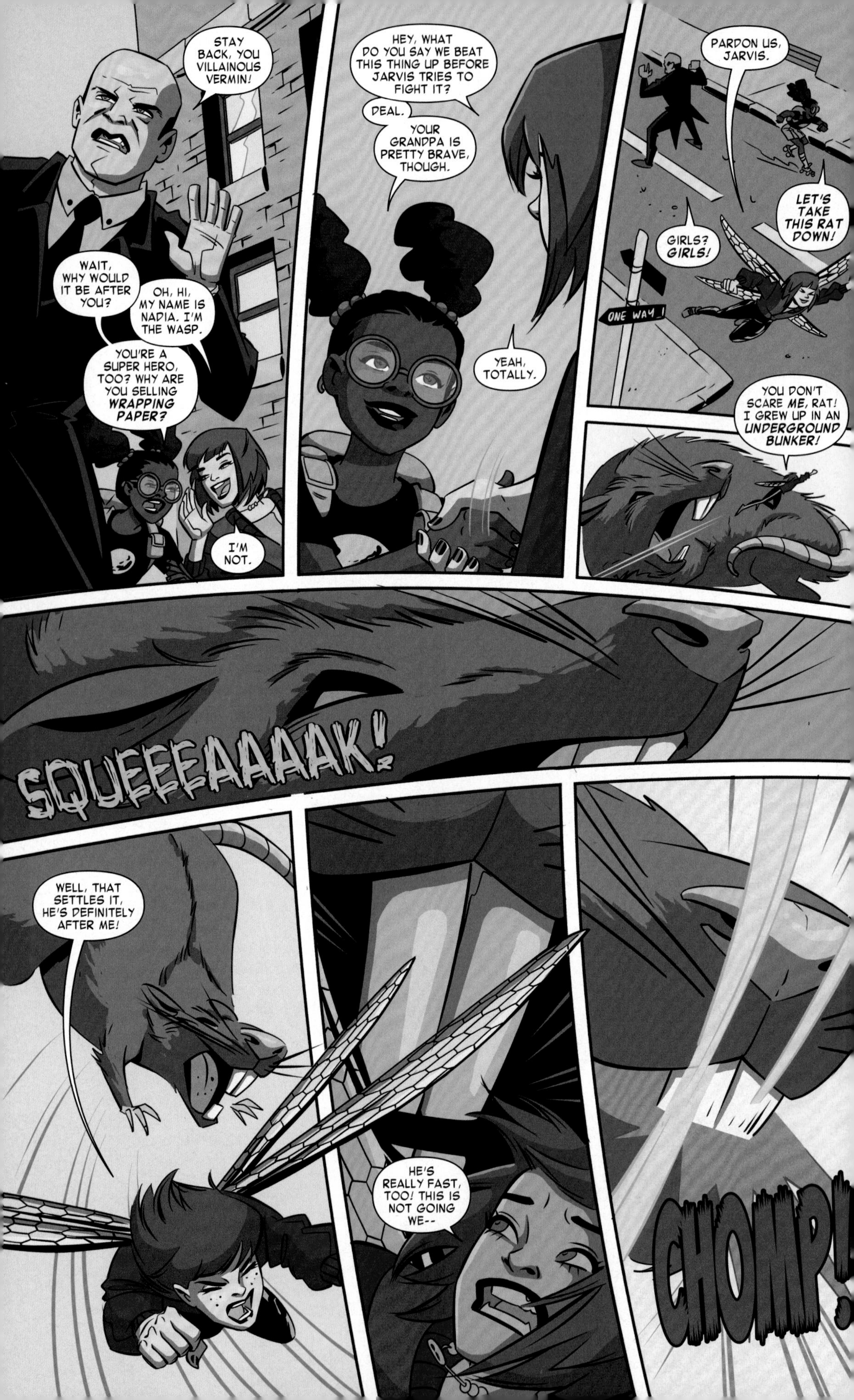
STAY BACK, YOU VILLAINOUS VERMIN!
WAIT, WHY WOULD IT BE AFTER YOU?
OH, HI, MY NAME IS NADIA. I'M THE WASP.
YOU'RE A SUPER HERO, TOO? WHY ARE YOU SELLING WRAPPING PAPER?
I'M NOT.
HEY, WHAT DO YOU SAY WE BEAT THIS THING UP BEFORE JARVIS TRIES TO FIGHT IT?
DEAL.
YOUR GRANDPA IS PRETTY BRAVE, THOUGH.
YEAH, TOTALLY.
PARDON US, JARVIS.
GIRLS? GIRLS!
LET'S TAKE THIS RAT DOWN!
ONE WAY
YOU DON'T SCARE ME, RAT! I GREW UP IN AN UNDERGROUND BUNKER!
SQUEEEAAAAK!
WELL, THAT SETTLES IT, HE'S DEFINITELY AFTER ME!
HE'S REALLY FAST, TOO! THIS IS NOT GOING WE--
CHOMP!

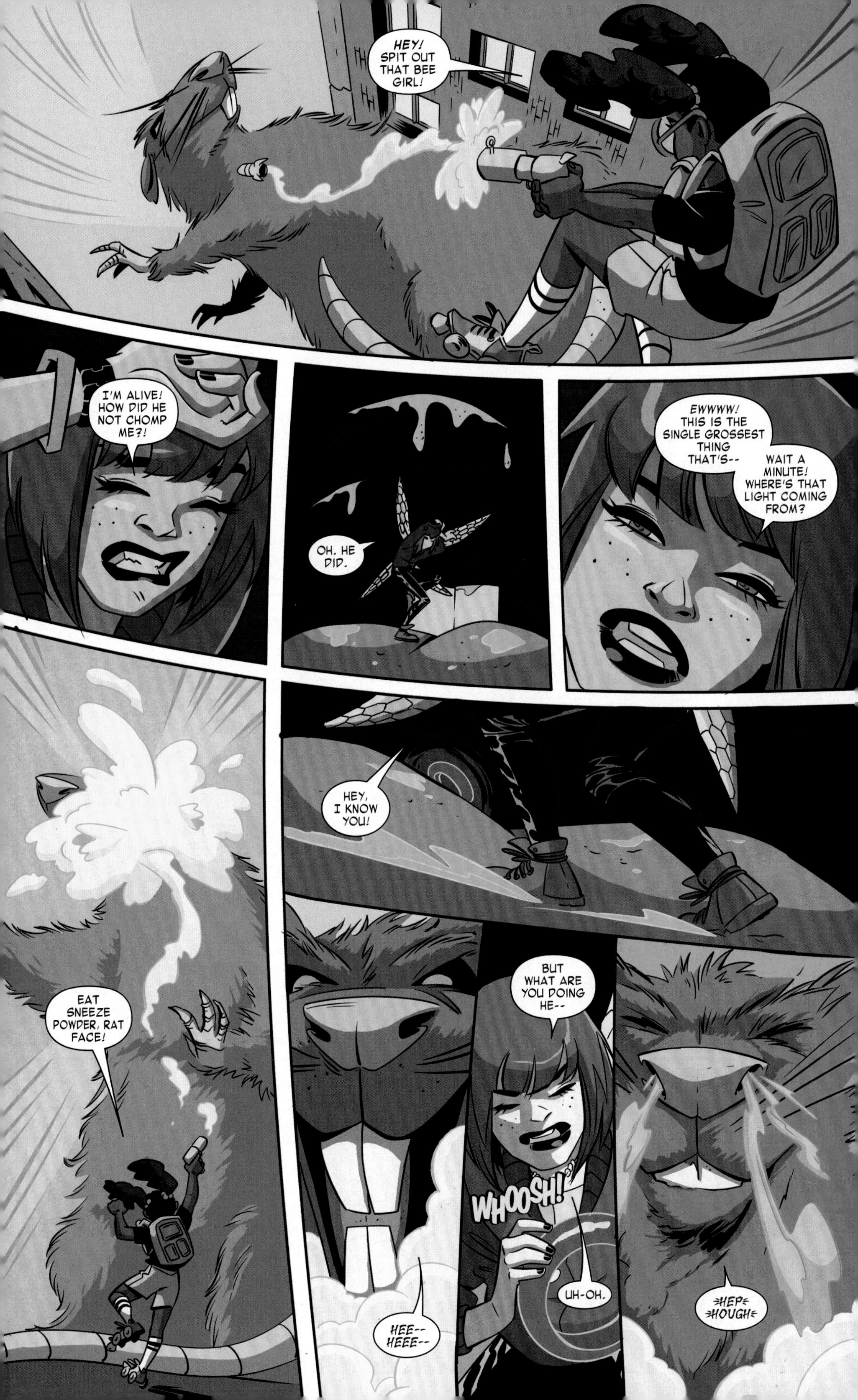

HEY! SPIT OUT THAT BEE GIRL!
I'M ALIVE! HOW DID HE NOT CHOMP ME?!
OH. HE DID.
EWWWW! THIS IS THE SINGLE GROSSEST THING THAT'S--
WAIT A MINUTE! WHERE'S THAT LIGHT COMING FROM?
EAT SNEEZE POWDER, RAT FACE!
HEY, I KNOW YOU!
BUT WHAT ARE YOU DOING HE--
WHOOSH!
HEE-- HEEE--
UH-OH.
HEP HOUGH

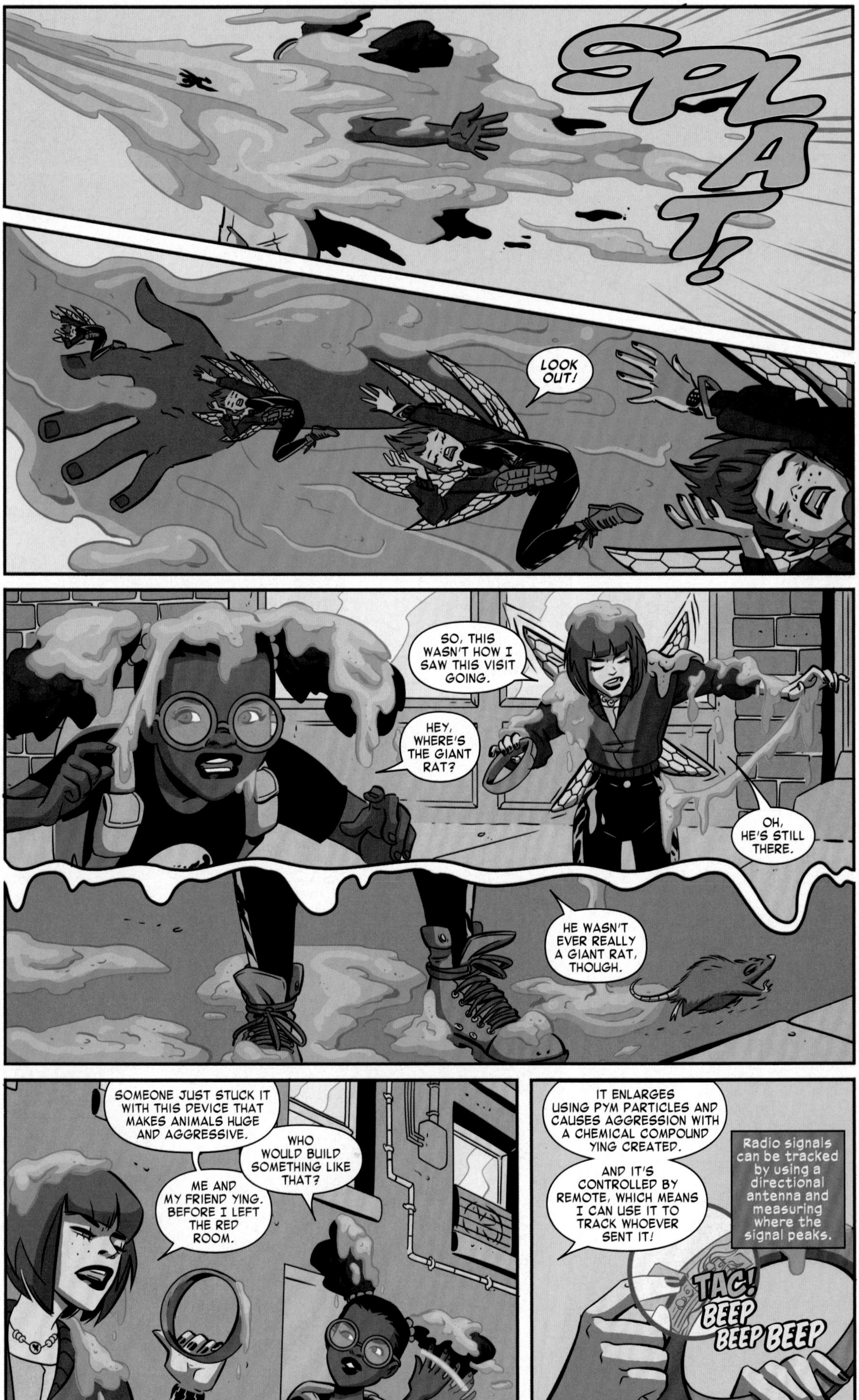
SPLAT!
LOOK OUT!
SO, THIS WASN'T HOW I SAW THIS VISIT GOING.
HEY, WHERE'S THE GIANT RAT?
OH, HE'S STILL THERE.
HE WASN'T EVER REALLY A GIANT RAT, THOUGH.
SOMEONE JUST STUCK IT WITH THIS DEVICE THAT MAKES ANIMALS HUGE AND AGGRESSIVE.
WHO WOULD BUILD SOMETHING LIKE THAT?
ME AND MY FRIEND YING. BEFORE I LEFT THE RED ROOM.
IT ENLARGES USING PYM PARTICLES AND CAUSES AGGRESSION WITH A CHEMICAL COMPOUND YING CREATED.
AND IT'S CONTROLLED BY REMOTE, WHICH MEANS I CAN USE IT TO TRACK WHOEVER SENT IT!
Radio signals can be tracked by using a directional antenna and measuring where the signal peaks.
TAC!
BEEP
BEEP BEEP

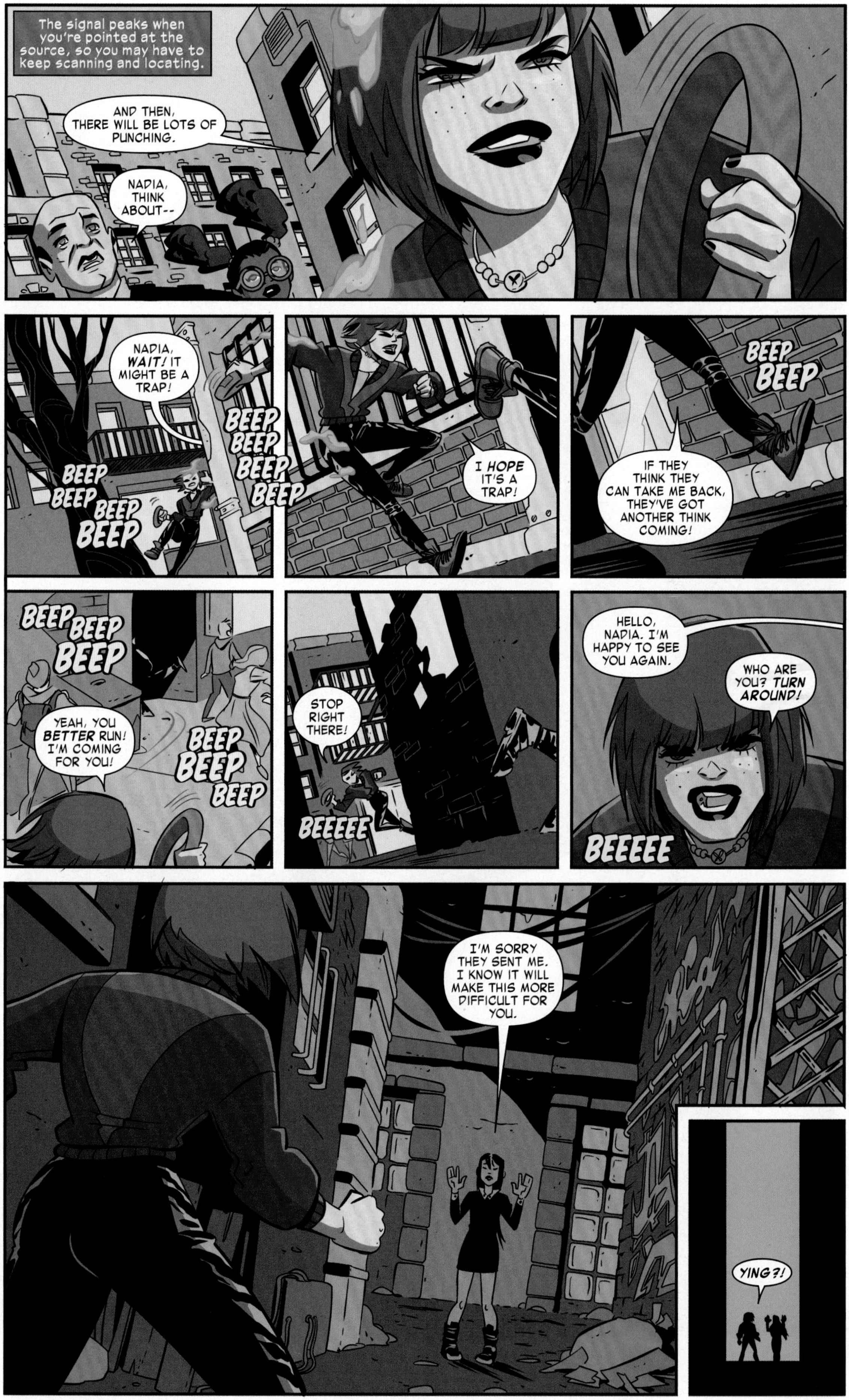
The signal peaks when you're pointed at the source, so you may have to keep scanning and locating.
AND THEN, THERE WILL BE LOTS OF PUNCHING.
NADIA, THINK ABOUT--
NADIA, WAIT! IT MIGHT BE A TRAP!
BEEP BEEP BEEP BEEP
BEEP BEEP BEEP BEEP
I HOPE IT'S A TRAP!
BEEP BEEP
IF THEY THINK THEY CAN TAKE ME BACK, THEY'VE GOT ANOTHER THINK COMING!
BEEP BEEP BEEP
YEAH, YOU BETTER RUN! I'M COMING FOR YOU!
BEEP BEEP BEEP
STOP RIGHT THERE!
BEEEEE
HELLO, NADIA. I'M HAPPY TO SEE YOU AGAIN.
WHO ARE YOU? TURN AROUND!
BEEEEE
I'M SORRY THEY SENT ME. I KNOW IT WILL MAKE THIS MORE DIFFICULT FOR YOU.
YING?!

3

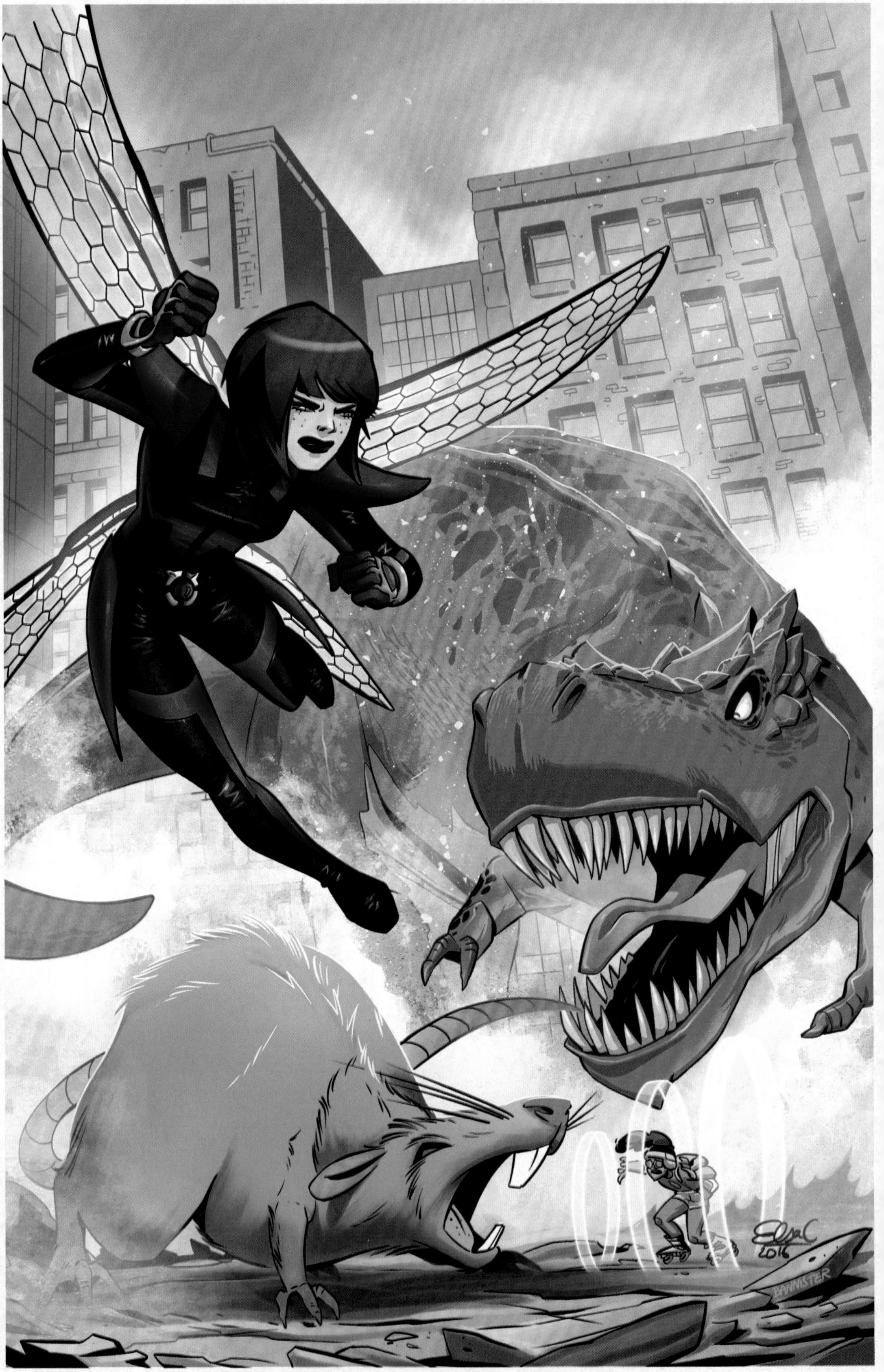

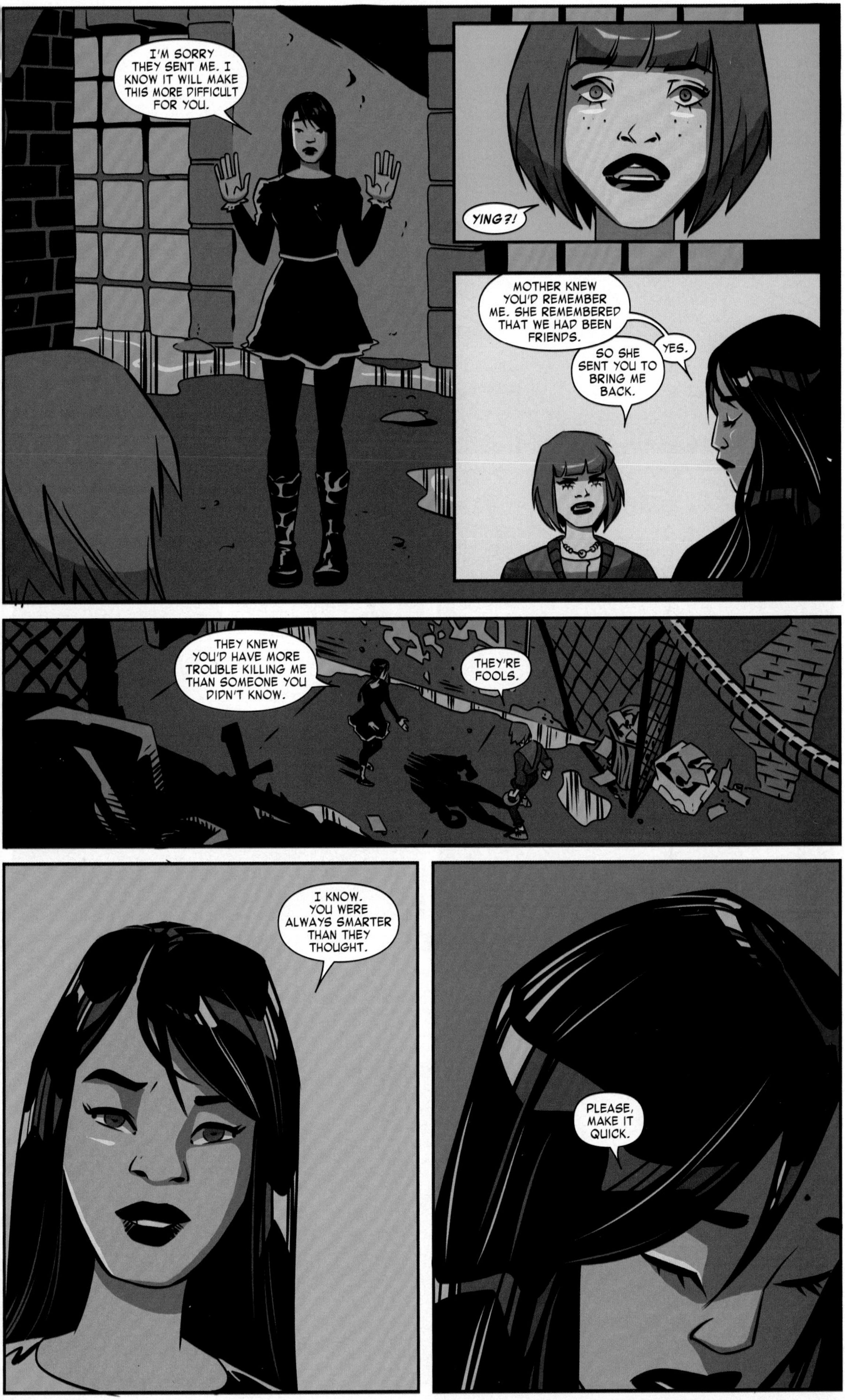
I'M SORRY THEY SENT ME. I KNOW IT WILL MAKE THIS MORE DIFFICULT FOR YOU.
YING?!
MOTHER KNEW YOU'D REMEMBER ME. SHE REMEMBERED THAT WE HAD BEEN FRIENDS.
SO SHE SENT YOU TO BRING ME BACK.
YES.
THEY KNEW YOU'D HAVE MORE TROUBLE KILLING ME THAN SOMEONE YOU DIDN'T KNOW.
THEY'RE FOOLS.
I KNOW. YOU WERE ALWAYS SMARTER THAN THEY THOUGHT.
PLEASE, MAKE IT QUICK.

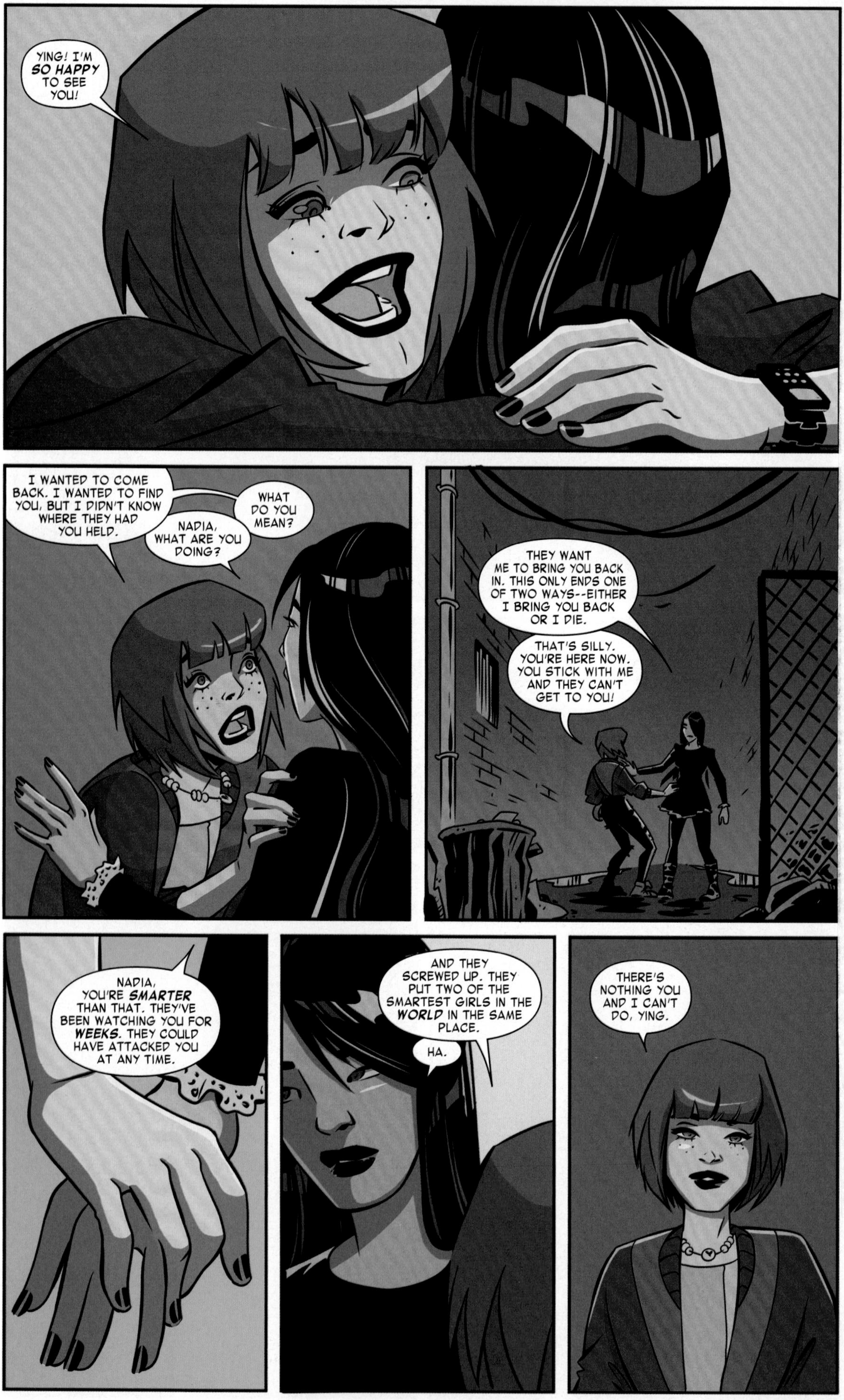
YING! I'M SO HAPPY TO SEE YOU!
I WANTED TO COME BACK. I WANTED TO FIND YOU, BUT I DIDN'T KNOW WHERE THEY HAD YOU HELD.
WHAT DO YOU MEAN?
NADIA, WHAT ARE YOU DOING?
THEY WANT ME TO BRING YOU BACK IN. THIS ONLY ENDS ONE OF TWO WAYS--EITHER I BRING YOU BACK OR I DIE.
THAT'S SILLY. YOU'RE HERE NOW. YOU STICK WITH ME AND THEY CAN'T GET TO YOU!
NADIA, YOU'RE SMARTER THAN THAT. THEY'VE BEEN WATCHING YOU FOR WEEKS. THEY COULD HAVE ATTACKED YOU AT ANY TIME.
AND THEY SCREWED UP. THEY PUT TWO OF THE SMARTEST GIRLS IN THE WORLD IN THE SAME PLACE.
HA.
THERE'S NOTHING YOU AND I CAN'T DO, YING.

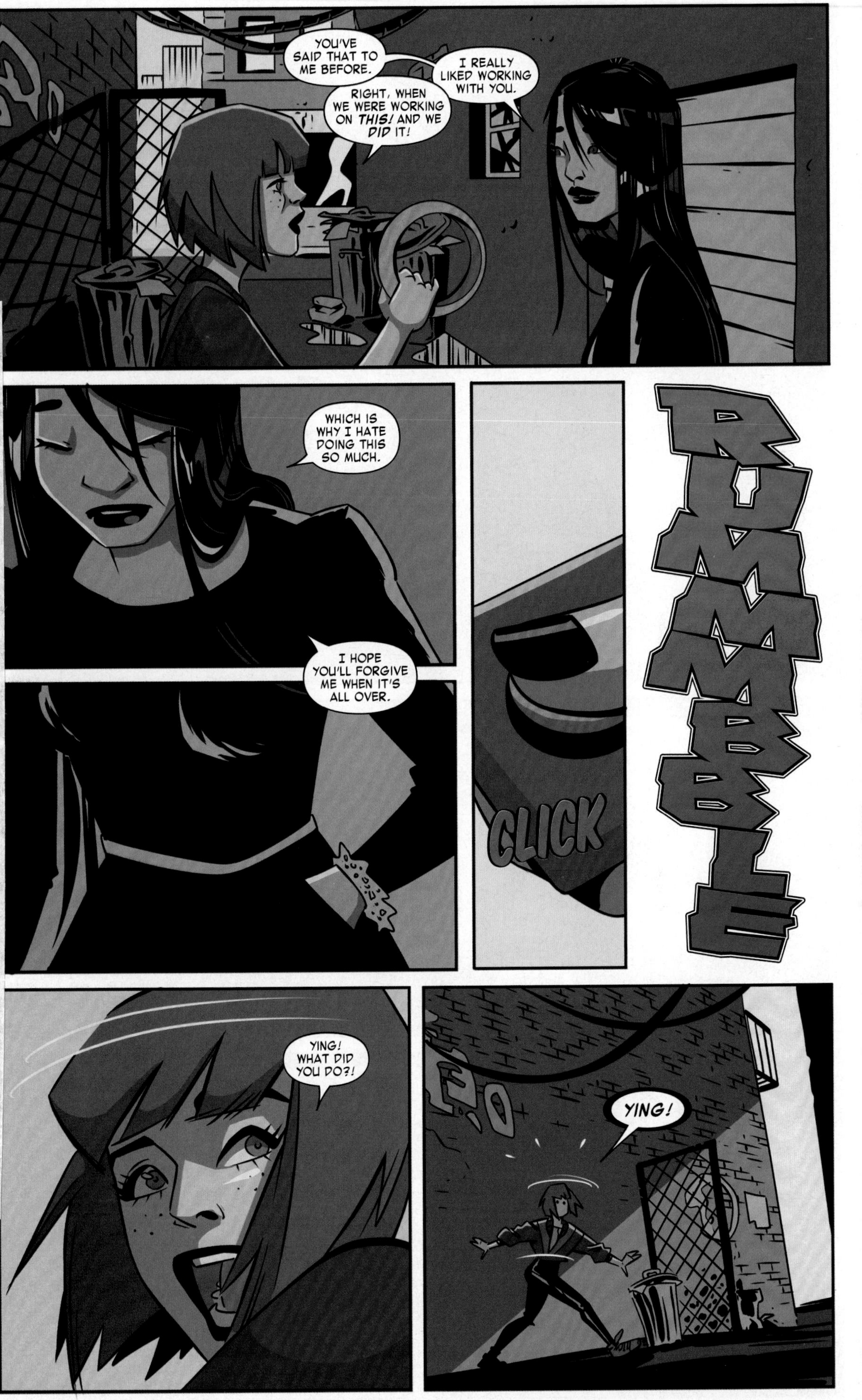
YOU'VE SAID THAT TO ME BEFORE.
I REALLY LIKED WORKING WITH YOU.
RIGHT, WHEN WE WERE WORKING ON *THIS!* AND WE *DID* IT!
WHICH IS WHY I HATE DOING THIS SO MUCH.
I HOPE YOU'LL FORGIVE ME WHEN IT'S ALL OVER.
CLICK
RUMMMBBLE
YING! WHAT DID YOU DO?!
YING!

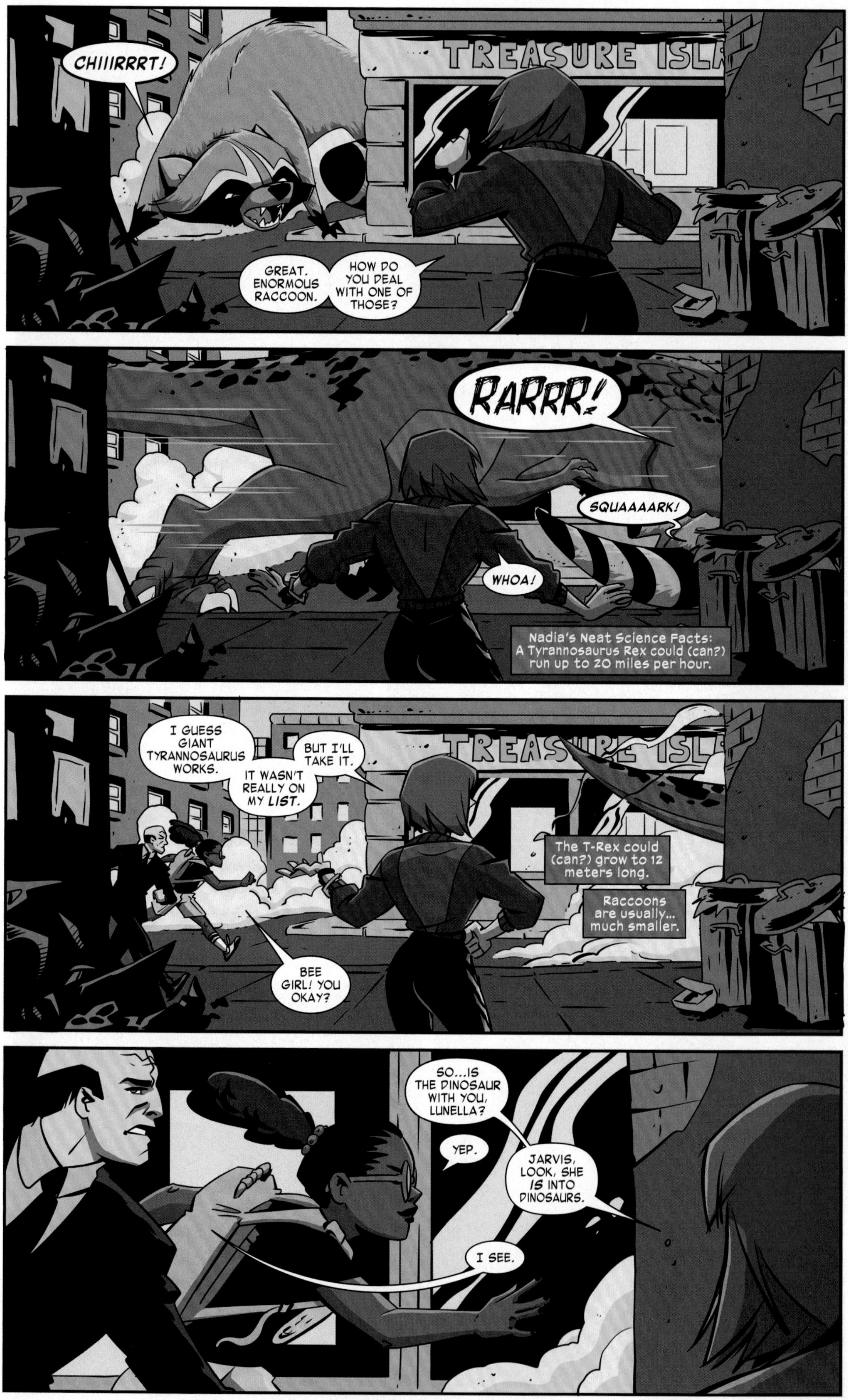
CHIIIRRRT!
TREASURE ISLA
GREAT. ENORMOUS RACCOON.
HOW DO YOU DEAL WITH ONE OF THOSE?
RARRR!
SQUAAAARK!
WHOA!
Nadia's Neat Science Facts: A Tyrannosaurus Rex could (can?) run up to 20 miles per hour.
I GUESS GIANT TYRANNOSAURUS WORKS.
IT WASN'T REALLY ON MY LIST.
BUT I'LL TAKE IT.
The T-Rex could (can?) grow to 12 meters long.
Raccoons are usually... much smaller.
BEE GIRL! YOU OKAY?
SO...IS THE DINOSAUR WITH YOU, LUNELLA?
YEP.
JARVIS, LOOK, SHE IS INTO DINOSAURS.
I SEE.

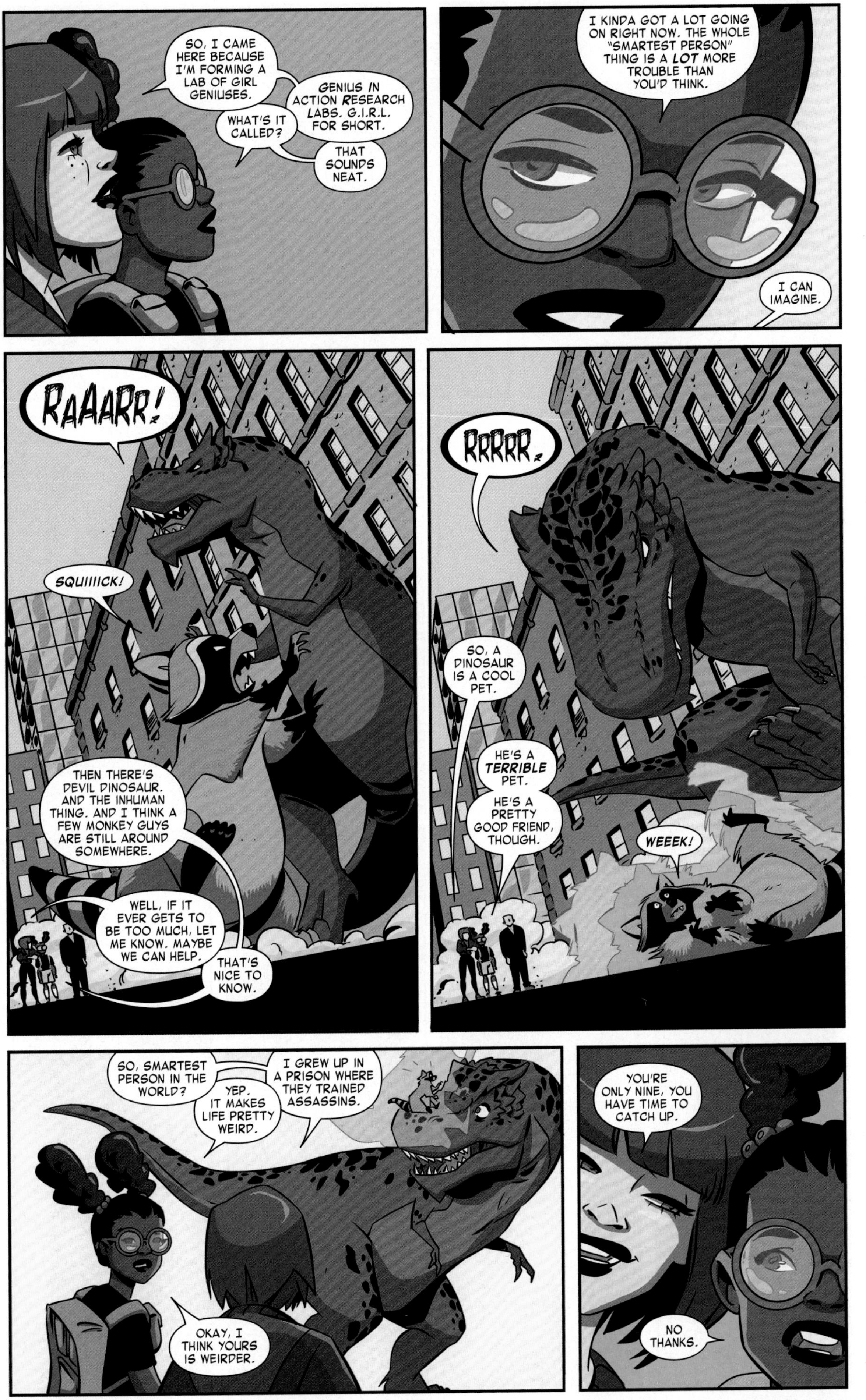
SO, I CAME HERE BECAUSE I'M FORMING A LAB OF GIRL GENIUSES.
WHAT'S IT CALLED?
GENIUS IN ACTION RESEARCH LABS. G.I.R.L. FOR SHORT.
THAT SOUNDS NEAT.
I KINDA GOT A LOT GOING ON RIGHT NOW. THE WHOLE "SMARTEST PERSON" THING IS A LOT MORE TROUBLE THAN YOU'D THINK.
I CAN IMAGINE.
RAAARR!
SQUIIIICK!
THEN THERE'S DEVIL DINOSAUR. AND THE INHUMAN THING. AND I THINK A FEW MONKEY GUYS ARE STILL AROUND SOMEWHERE.
WELL, IF IT EVER GETS TO BE TOO MUCH, LET ME KNOW. MAYBE WE CAN HELP.
THAT'S NICE TO KNOW.
RRRRR.
SO, A DINOSAUR IS A COOL PET.
HE'S A TERRIBLE PET.
HE'S A PRETTY GOOD FRIEND, THOUGH.
WEEEK!
SO, SMARTEST PERSON IN THE WORLD?
YEP. IT MAKES LIFE PRETTY WEIRD.
I GREW UP IN A PRISON WHERE THEY TRAINED ASSASSINS.
OKAY, I THINK YOURS IS WEIRDER.
YOU'RE ONLY NINE, YOU HAVE TIME TO CATCH UP.
NO THANKS.

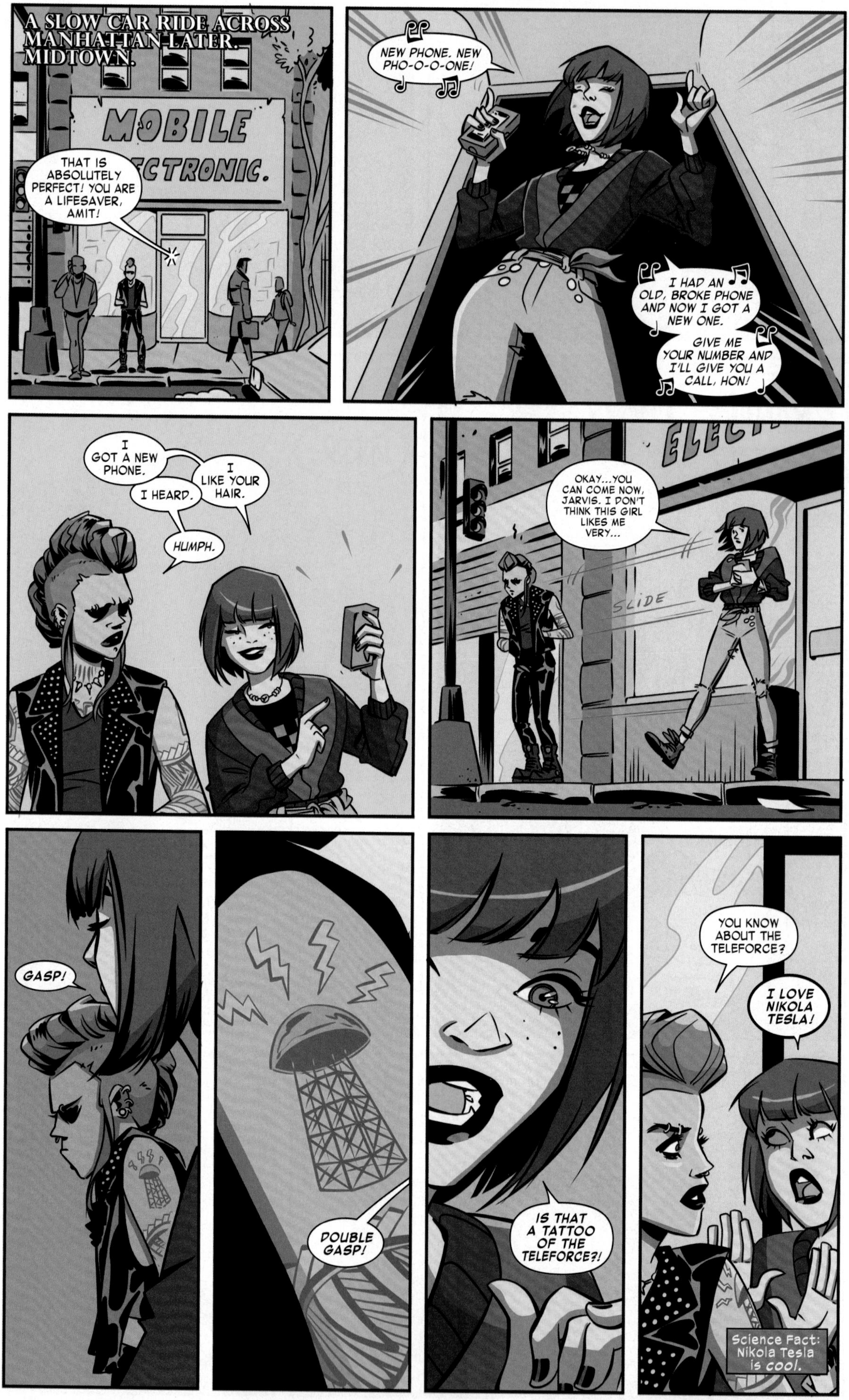

A SLOW CAR RIDE ACROSS MANHATTAN LATER. MIDTOWN.
MOBILE ...CTRONIC.
THAT IS ABSOLUTELY PERFECT! YOU ARE A LIFESAVER, AMIT!
NEW PHONE. NEW PHO-O-O-ONE!
I HAD AN OLD, BROKE PHONE AND NOW I GOT A NEW ONE.
GIVE ME YOUR NUMBER AND I'LL GIVE YOU A CALL, HON!
I GOT A NEW PHONE.
I HEARD.
I LIKE YOUR HAIR.
HUMPH.
ELEC...
OKAY...YOU CAN COME NOW, JARVIS. I DON'T THINK THIS GIRL LIKES ME VERY...
SLIDE
GASP!
DOUBLE GASP!
IS THAT A TATTOO OF THE TELEFORCE?!
YOU KNOW ABOUT THE TELEFORCE?
I LOVE NIKOLA TESLA!
Science Fact: Nikola Tesla is cool.

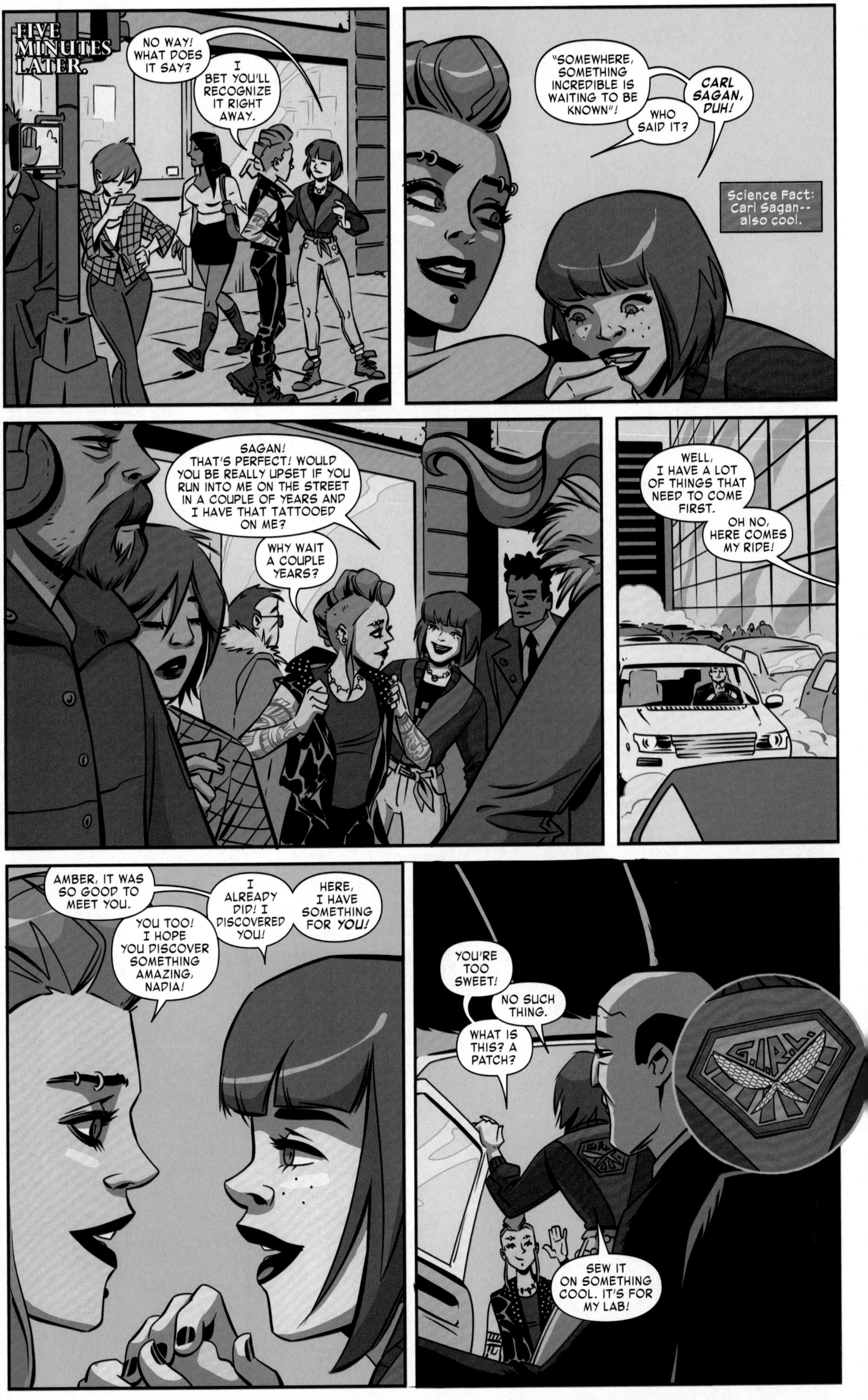
FIVE MINUTES LATER.
NO WAY! WHAT DOES IT SAY?
I BET YOU'LL RECOGNIZE IT RIGHT AWAY.
"SOMEWHERE, SOMETHING INCREDIBLE IS WAITING TO BE KNOWN"!
WHO SAID IT?
CARL SAGAN, DUH!
Science Fact: Carl Sagan-- also cool.
SAGAN! THAT'S PERFECT! WOULD YOU BE REALLY UPSET IF YOU RUN INTO ME ON THE STREET IN A COUPLE OF YEARS AND I HAVE THAT TATTOOED ON ME?
WHY WAIT A COUPLE YEARS?
WELL, I HAVE A LOT OF THINGS THAT NEED TO COME FIRST.
OH NO, HERE COMES MY RIDE!
AMBER, IT WAS SO GOOD TO MEET YOU.
YOU TOO! I HOPE YOU DISCOVER SOMETHING AMAZING, NADIA!
I ALREADY DID! I DISCOVERED YOU!
HERE, I HAVE SOMETHING FOR YOU!
YOU'RE TOO SWEET!
NO SUCH THING.
WHAT IS THIS? A PATCH?
SEW IT ON SOMETHING COOL. IT'S FOR MY LAB!

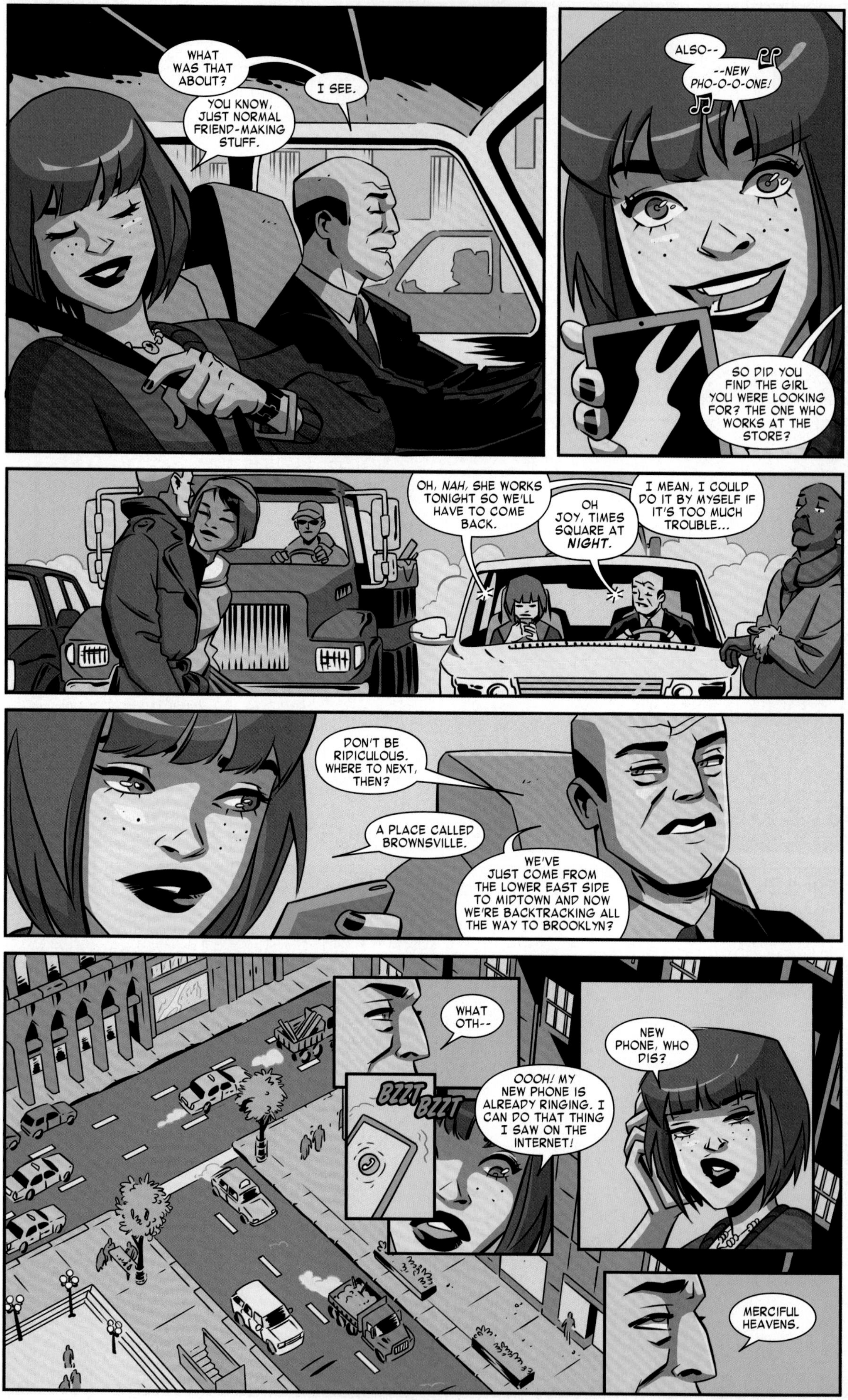
WHAT WAS THAT ABOUT?
YOU KNOW, JUST NORMAL FRIEND-MAKING STUFF.
I SEE.
ALSO--
--NEW PHO-O-O-ONE!
SO DID YOU FIND THE GIRL YOU WERE LOOKING FOR? THE ONE WHO WORKS AT THE STORE?
OH, NAH, SHE WORKS TONIGHT SO WE'LL HAVE TO COME BACK.
OH JOY, TIMES SQUARE AT NIGHT.
I MEAN, I COULD DO IT BY MYSELF IF IT'S TOO MUCH TROUBLE...
DON'T BE RIDICULOUS. WHERE TO NEXT, THEN?
A PLACE CALLED BROWNSVILLE.
WE'VE JUST COME FROM THE LOWER EAST SIDE TO MIDTOWN AND NOW WE'RE BACKTRACKING ALL THE WAY TO BROOKLYN?
WHAT OTH--
BZZT BZZT
OOOH! MY NEW PHONE IS ALREADY RINGING. I CAN DO THAT THING I SAW ON THE INTERNET!
NEW PHONE, WHO DIS?
MERCIFUL HEAVENS.

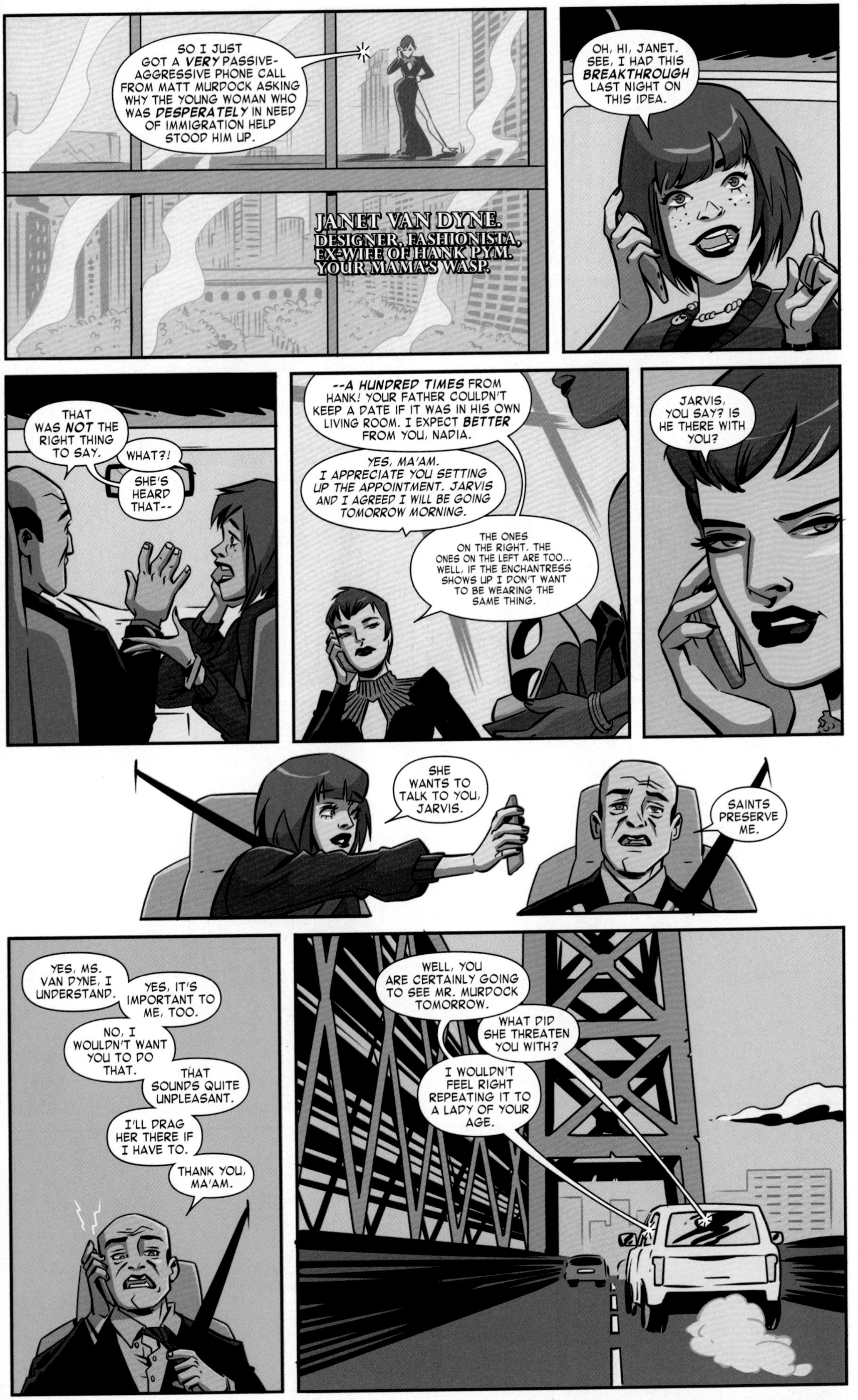
SO I JUST GOT A VERY PASSIVE-AGGRESSIVE PHONE CALL FROM MATT MURDOCK ASKING WHY THE YOUNG WOMAN WHO WAS DESPERATELY IN NEED OF IMMIGRATION HELP STOOD HIM UP.
JANET VAN DYNE. DESIGNER, FASHIONISTA, EX-WIFE OF HANK PYM. YOUR MAMA'S WASP.
OH, HI, JANET. SEE, I HAD THIS BREAKTHROUGH LAST NIGHT ON THIS IDEA.
THAT WAS NOT THE RIGHT THING TO SAY.
WHAT?!
SHE'S HEARD THAT--
--A HUNDRED TIMES FROM HANK! YOUR FATHER COULDN'T KEEP A DATE IF IT WAS IN HIS OWN LIVING ROOM. I EXPECT BETTER FROM YOU, NADIA.
YES, MA'AM. I APPRECIATE YOU SETTING UP THE APPOINTMENT. JARVIS AND I AGREED I WILL BE GOING TOMORROW MORNING.
THE ONES ON THE RIGHT. THE ONES ON THE LEFT ARE TOO... WELL, IF THE ENCHANTRESS SHOWS UP I DON'T WANT TO BE WEARING THE SAME THING.
JARVIS, YOU SAY? IS HE THERE WITH YOU?
SHE WANTS TO TALK TO YOU, JARVIS.
SAINTS PRESERVE ME.
YES, MS. VAN DYNE, I UNDERSTAND.
YES, IT'S IMPORTANT TO ME, TOO.
NO, I WOULDN'T WANT YOU TO DO THAT.
THAT SOUNDS QUITE UNPLEASANT.
I'LL DRAG HER THERE IF I HAVE TO.
THANK YOU, MA'AM.
WELL, YOU ARE CERTAINLY GOING TO SEE MR. MURDOCK TOMORROW.
WHAT DID SHE THREATEN YOU WITH?
I WOULDN'T FEEL RIGHT REPEATING IT TO A LADY OF YOUR AGE.

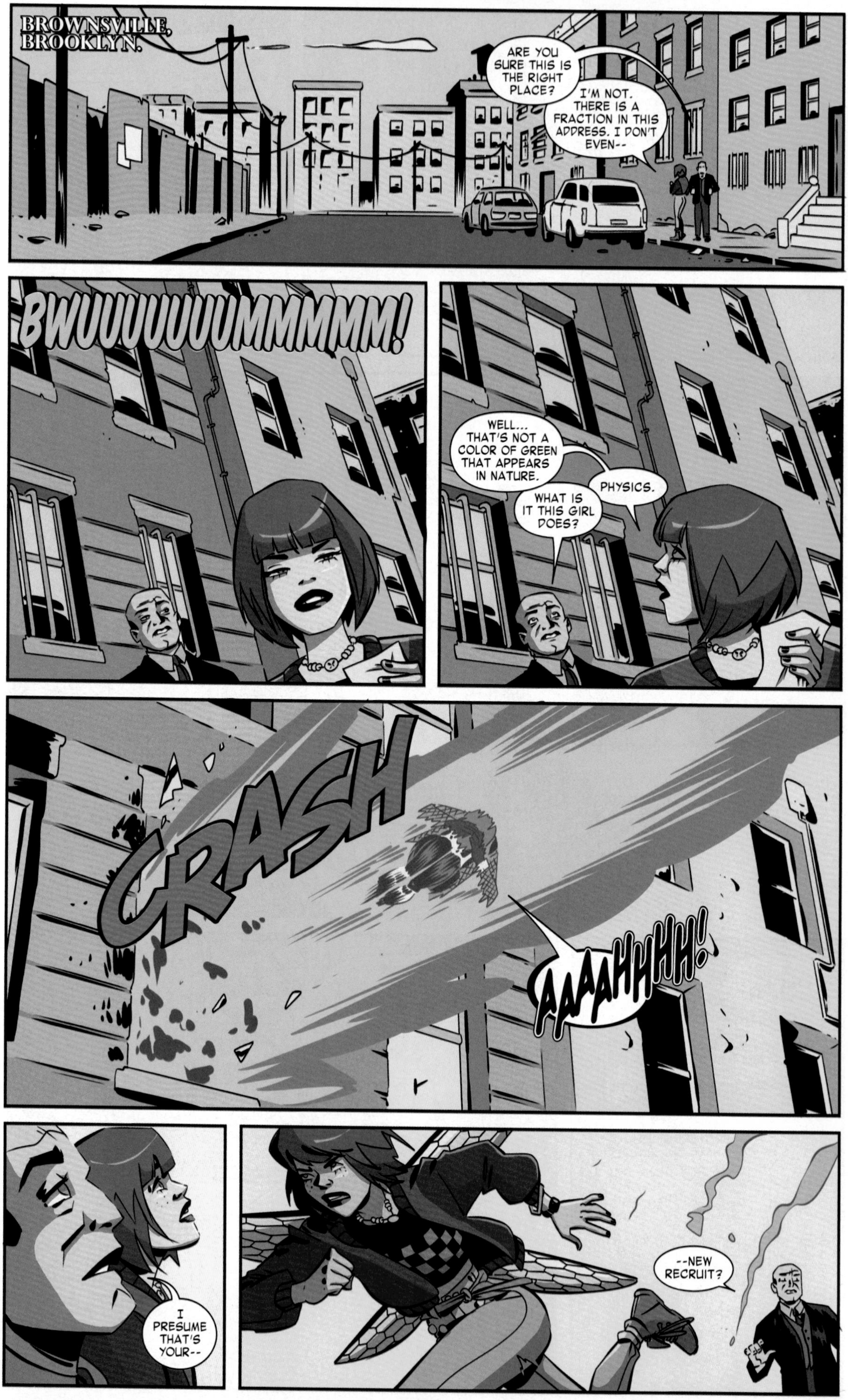
BROWNSVILLE, BROOKLYN.
ARE YOU SURE THIS IS THE RIGHT PLACE?
I'M NOT. THERE IS A FRACTION IN THIS ADDRESS. I DON'T EVEN--
BWUUUUUUUMMMMMM!
WELL... THAT'S NOT A COLOR OF GREEN THAT APPEARS IN NATURE.
PHYSICS.
WHAT IS IT THIS GIRL DOES?
CRASH
AAAAHHHH!
I PRESUME THAT'S YOUR--
--NEW RECRUIT?

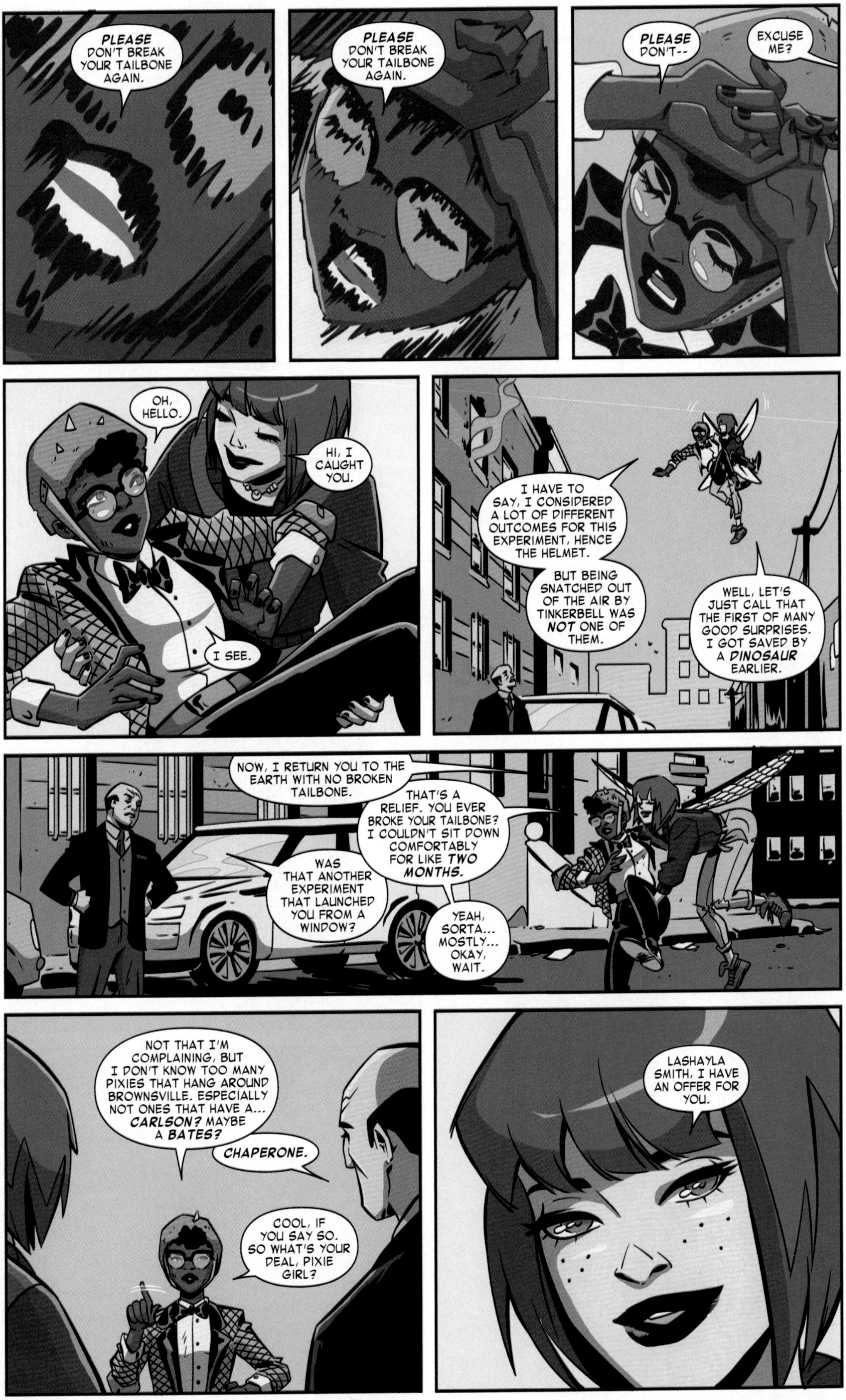
PLEASE DON'T BREAK YOUR TAILBONE AGAIN.
PLEASE DON'T BREAK YOUR TAILBONE AGAIN.
PLEASE DON'T--
EXCUSE ME?
OH, HELLO.
HI, I CAUGHT YOU.
I SEE.
I HAVE TO SAY, I CONSIDERED A LOT OF DIFFERENT OUTCOMES FOR THIS EXPERIMENT, HENCE THE HELMET.
BUT BEING SNATCHED OUT OF THE AIR BY TINKERBELL WAS NOT ONE OF THEM.
WELL, LET'S JUST CALL THAT THE FIRST OF MANY GOOD SURPRISES. I GOT SAVED BY A DINOSAUR EARLIER.
NOW, I RETURN YOU TO THE EARTH WITH NO BROKEN TAILBONE.
THAT'S A RELIEF. YOU EVER BROKE YOUR TAILBONE? I COULDN'T SIT DOWN COMFORTABLY FOR LIKE TWO MONTHS.
WAS THAT ANOTHER EXPERIMENT THAT LAUNCHED YOU FROM A WINDOW?
YEAH, SORTA... MOSTLY... OKAY, WAIT.
NOT THAT I'M COMPLAINING, BUT I DON'T KNOW TOO MANY PIXIES THAT HANG AROUND BROWNSVILLE. ESPECIALLY NOT ONES THAT HAVE A... CARLSON? MAYBE A BATES?
CHAPERONE.
COOL, IF YOU SAY SO. SO WHAT'S YOUR DEAL, PIXIE GIRL?
LASHAYLA SMITH, I HAVE AN OFFER FOR YOU.

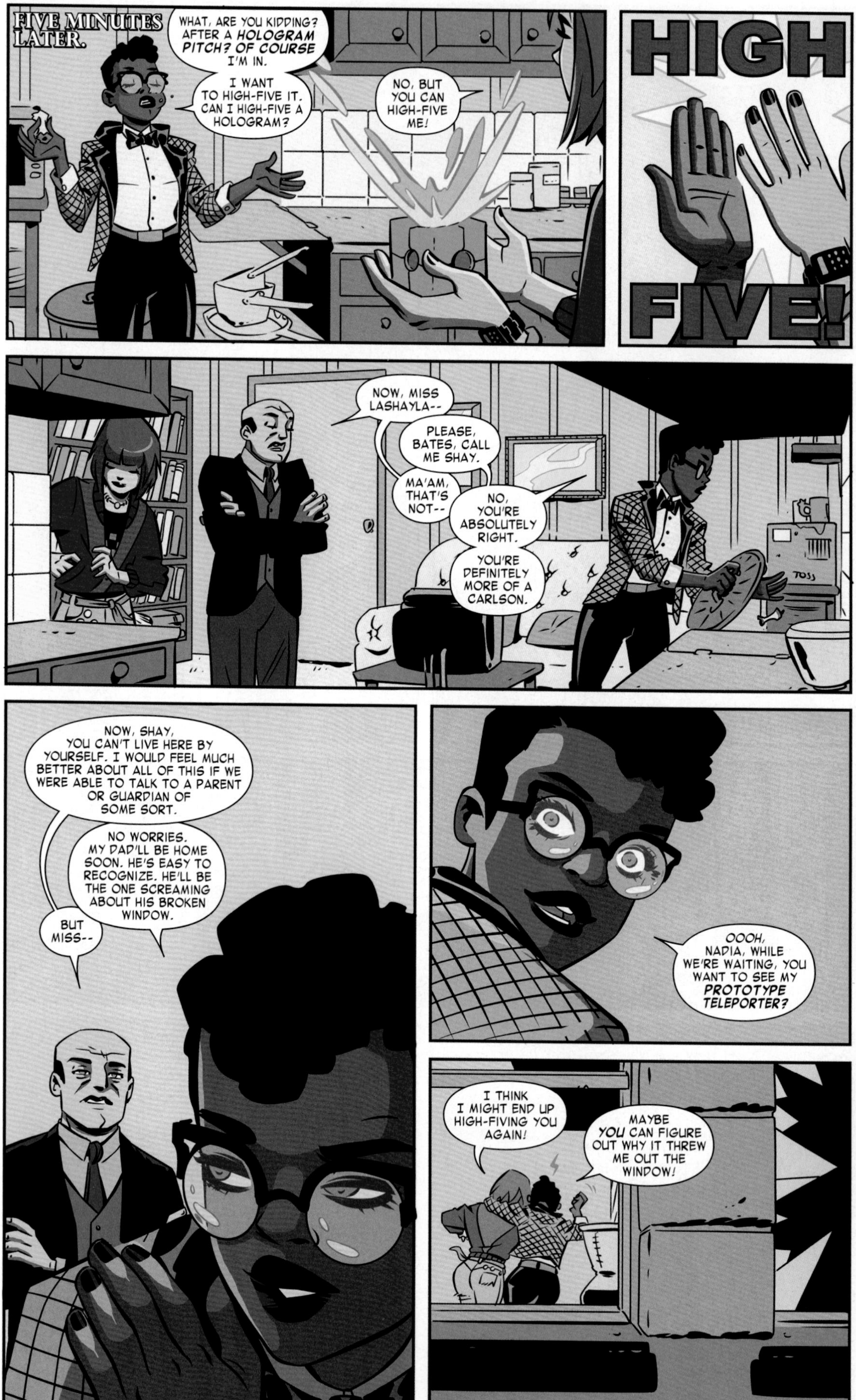

FIVE MINUTES LATER.
WHAT, ARE YOU KIDDING? AFTER A HOLOGRAM PITCH? OF COURSE I'M IN.
I WANT TO HIGH-FIVE IT. CAN I HIGH-FIVE A HOLOGRAM?
NO, BUT YOU CAN HIGH-FIVE ME!
HIGH FIVE!
NOW, MISS LASHAYLA--
PLEASE, BATES, CALL ME SHAY.
MA'AM, THAT'S NOT--
NO, YOU'RE ABSOLUTELY RIGHT.
YOU'RE DEFINITELY MORE OF A CARLSON.
NOW, SHAY, YOU CAN'T LIVE HERE BY YOURSELF. I WOULD FEEL MUCH BETTER ABOUT ALL OF THIS IF WE WERE ABLE TO TALK TO A PARENT OR GUARDIAN OF SOME SORT.
NO WORRIES. MY DAD'LL BE HOME SOON. HE'S EASY TO RECOGNIZE. HE'LL BE THE ONE SCREAMING ABOUT HIS BROKEN WINDOW.
BUT MISS--
OOOH, NADIA, WHILE WE'RE WAITING, YOU WANT TO SEE MY PROTOTYPE TELEPORTER?
I THINK I MIGHT END UP HIGH-FIVING YOU AGAIN!
MAYBE YOU CAN FIGURE OUT WHY IT THREW ME OUT THE WINDOW!

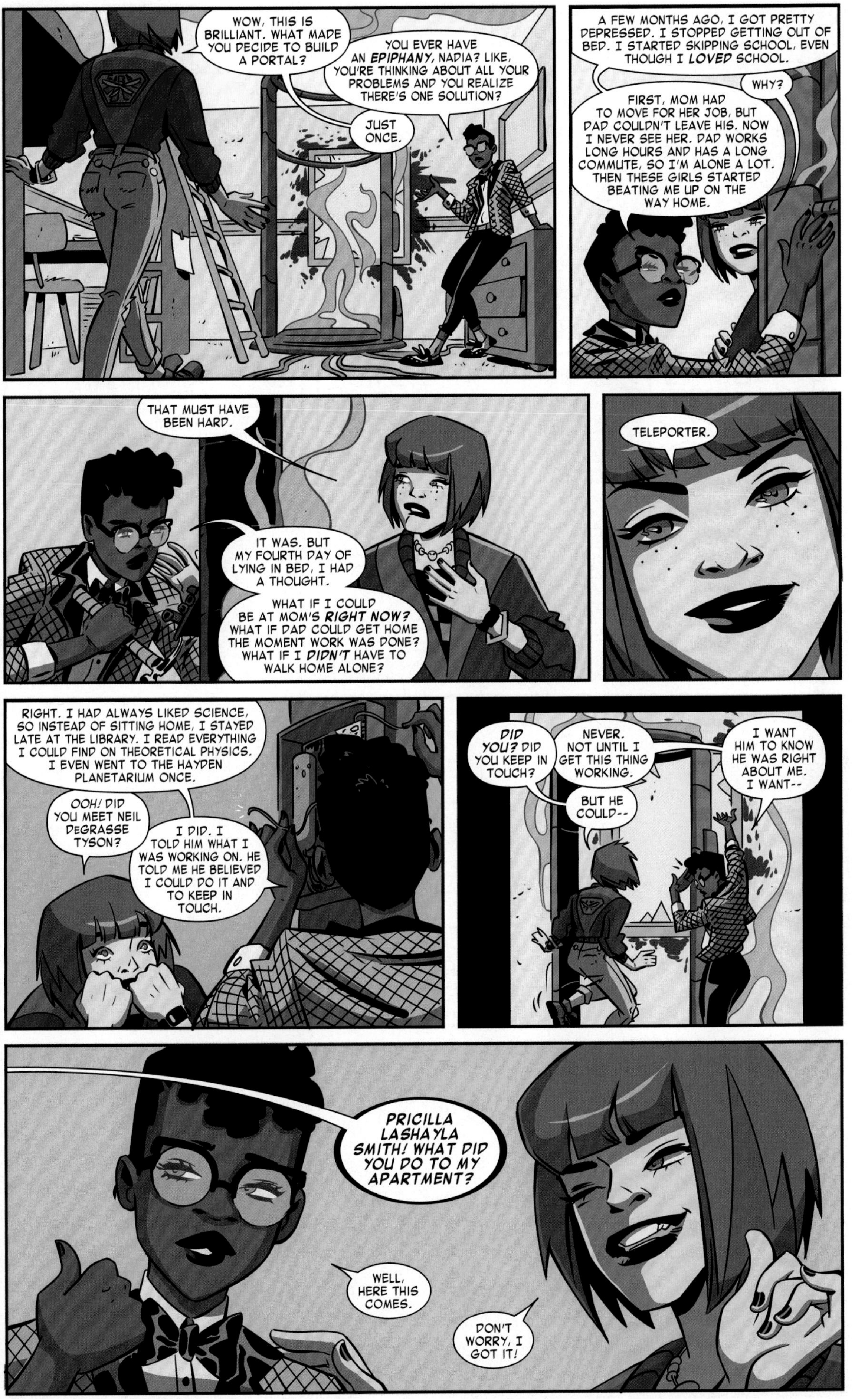
WOW, THIS IS BRILLIANT. WHAT MADE YOU DECIDE TO BUILD A PORTAL?
YOU EVER HAVE AN EPIPHANY, NADIA? LIKE, YOU'RE THINKING ABOUT ALL YOUR PROBLEMS AND YOU REALIZE THERE'S ONE SOLUTION?
JUST ONCE.
A FEW MONTHS AGO, I GOT PRETTY DEPRESSED. I STOPPED GETTING OUT OF BED. I STARTED SKIPPING SCHOOL, EVEN THOUGH I LOVED SCHOOL.
WHY?
FIRST, MOM HAD TO MOVE FOR HER JOB, BUT DAD COULDN'T LEAVE HIS. NOW I NEVER SEE HER. DAD WORKS LONG HOURS AND HAS A LONG COMMUTE, SO I'M ALONE A LOT. THEN THESE GIRLS STARTED BEATING ME UP ON THE WAY HOME.
THAT MUST HAVE BEEN HARD.
IT WAS. BUT MY FOURTH DAY OF LYING IN BED, I HAD A THOUGHT.
WHAT IF I COULD BE AT MOM'S RIGHT NOW? WHAT IF DAD COULD GET HOME THE MOMENT WORK WAS DONE? WHAT IF I DIDN'T HAVE TO WALK HOME ALONE?
TELEPORTER.
RIGHT. I HAD ALWAYS LIKED SCIENCE, SO INSTEAD OF SITTING HOME, I STAYED LATE AT THE LIBRARY. I READ EVERYTHING I COULD FIND ON THEORETICAL PHYSICS. I EVEN WENT TO THE HAYDEN PLANETARIUM ONCE.
OOH! DID YOU MEET NEIL DEGRASSE TYSON?
I DID. I TOLD HIM WHAT I WAS WORKING ON. HE TOLD ME HE BELIEVED I COULD DO IT AND TO KEEP IN TOUCH.
DID YOU? DID YOU KEEP IN TOUCH?
NEVER. NOT UNTIL I GET THIS THING WORKING.
BUT HE COULD--
I WANT HIM TO KNOW HE WAS RIGHT ABOUT ME. I WANT--
PRICILLA LASHAYLA SMITH! WHAT DID YOU DO TO MY APARTMENT?
WELL, HERE THIS COMES.
DON'T WORRY, I GOT IT!

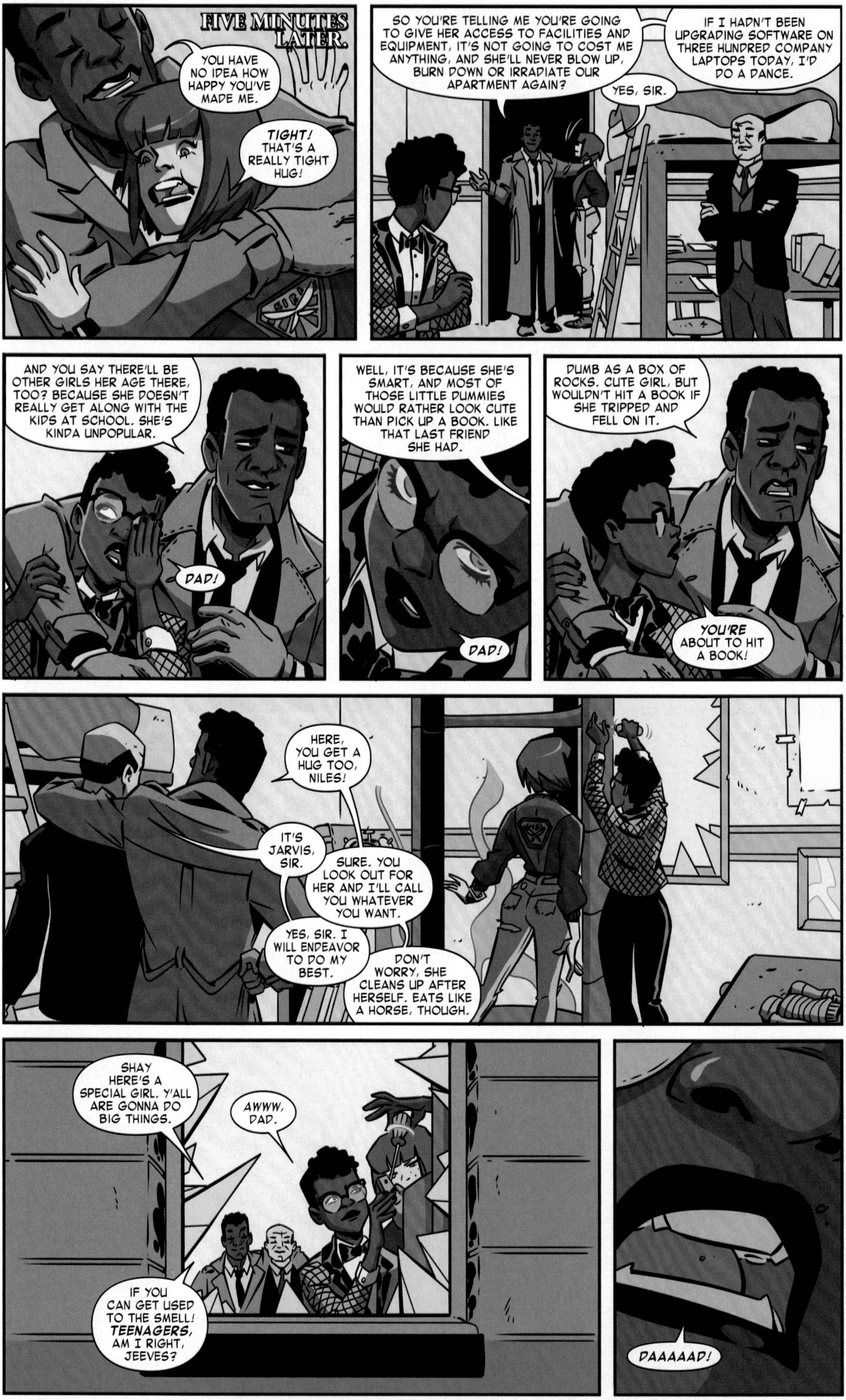
FIVE MINUTES LATER.
YOU HAVE NO IDEA HOW HAPPY YOU'VE MADE ME.
TIGHT! THAT'S A REALLY TIGHT HUG!
SO YOU'RE TELLING ME YOU'RE GOING TO GIVE HER ACCESS TO FACILITIES AND EQUIPMENT, IT'S NOT GOING TO COST ME ANYTHING, AND SHE'LL NEVER BLOW UP, BURN DOWN OR IRRADIATE OUR APARTMENT AGAIN?
IF I HADN'T BEEN UPGRADING SOFTWARE ON THREE HUNDRED COMPANY LAPTOPS TODAY, I'D DO A DANCE.
YES, SIR.
AND YOU SAY THERE'LL BE OTHER GIRLS HER AGE THERE, TOO? BECAUSE SHE DOESN'T REALLY GET ALONG WITH THE KIDS AT SCHOOL. SHE'S KINDA UNPOPULAR.
DAD!
WELL, IT'S BECAUSE SHE'S SMART, AND MOST OF THOSE LITTLE DUMMIES WOULD RATHER LOOK CUTE THAN PICK UP A BOOK. LIKE THAT LAST FRIEND SHE HAD.
DAD!
DUMB AS A BOX OF ROCKS. CUTE GIRL, BUT WOULDN'T HIT A BOOK IF SHE TRIPPED AND FELL ON IT.
YOU'RE ABOUT TO HIT A BOOK!
HERE, YOU GET A HUG TOO, NILES!
IT'S JARVIS, SIR.
SURE. YOU LOOK OUT FOR HER AND I'LL CALL YOU WHATEVER YOU WANT.
YES, SIR. I WILL ENDEAVOR TO DO MY BEST.
DON'T WORRY, SHE CLEANS UP AFTER HERSELF. EATS LIKE A HORSE, THOUGH.
SHAY HERE'S A SPECIAL GIRL. Y'ALL ARE GONNA DO BIG THINGS.
AWWW, DAD.
IF YOU CAN GET USED TO THE SMELL! TEENAGERS, AM I RIGHT, JEEVES?
DAAAAAD!

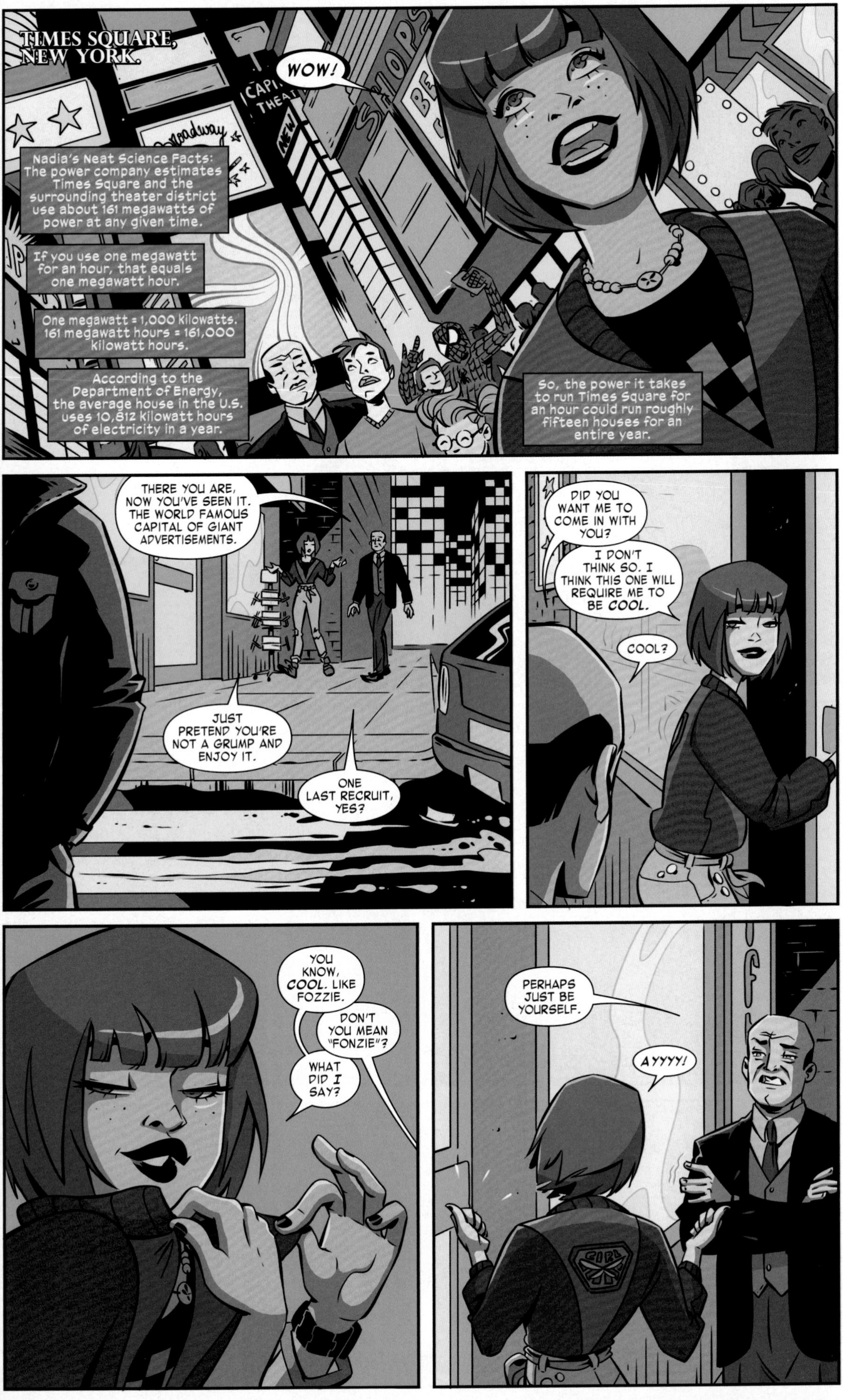
TIMES SQUARE, NEW YORK.
WOW!
Nadia's Neat Science Facts: The power company estimates Times Square and the surrounding theater district use about 161 megawatts of power at any given time.
If you use one megawatt for an hour, that equals one megawatt hour.
One megawatt = 1,000 kilowatts. 161 megawatt hours = 161,000 kilowatt hours.
According to the Department of Energy, the average house in the U.S. uses 10,812 kilowatt hours of electricity in a year.
So, the power it takes to run Times Square for an hour could run roughly fifteen houses for an entire year.
THERE YOU ARE, NOW YOU'VE SEEN IT. THE WORLD FAMOUS CAPITAL OF GIANT ADVERTISEMENTS.
JUST PRETEND YOU'RE NOT A GRUMP AND ENJOY IT.
ONE LAST RECRUIT, YES?
DID YOU WANT ME TO COME IN WITH YOU?
I DON'T THINK SO. I THINK THIS ONE WILL REQUIRE ME TO BE COOL.
COOL?
YOU KNOW, COOL. LIKE FOZZIE.
DON'T YOU MEAN "FONZIE"?
WHAT DID I SAY?
PERHAPS JUST BE YOURSELF.
AYYYY!

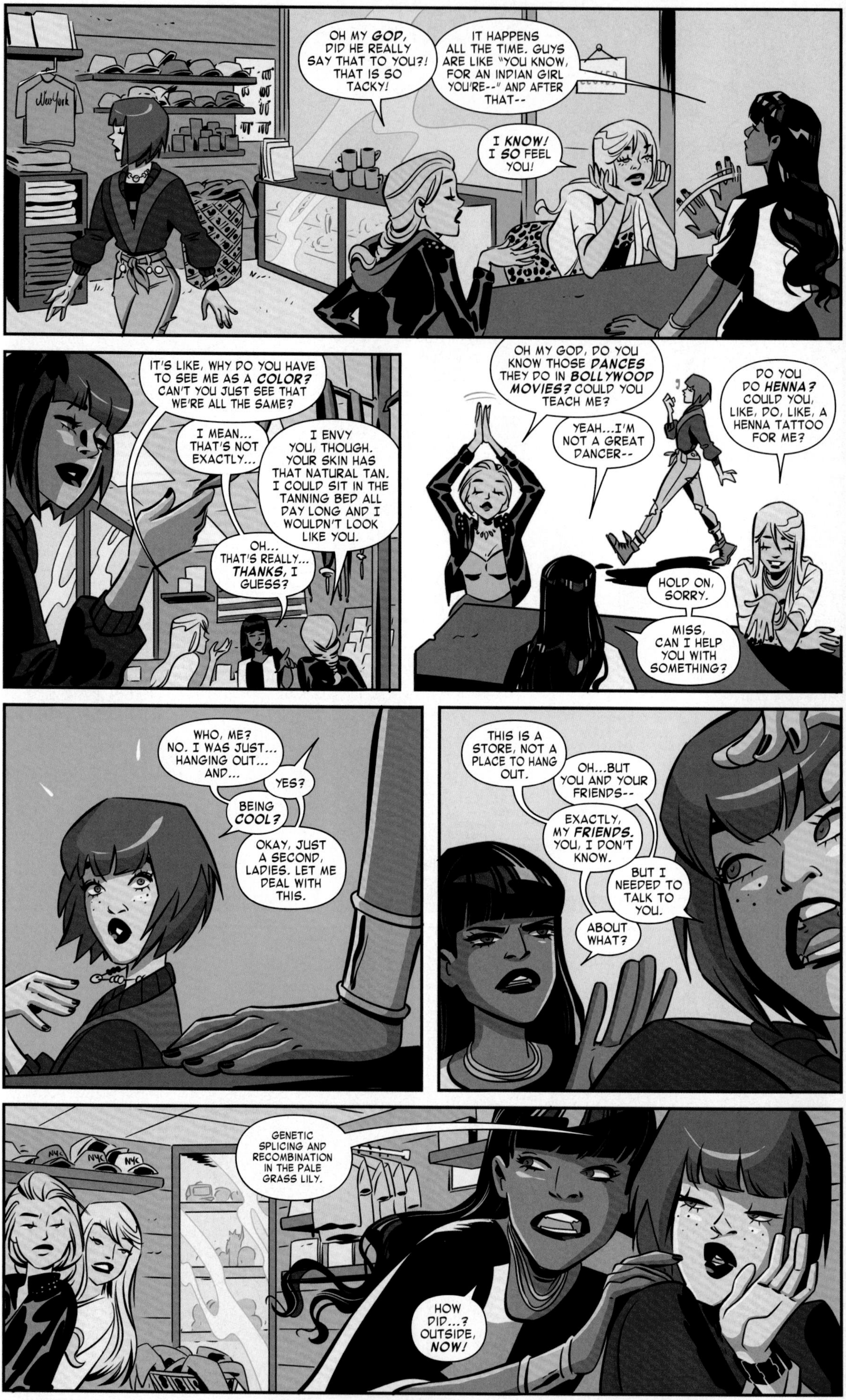
OH MY GOD, DID HE REALLY SAY THAT TO YOU?! THAT IS SO TACKY!
IT HAPPENS ALL THE TIME. GUYS ARE LIKE "YOU KNOW, FOR AN INDIAN GIRL YOU'RE--" AND AFTER THAT--
I KNOW! I SO FEEL YOU!
IT'S LIKE, WHY DO YOU HAVE TO SEE ME AS A COLOR? CAN'T YOU JUST SEE THAT WE'RE ALL THE SAME?
I MEAN... THAT'S NOT EXACTLY...
I ENVY YOU, THOUGH. YOUR SKIN HAS THAT NATURAL TAN. I COULD SIT IN THE TANNING BED ALL DAY LONG AND I WOULDN'T LOOK LIKE YOU.
OH... THAT'S REALLY... THANKS, I GUESS?
OH MY GOD, DO YOU KNOW THOSE DANCES THEY DO IN BOLLYWOOD MOVIES? COULD YOU TEACH ME?
YEAH...I'M NOT A GREAT DANCER--
DO YOU DO HENNA? COULD YOU, LIKE, DO, LIKE, A HENNA TATTOO FOR ME?
HOLD ON, SORRY.
MISS, CAN I HELP YOU WITH SOMETHING?
WHO, ME? NO. I WAS JUST... HANGING OUT... AND...
YES?
BEING COOL?
OKAY, JUST A SECOND, LADIES. LET ME DEAL WITH THIS.
THIS IS A STORE, NOT A PLACE TO HANG OUT.
OH...BUT YOU AND YOUR FRIENDS--
EXACTLY, MY FRIENDS. YOU, I DON'T KNOW.
BUT I NEEDED TO TALK TO YOU.
ABOUT WHAT?
GENETIC SPLICING AND RECOMBINATION IN THE PALE GRASS LILY.
HOW DID...? OUTSIDE, NOW!

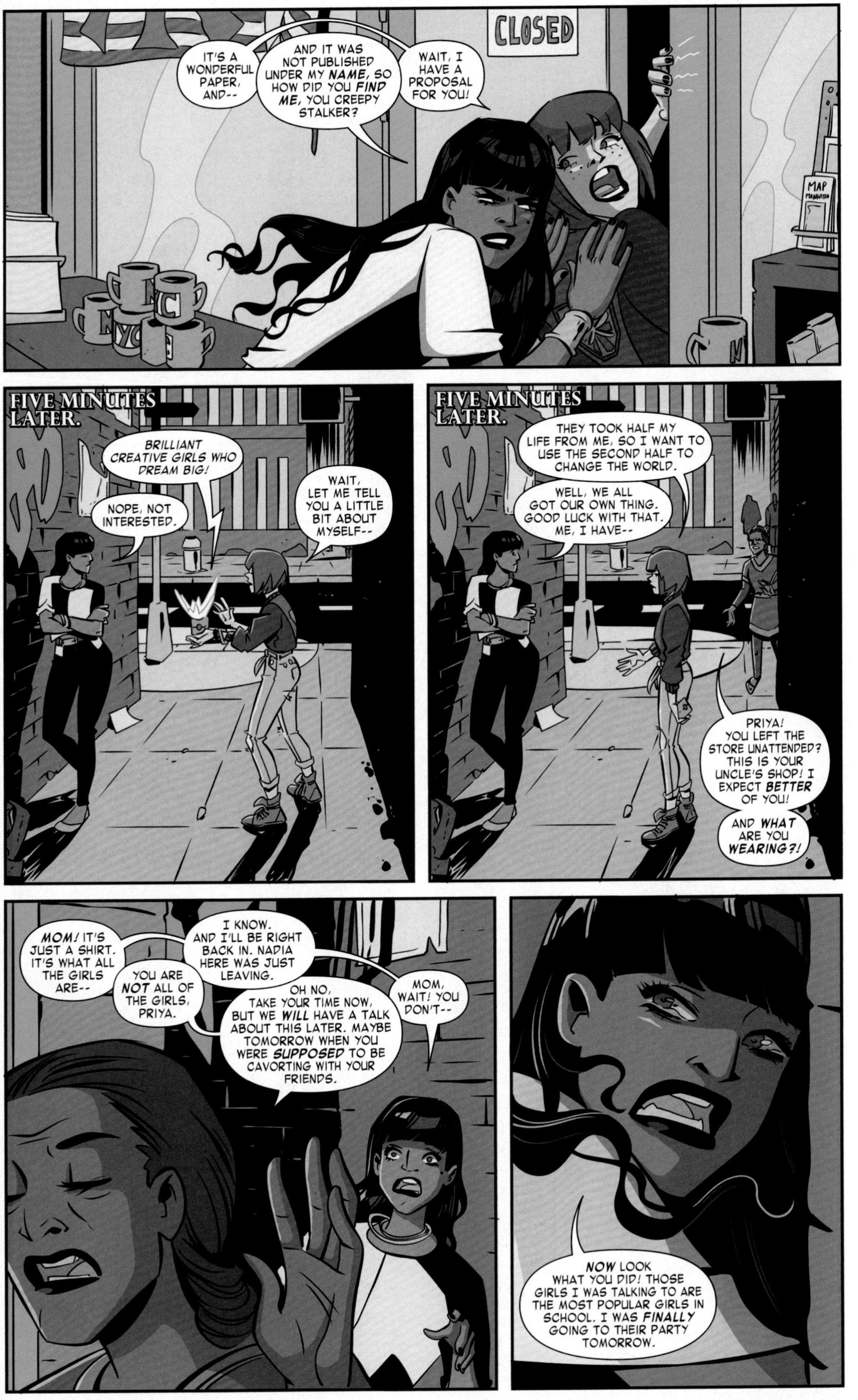
CLOSED
IT'S A WONDERFUL PAPER, AND--
AND IT WAS NOT PUBLISHED UNDER MY NAME, SO HOW DID YOU FIND ME, YOU CREEPY STALKER?
WAIT, I HAVE A PROPOSAL FOR YOU!
MAP
FIVE MINUTES LATER.
BRILLIANT CREATIVE GIRLS WHO DREAM BIG!
NOPE, NOT INTERESTED.
WAIT, LET ME TELL YOU A LITTLE BIT ABOUT MYSELF--
FIVE MINUTES LATER.
THEY TOOK HALF MY LIFE FROM ME, SO I WANT TO USE THE SECOND HALF TO CHANGE THE WORLD.
WELL, WE ALL GOT OUR OWN THING. GOOD LUCK WITH THAT. ME, I HAVE--
PRIYA! YOU LEFT THE STORE UNATTENDED? THIS IS YOUR UNCLE'S SHOP! I EXPECT BETTER OF YOU!
AND WHAT ARE YOU WEARING?!
MOM! IT'S JUST A SHIRT. IT'S WHAT ALL THE GIRLS ARE--
YOU ARE NOT ALL OF THE GIRLS, PRIYA.
I KNOW. AND I'LL BE RIGHT BACK IN. NADIA HERE WAS JUST LEAVING.
OH NO, TAKE YOUR TIME NOW, BUT WE WILL HAVE A TALK ABOUT THIS LATER. MAYBE TOMORROW WHEN YOU WERE SUPPOSED TO BE CAVORTING WITH YOUR FRIENDS.
MOM, WAIT! YOU DON'T--
NOW LOOK WHAT YOU DID! THOSE GIRLS I WAS TALKING TO ARE THE MOST POPULAR GIRLS IN SCHOOL. I WAS FINALLY GOING TO THEIR PARTY TOMORROW.

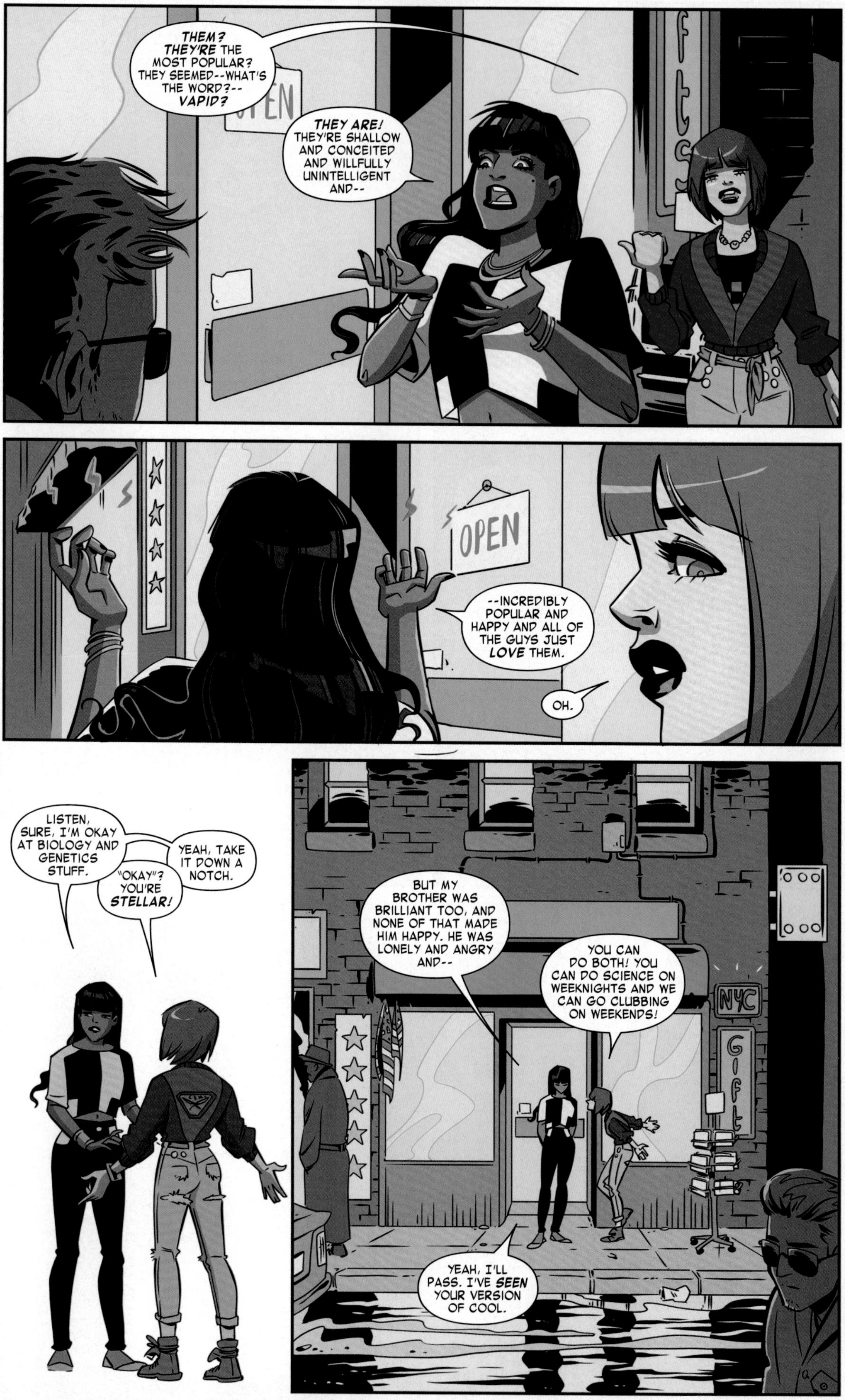
THEM? THEY'RE THE MOST POPULAR? THEY SEEMED--WHAT'S THE WORD?--VAPID?
OPEN
THEY ARE! THEY'RE SHALLOW AND CONCEITED AND WILLFULLY UNINTELLIGENT AND--
OPEN
--INCREDIBLY POPULAR AND HAPPY AND ALL OF THE GUYS JUST LOVE THEM.
OH.
LISTEN, SURE, I'M OKAY AT BIOLOGY AND GENETICS STUFF.
"OKAY"? YOU'RE STELLAR!
YEAH, TAKE IT DOWN A NOTCH.
BUT MY BROTHER WAS BRILLIANT TOO, AND NONE OF THAT MADE HIM HAPPY. HE WAS LONELY AND ANGRY AND--
YOU CAN DO BOTH! YOU CAN DO SCIENCE ON WEEKNIGHTS AND WE CAN GO CLUBBING ON WEEKENDS!
NYC
GIFT
YEAH, I'LL PASS. I'VE SEEN YOUR VERSION OF COOL.

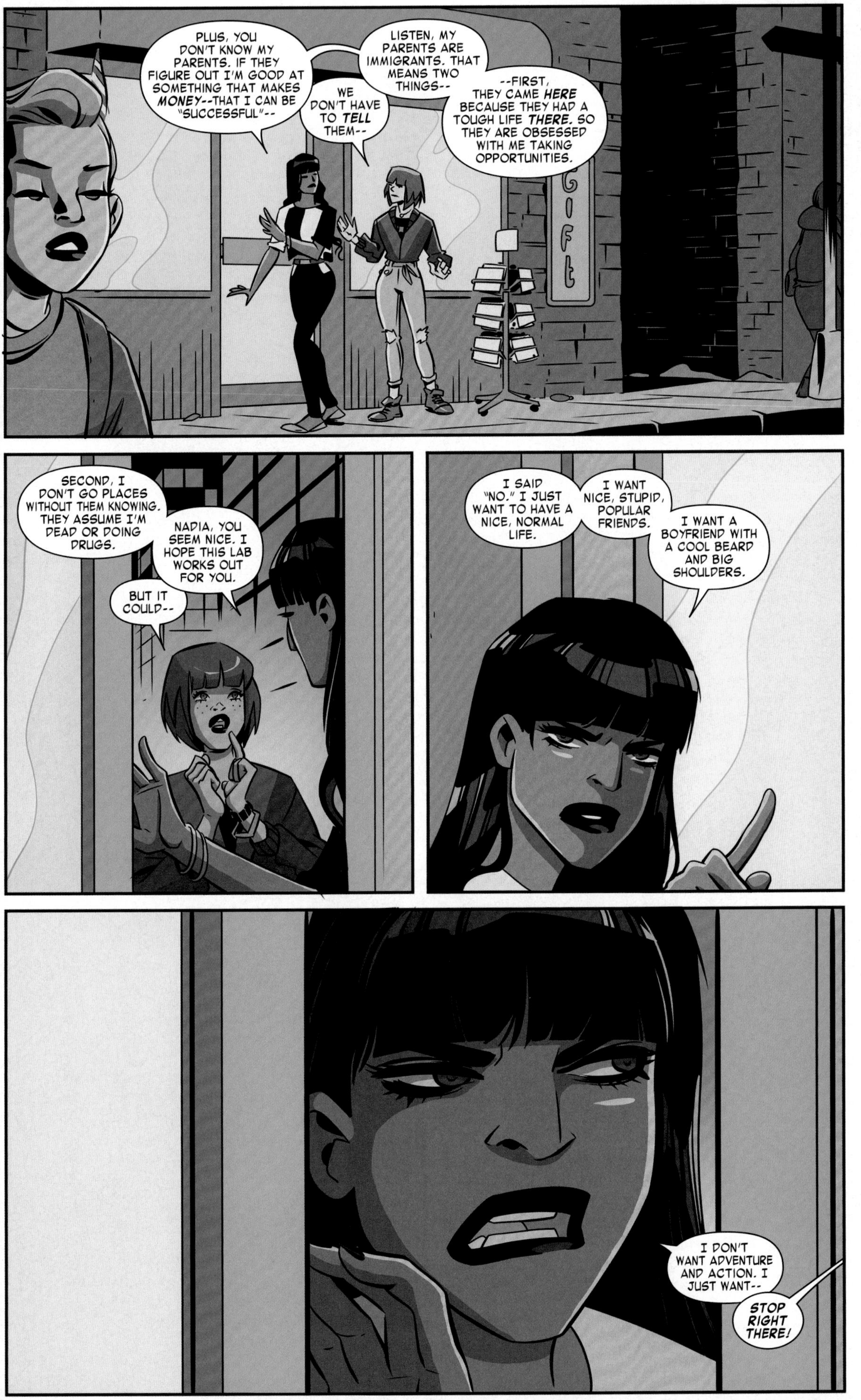
PLUS, YOU DON'T KNOW MY PARENTS. IF THEY FIGURE OUT I'M GOOD AT SOMETHING THAT MAKES MONEY--THAT I CAN BE "SUCCESSFUL"--
WE DON'T HAVE TO TELL THEM--
LISTEN, MY PARENTS ARE IMMIGRANTS. THAT MEANS TWO THINGS--
--FIRST, THEY CAME HERE BECAUSE THEY HAD A TOUGH LIFE THERE. SO THEY ARE OBSESSED WITH ME TAKING OPPORTUNITIES.
GIFT
SECOND, I DON'T GO PLACES WITHOUT THEM KNOWING. THEY ASSUME I'M DEAD OR DOING DRUGS.
NADIA, YOU SEEM NICE. I HOPE THIS LAB WORKS OUT FOR YOU.
BUT IT COULD--
I SAID "NO." I JUST WANT TO HAVE A NICE, NORMAL LIFE.
I WANT NICE, STUPID, POPULAR FRIENDS.
I WANT A BOYFRIEND WITH A COOL BEARD AND BIG SHOULDERS.
I DON'T WANT ADVENTURE AND ACTION. I JUST WANT--
STOP RIGHT THERE!

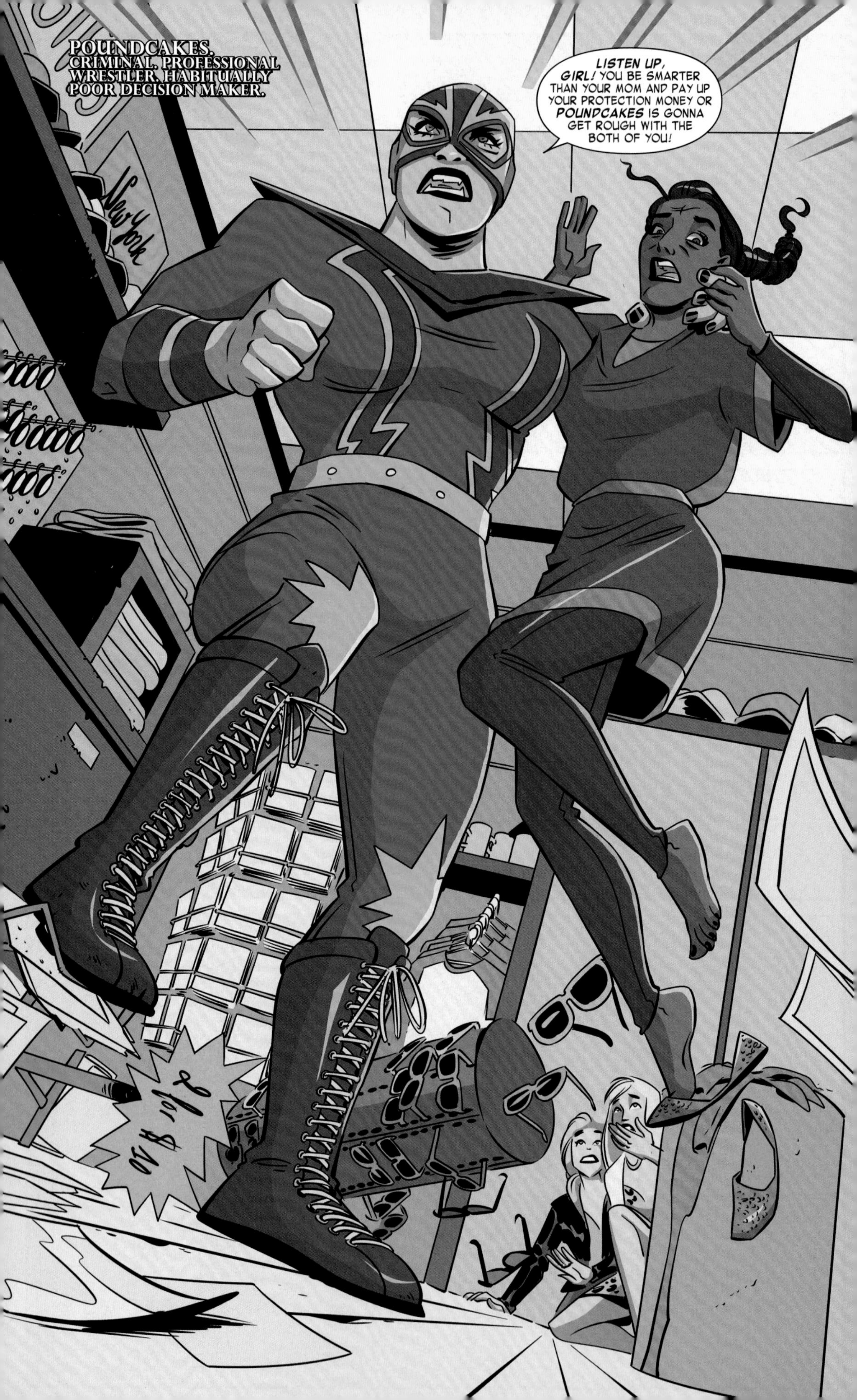
POUNDCAKES.
CRIMINAL. PROFESSIONAL WRESTLER. HABITUALLY POOR DECISION MAKER.
LISTEN UP, GIRL! YOU BE SMARTER THAN YOUR MOM AND PAY UP YOUR PROTECTION MONEY OR POUNDCAKES IS GONNA GET ROUGH WITH THE BOTH OF YOU!

4

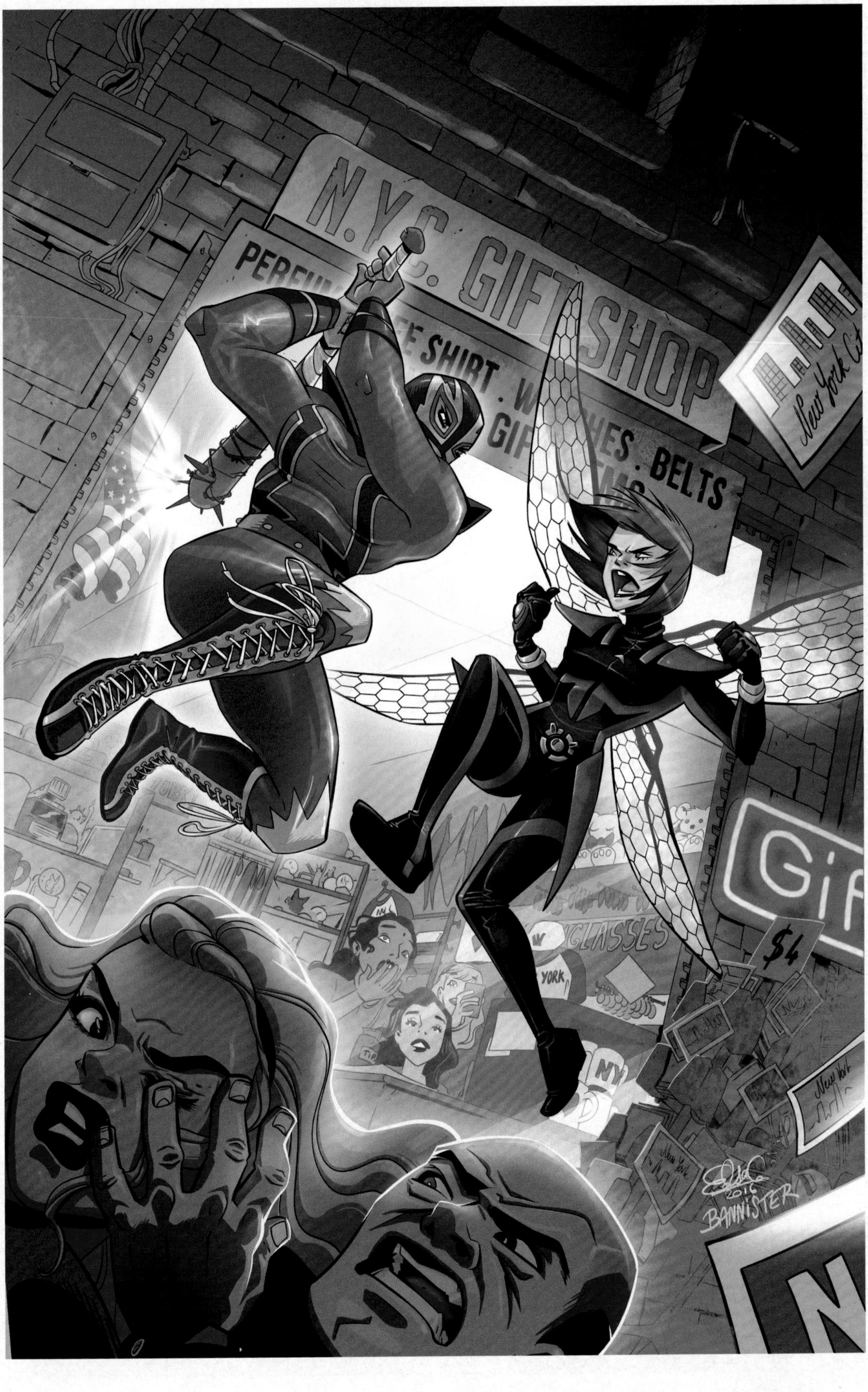

N.Y.C. GIFTSHOP
SHIRT . W
HES . BELTS
New York City
Gif
$4
YORK
NY
2016
BANNISTER

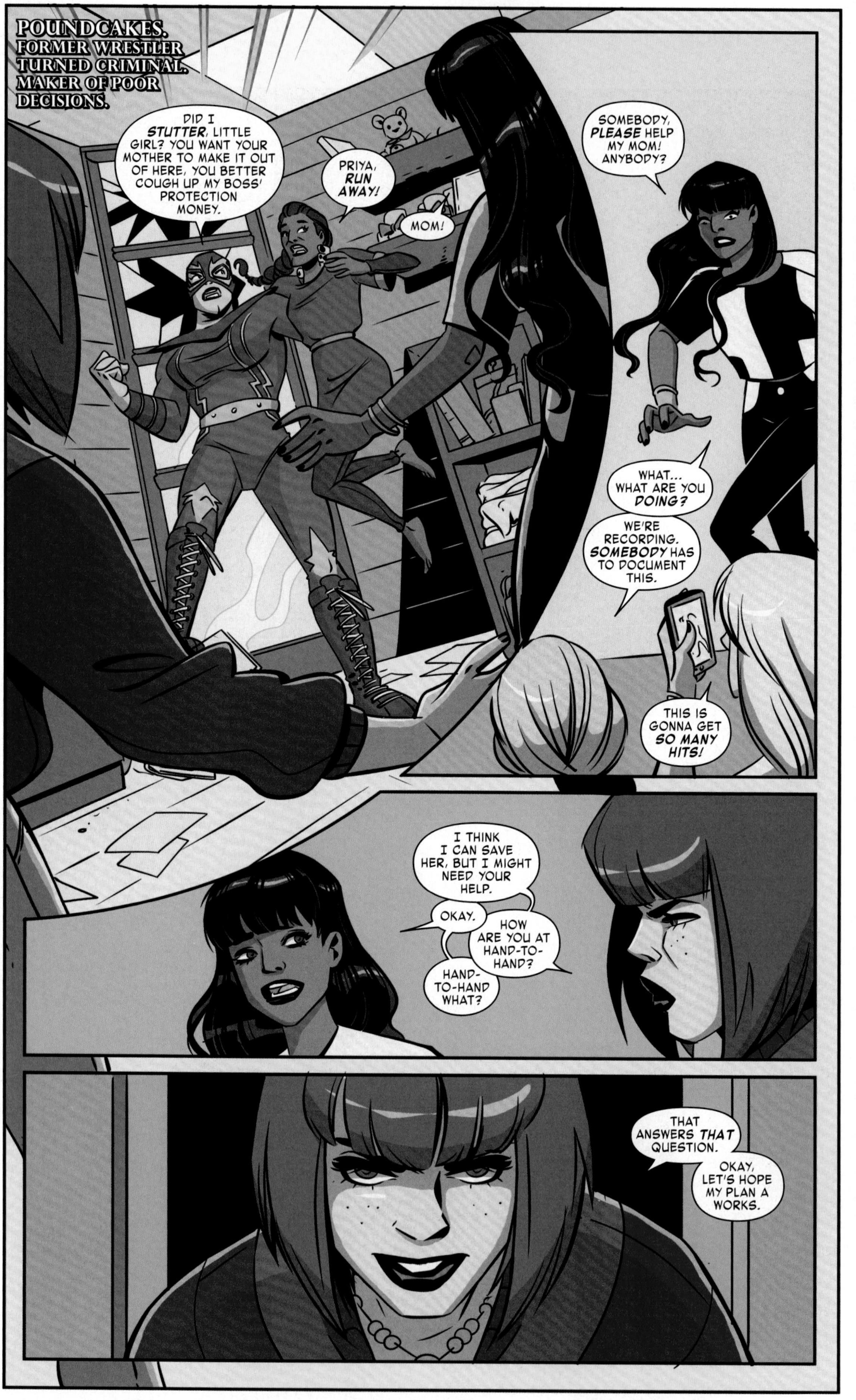
POUNDCAKES. FORMER WRESTLER TURNED CRIMINAL. MAKER OF POOR DECISIONS.
DID I STUTTER, LITTLE GIRL? YOU WANT YOUR MOTHER TO MAKE IT OUT OF HERE, YOU BETTER COUGH UP MY BOSS' PROTECTION MONEY.
PRIYA, RUN AWAY!
MOM!
SOMEBODY, PLEASE HELP MY MOM! ANYBODY?
WHAT... WHAT ARE YOU DOING?
WE'RE RECORDING. SOMEBODY HAS TO DOCUMENT THIS.
THIS IS GONNA GET SO MANY HITS!
I THINK I CAN SAVE HER, BUT I MIGHT NEED YOUR HELP.
OKAY.
HOW ARE YOU AT HAND-TO-HAND?
HAND-TO-HAND WHAT?
THAT ANSWERS THAT QUESTION.
OKAY, LET'S HOPE MY PLAN A WORKS.

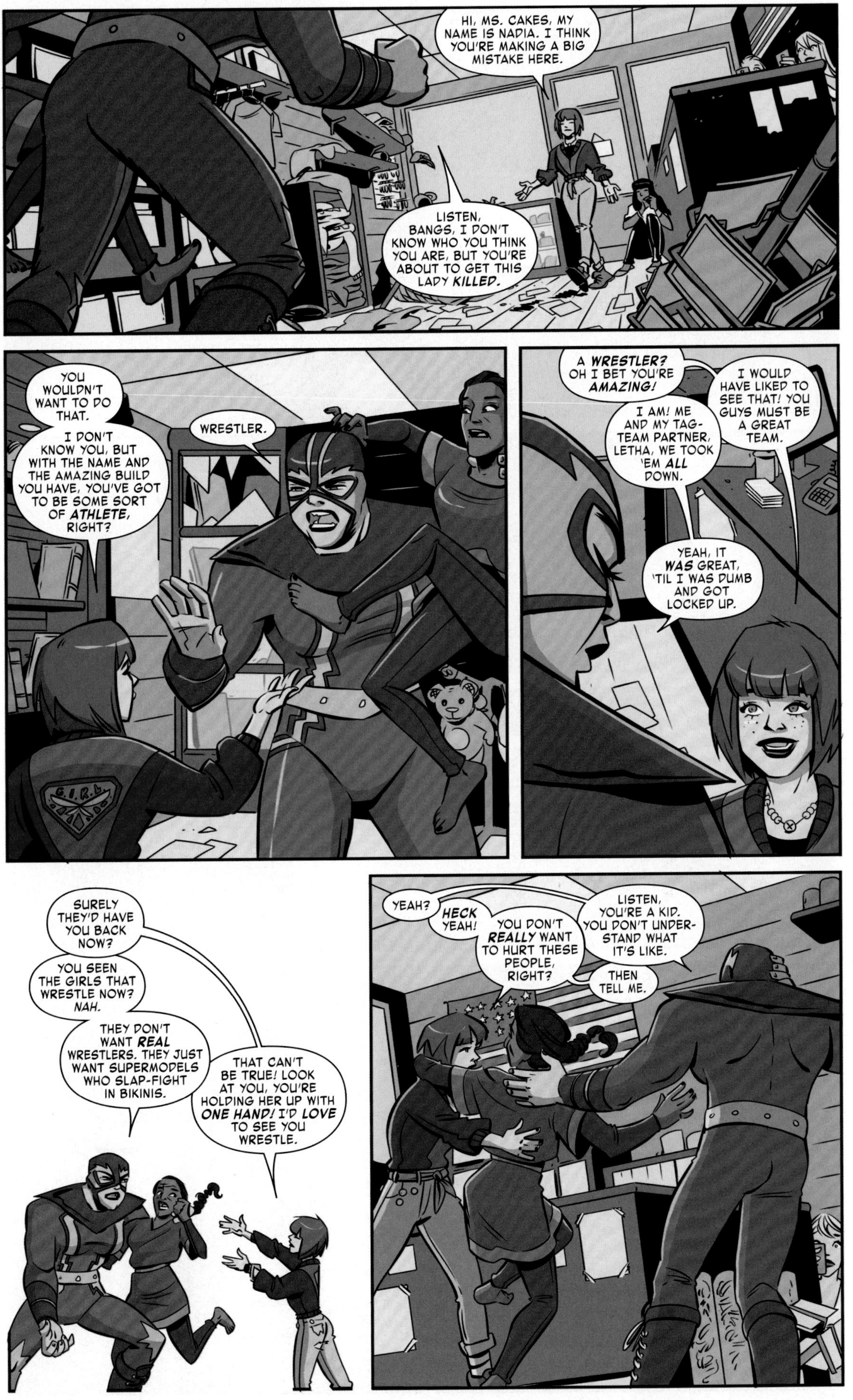
HI, MS. CAKES, MY NAME IS NADIA. I THINK YOU'RE MAKING A BIG MISTAKE HERE.
LISTEN, BANGS, I DON'T KNOW WHO YOU THINK YOU ARE, BUT YOU'RE ABOUT TO GET THIS LADY KILLED.
YOU WOULDN'T WANT TO DO THAT.
I DON'T KNOW YOU, BUT WITH THE NAME AND THE AMAZING BUILD YOU HAVE, YOU'VE GOT TO BE SOME SORT OF ATHLETE, RIGHT?
WRESTLER.
A WRESTLER? OH I BET YOU'RE AMAZING!
I AM! ME AND MY TAG-TEAM PARTNER, LETHA, WE TOOK 'EM ALL DOWN.
I WOULD HAVE LIKED TO SEE THAT! YOU GUYS MUST BE A GREAT TEAM.
YEAH, IT WAS GREAT, 'TIL I WAS DUMB AND GOT LOCKED UP.
SURELY THEY'D HAVE YOU BACK NOW?
YOU SEEN THE GIRLS THAT WRESTLE NOW? NAH.
THEY DON'T WANT REAL WRESTLERS. THEY JUST WANT SUPERMODELS WHO SLAP-FIGHT IN BIKINIS.
THAT CAN'T BE TRUE! LOOK AT YOU, YOU'RE HOLDING HER UP WITH ONE HAND! I'D LOVE TO SEE YOU WRESTLE.
LISTEN, YOU'RE A KID. YOU DON'T UNDERSTAND WHAT IT'S LIKE.
THEN TELL ME.
YOU DON'T REALLY WANT TO HURT THESE PEOPLE, RIGHT?
YEAH?
HECK YEAH!

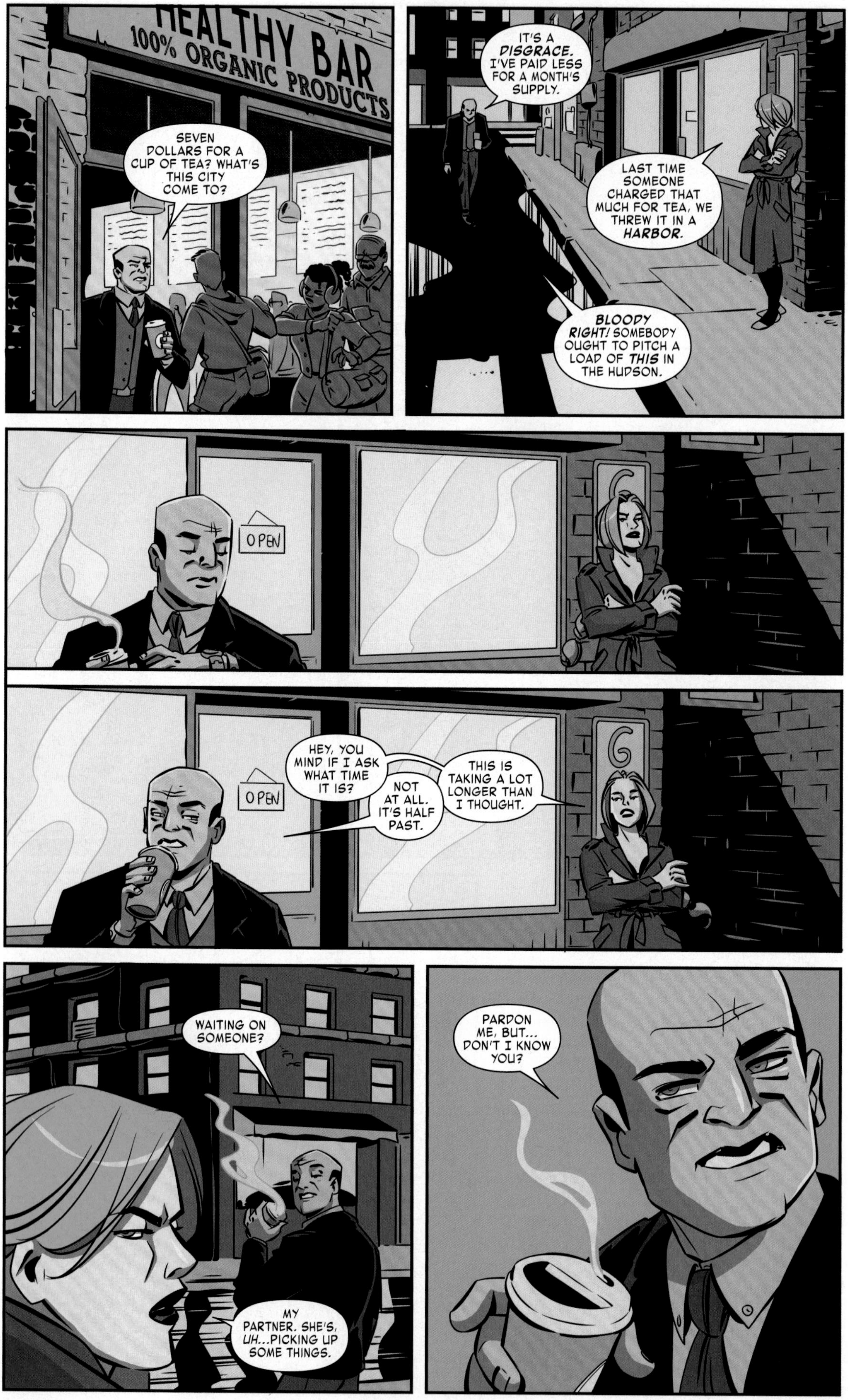
HEALTHY BAR
100% ORGANIC PRODUCTS
SEVEN DOLLARS FOR A CUP OF TEA? WHAT'S THIS CITY COME TO?
IT'S A DISGRACE. I'VE PAID LESS FOR A MONTH'S SUPPLY.
LAST TIME SOMEONE CHARGED THAT MUCH FOR TEA, WE THREW IT IN A HARBOR.
BLOODY RIGHT! SOMEBODY OUGHT TO PITCH A LOAD OF THIS IN THE HUDSON.
OPEN
OPEN
HEY, YOU MIND IF I ASK WHAT TIME IT IS?
NOT AT ALL. IT'S HALF PAST.
THIS IS TAKING A LOT LONGER THAN I THOUGHT.
WAITING ON SOMEONE?
MY PARTNER. SHE'S, UH...PICKING UP SOME THINGS.
PARDON ME, BUT... DON'T I KNOW YOU?

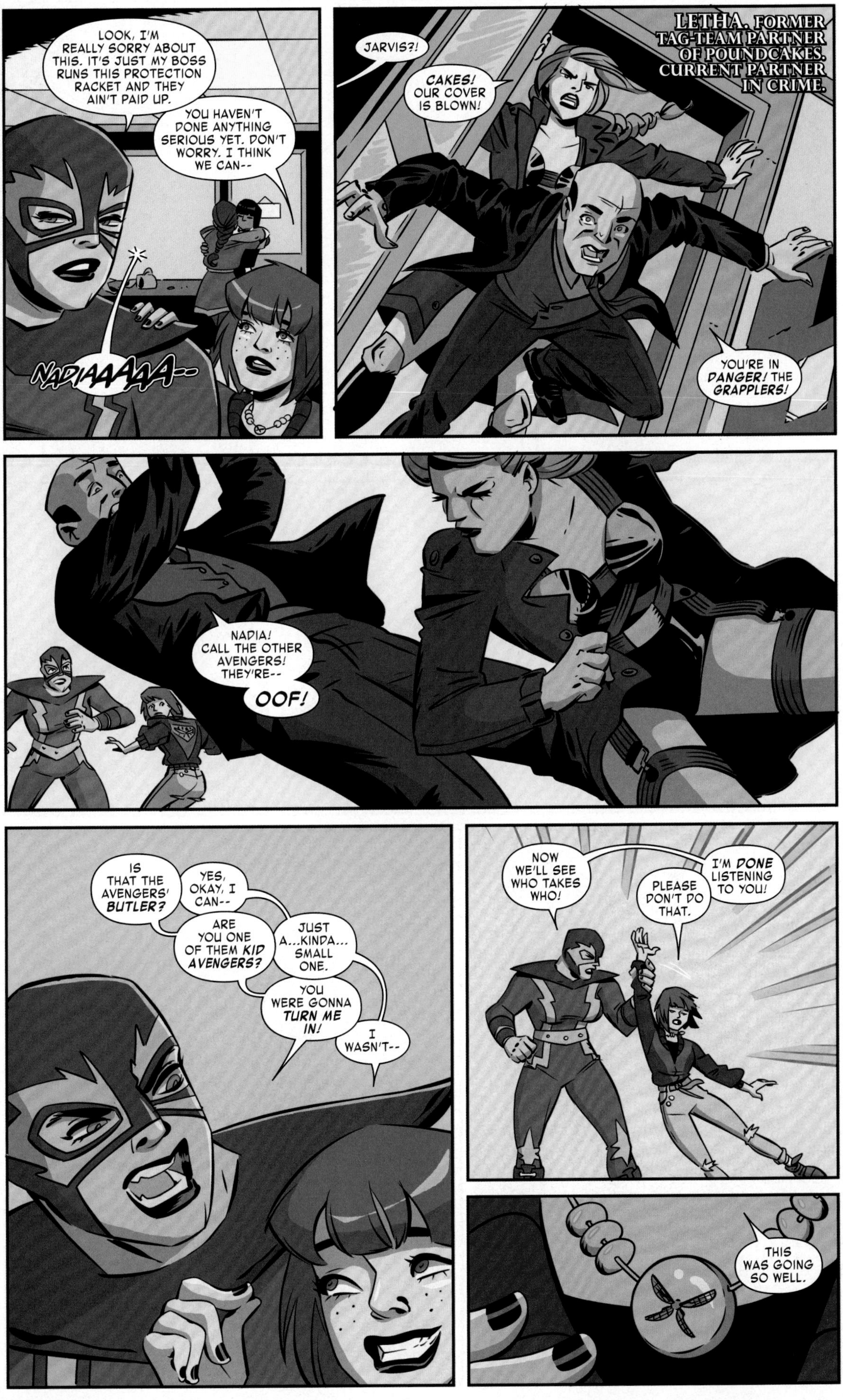
LOOK, I'M REALLY SORRY ABOUT THIS. IT'S JUST MY BOSS RUNS THIS PROTECTION RACKET AND THEY AIN'T PAID UP.
YOU HAVEN'T DONE ANYTHING SERIOUS YET. DON'T WORRY. I THINK WE CAN--
NADIAAAAA--
LETHA. FORMER TAG-TEAM PARTNER OF POUNDCAKES. CURRENT PARTNER IN CRIME.
JARVIS?!
CAKES! OUR COVER IS BLOWN!
YOU'RE IN DANGER! THE GRAPPLERS!
NADIA! CALL THE OTHER AVENGERS! THEY'RE--
OOF!
IS THAT THE AVENGERS' BUTLER?
YES, OKAY, I CAN--
ARE YOU ONE OF THEM KID AVENGERS?
JUST A...KINDA... SMALL ONE.
YOU WERE GONNA TURN ME IN!
I WASN'T--
NOW WE'LL SEE WHO TAKES WHO!
I'M DONE LISTENING TO YOU!
PLEASE DON'T DO THAT.
THIS WAS GOING SO WELL.

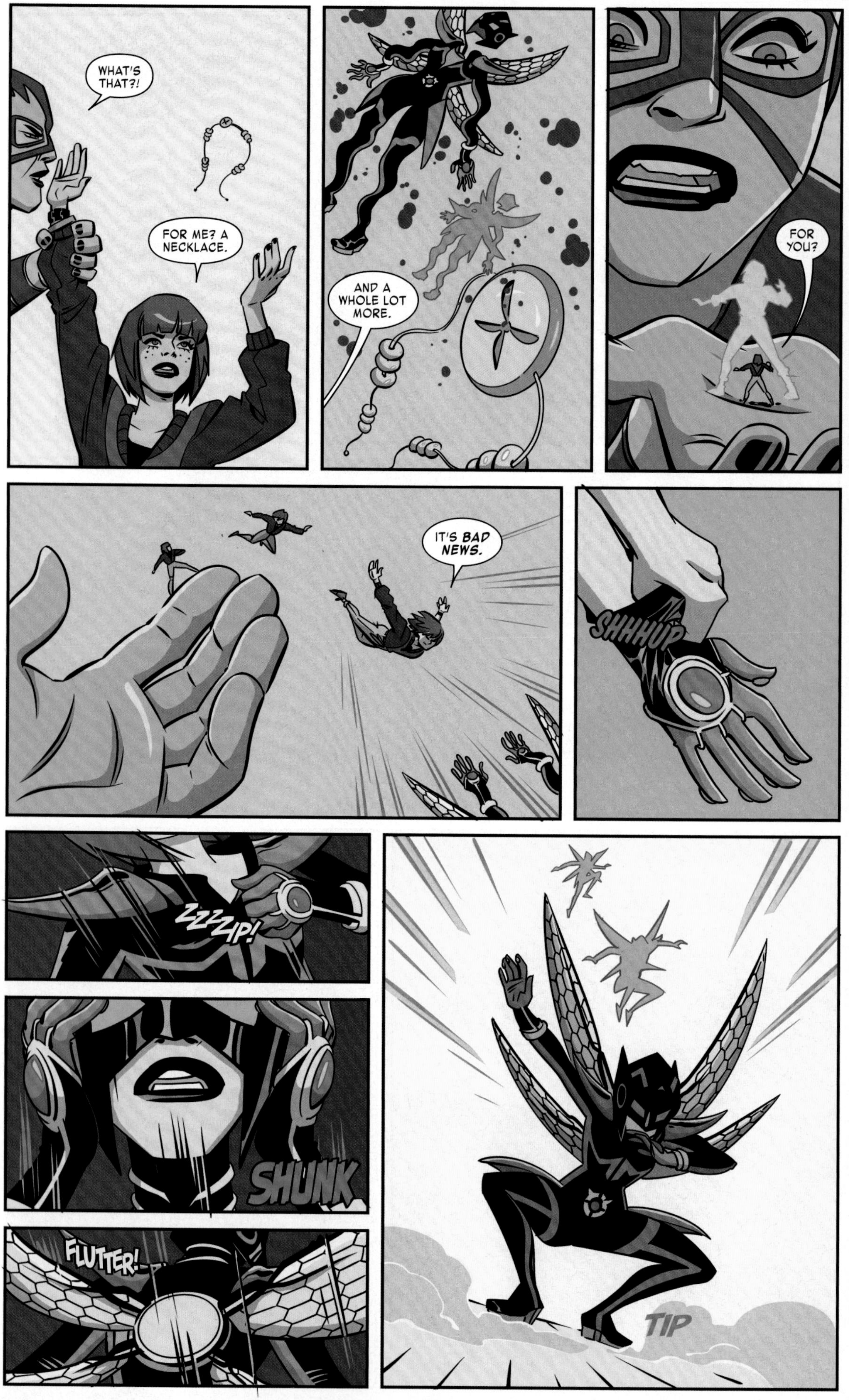
WHAT'S THAT?!
FOR ME? A NECKLACE.
AND A WHOLE LOT MORE.
FOR YOU?
IT'S BAD NEWS.
SHHHUP
ZZZZIP!
SHUNK
FLUTTER!
TIP

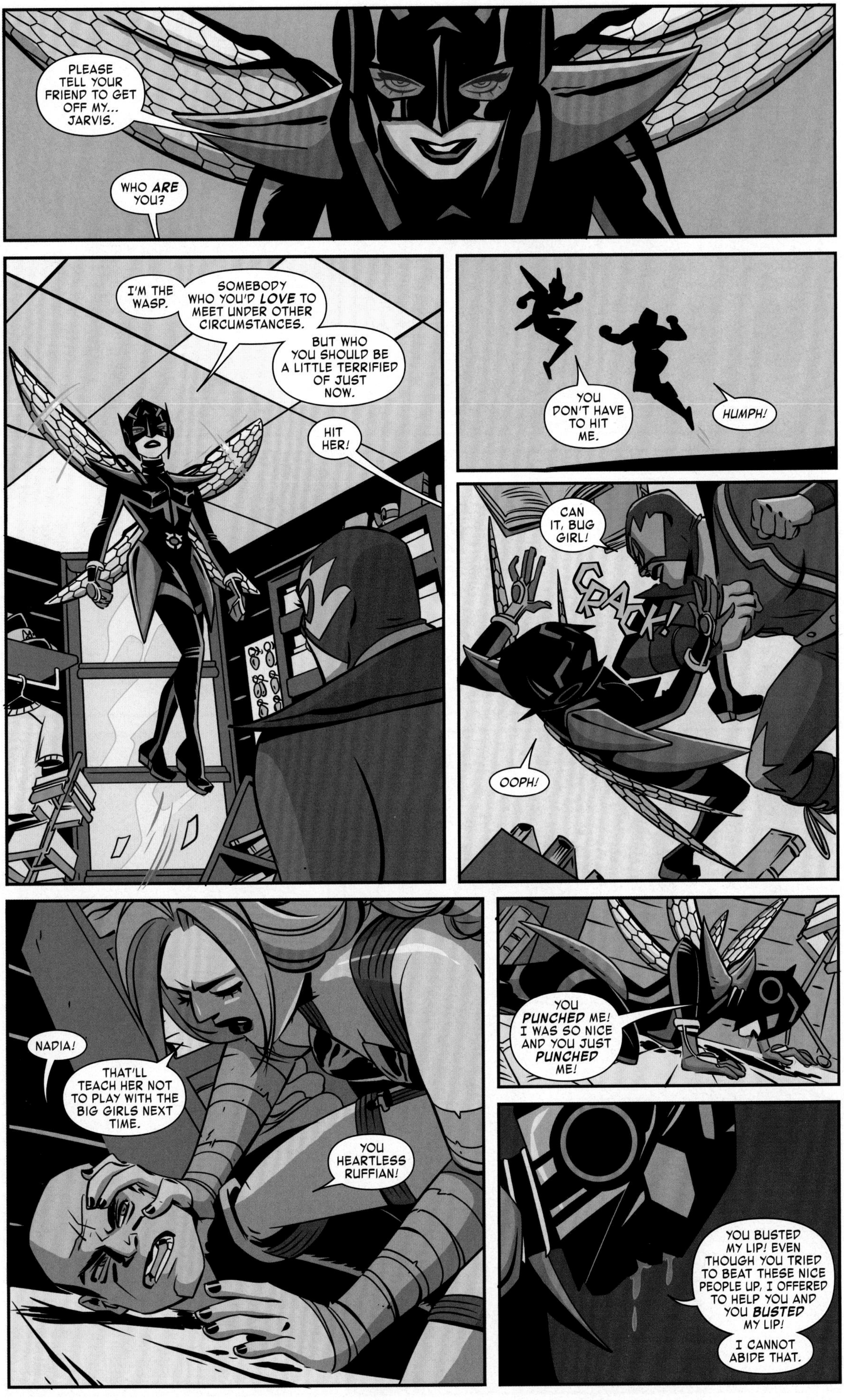
PLEASE TELL YOUR FRIEND TO GET OFF MY... JARVIS.
WHO ARE YOU?
I'M THE WASP.
SOMEBODY WHO YOU'D LOVE TO MEET UNDER OTHER CIRCUMSTANCES.
BUT WHO YOU SHOULD BE A LITTLE TERRIFIED OF JUST NOW.
HIT HER!
YOU DON'T HAVE TO HIT ME.
HUMPH!
CAN IT, BUG GIRL!
CRACK!
OOPH!
NADIA!
THAT'LL TEACH HER NOT TO PLAY WITH THE BIG GIRLS NEXT TIME.
YOU HEARTLESS RUFFIAN!
YOU PUNCHED ME! I WAS SO NICE AND YOU JUST PUNCHED ME!
YOU BUSTED MY LIP! EVEN THOUGH YOU TRIED TO BEAT THESE NICE PEOPLE UP, I OFFERED TO HELP YOU AND YOU BUSTED MY LIP!
I CANNOT ABIDE THAT.

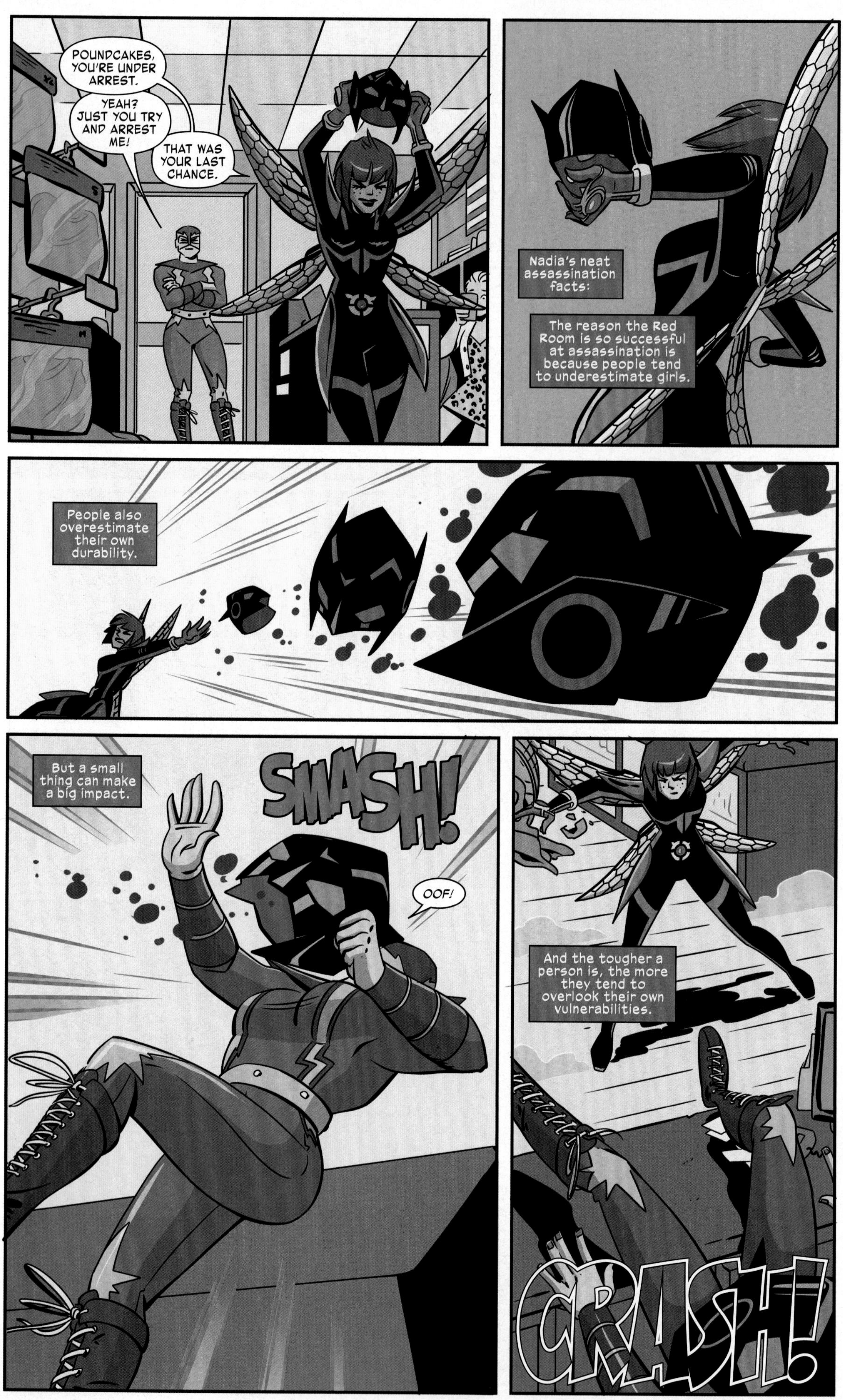
POUNDCAKES, YOU'RE UNDER ARREST.
YEAH? JUST YOU TRY AND ARREST ME!
THAT WAS YOUR LAST CHANCE.
Nadia's neat assassination facts:
The reason the Red Room is so successful at assassination is because people tend to underestimate girls.
People also overestimate their own durability.
But a small thing can make a big impact.
SMASH!
OOF!
And the tougher a person is, the more they tend to overlook their own vulnerabilities.
CRASH!

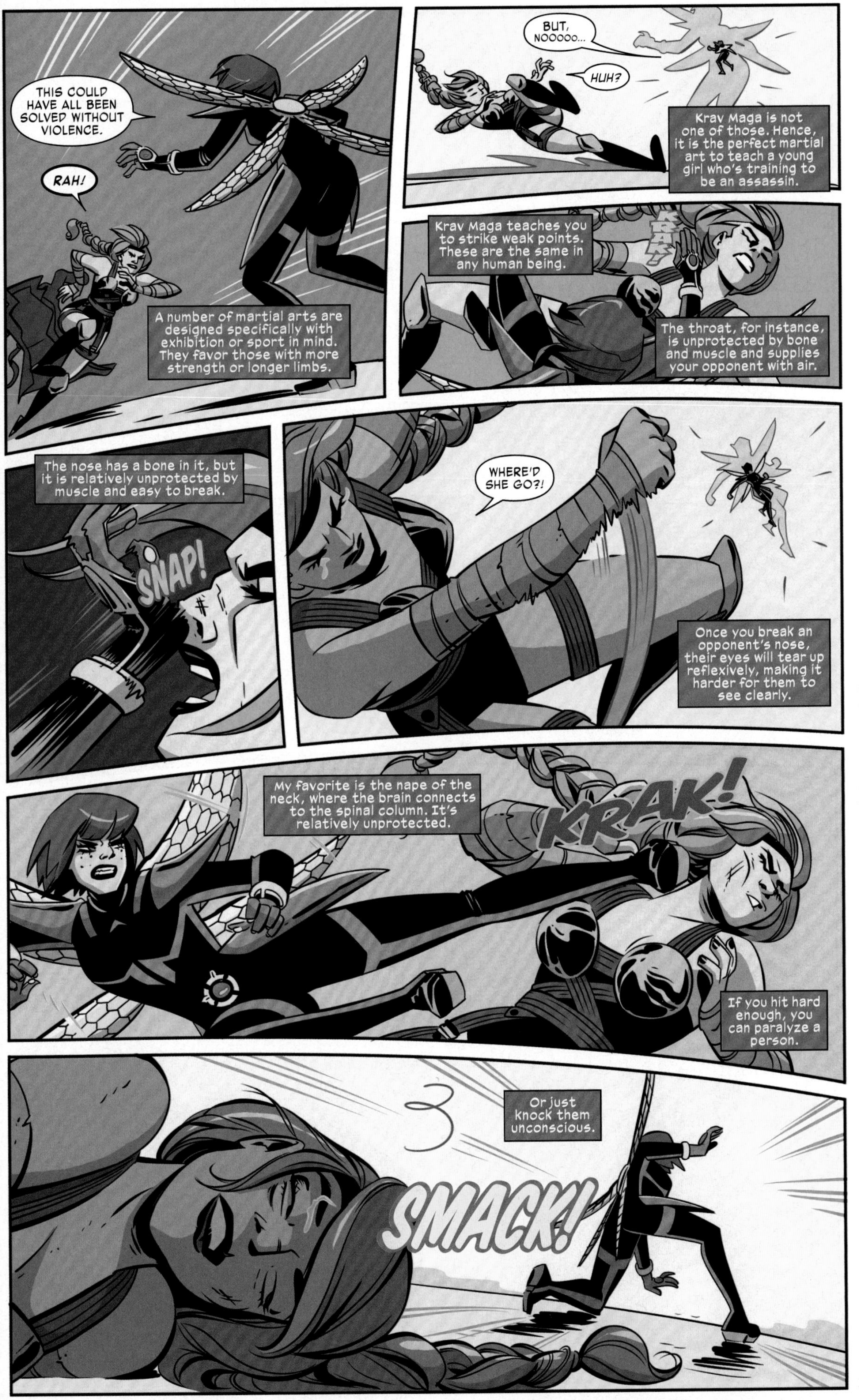
THIS COULD HAVE ALL BEEN SOLVED WITHOUT VIOLENCE.
RAH!
A number of martial arts are designed specifically with exhibition or sport in mind. They favor those with more strength or longer limbs.
BUT, NOOOOO...
HUH?
Krav Maga is not one of those. Hence, it is the perfect martial art to teach a young girl who's training to be an assassin.
Krav Maga teaches you to strike weak points. These are the same in any human being.
KRAK!
The throat, for instance, is unprotected by bone and muscle and supplies your opponent with air.
The nose has a bone in it, but it is relatively unprotected by muscle and easy to break.
SNAP!
WHERE'D SHE GO?!
Once you break an opponent's nose, their eyes will tear up reflexively, making it harder for them to see clearly.
My favorite is the nape of the neck, where the brain connects to the spinal column. It's relatively unprotected.
KRAK!
If you hit hard enough, you can paralyze a person.
Or just knock them unconscious.
SMACK!

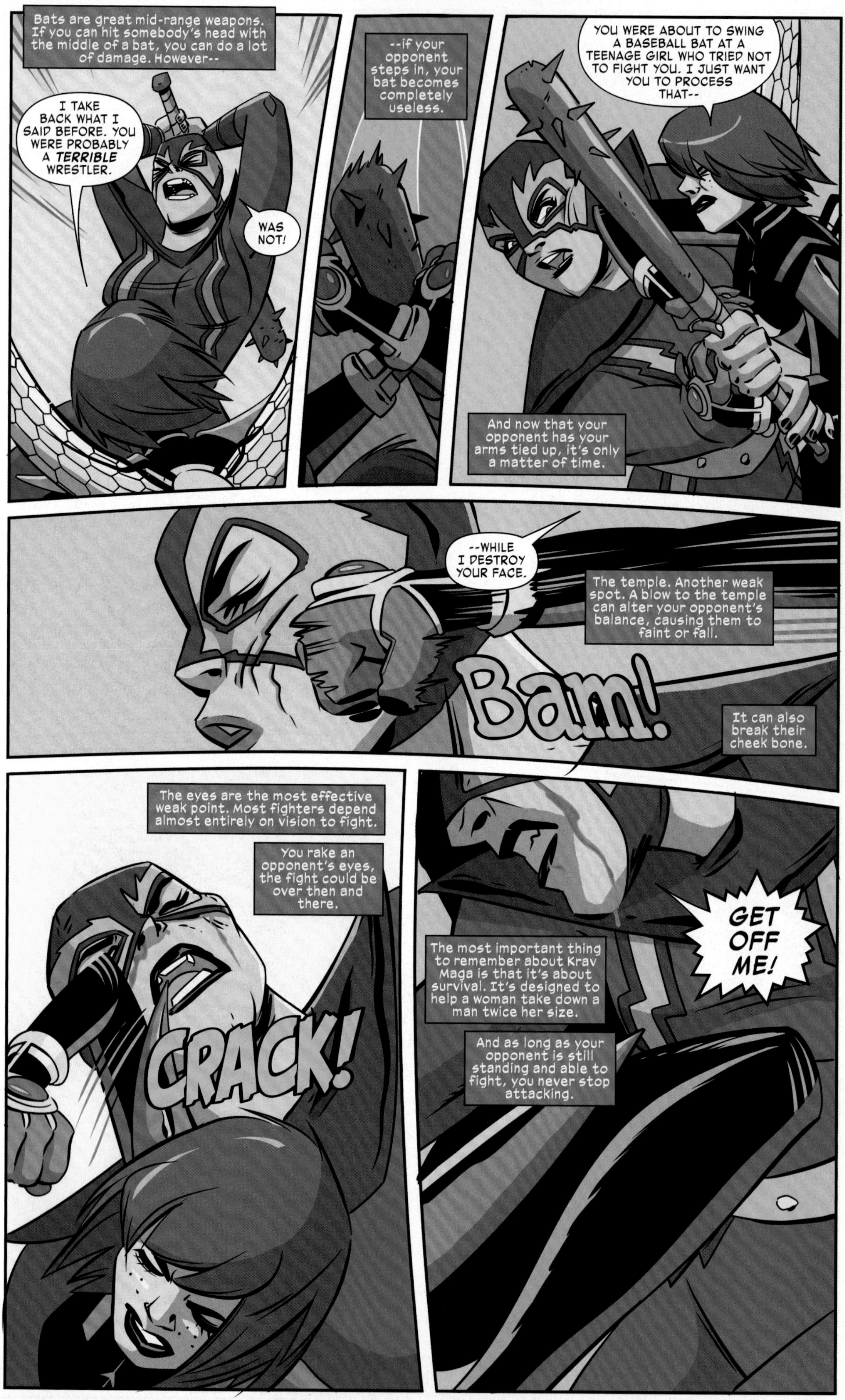
Bats are great mid-range weapons. If you can hit somebody's head with the middle of a bat, you can do a lot of damage. However--
I TAKE BACK WHAT I SAID BEFORE. YOU WERE PROBABLY A *TERRIBLE* WRESTLER.
WAS NOT!
--if your opponent steps in, your bat becomes completely useless.
YOU WERE ABOUT TO SWING A BASEBALL BAT AT A TEENAGE GIRL WHO TRIED NOT TO FIGHT YOU. I JUST WANT YOU TO PROCESS THAT--
And now that your opponent has your arms tied up, it's only a matter of time.
--WHILE I DESTROY YOUR FACE.
The temple. Another weak spot. A blow to the temple can alter your opponent's balance, causing them to faint or fall.
Bam!
It can also break their cheek bone.
The eyes are the most effective weak point. Most fighters depend almost entirely on vision to fight.
You rake an opponent's eyes, the fight could be over then and there.
CRACK!
GET OFF ME!
The most important thing to remember about Krav Maga is that it's about survival. It's designed to help a woman take down a man twice her size.
And as long as your opponent is still standing and able to fight, you never stop attacking.

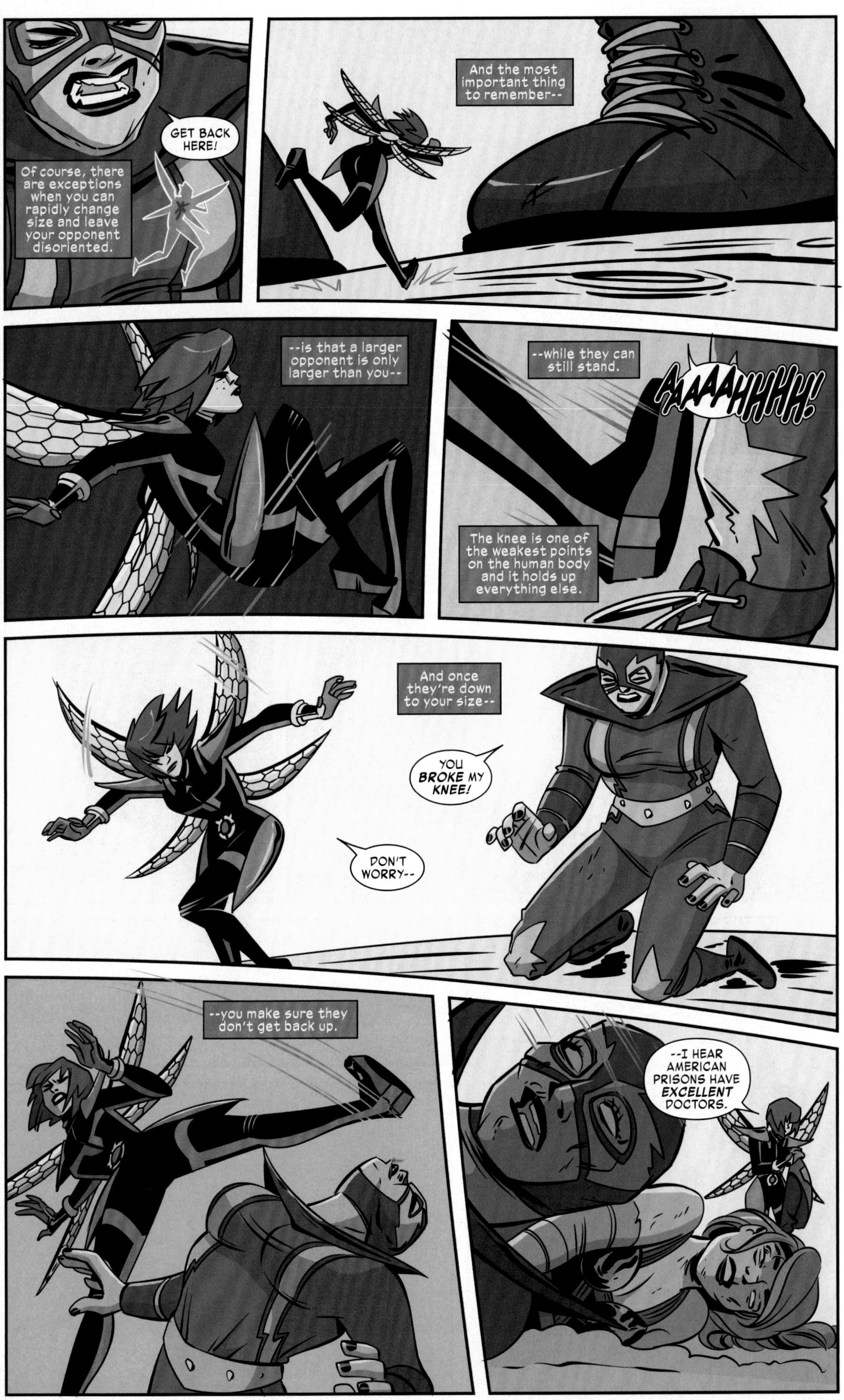
GET BACK HERE!
Of course, there are exceptions when you can rapidly change size and leave your opponent disoriented.
And the most important thing to remember--
--is that a larger opponent is only larger than you--
--while they can still stand.
AAAAAHHHH!
The knee is one of the weakest points on the human body and it holds up everything else.
And once they're down to your size--
YOU **BROKE** MY **KNEE!**
DON'T WORRY--
--you make sure they don't get back up.
--I HEAR AMERICAN PRISONS HAVE **EXCELLENT** DOCTORS.

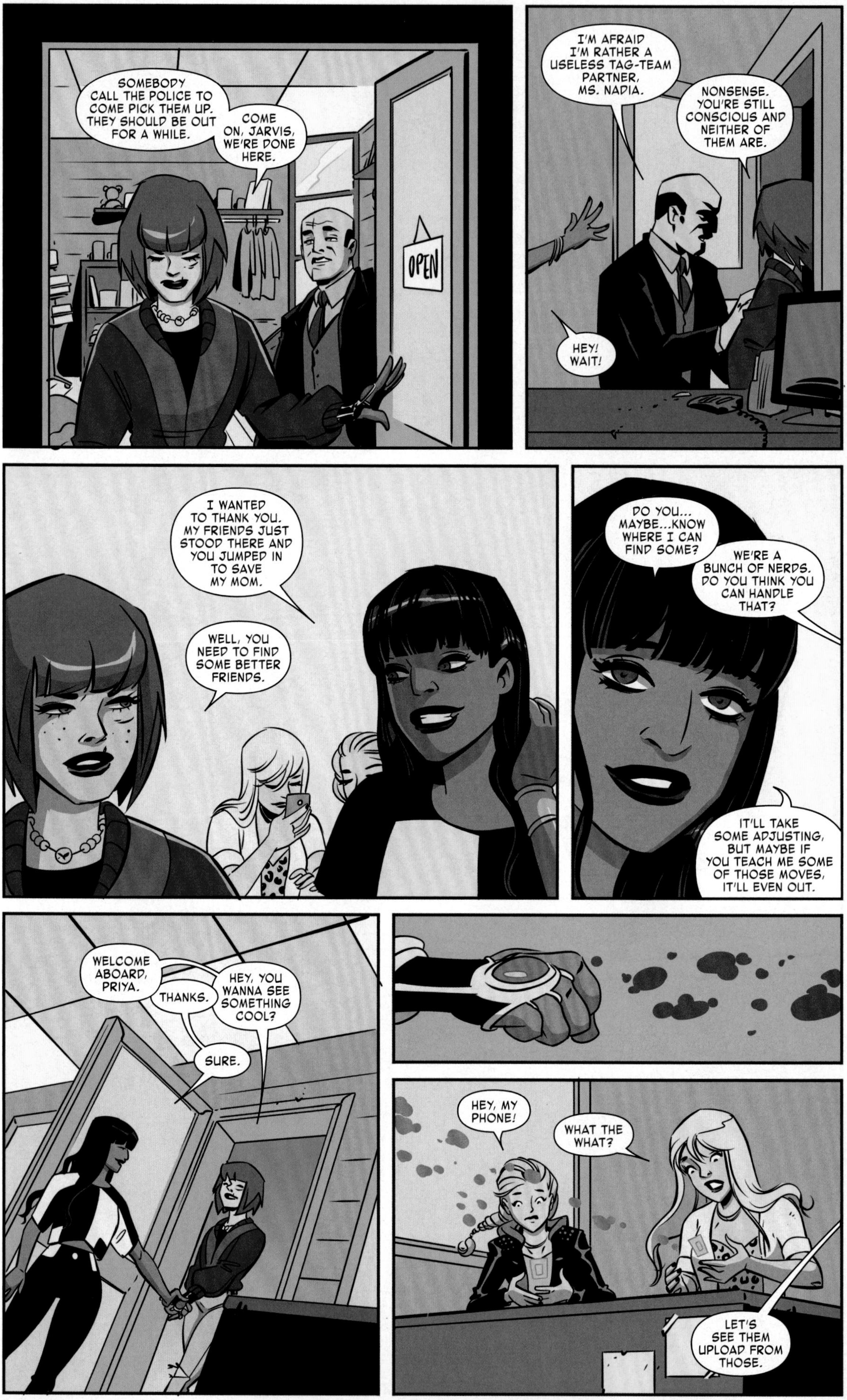
SOMEBODY CALL THE POLICE TO COME PICK THEM UP. THEY SHOULD BE OUT FOR A WHILE.
COME ON, JARVIS, WE'RE DONE HERE.
OPEN
I'M AFRAID I'M RATHER A USELESS TAG-TEAM PARTNER, MS. NADIA.
NONSENSE. YOU'RE STILL CONSCIOUS AND NEITHER OF THEM ARE.
HEY! WAIT!
I WANTED TO THANK YOU. MY FRIENDS JUST STOOD THERE AND YOU JUMPED IN TO SAVE MY MOM.
WELL, YOU NEED TO FIND SOME BETTER FRIENDS.
DO YOU... MAYBE...KNOW WHERE I CAN FIND SOME?
WE'RE A BUNCH OF NERDS. DO YOU THINK YOU CAN HANDLE THAT?
IT'LL TAKE SOME ADJUSTING, BUT MAYBE IF YOU TEACH ME SOME OF THOSE MOVES, IT'LL EVEN OUT.
WELCOME ABOARD, PRIYA.
THANKS.
HEY, YOU WANNA SEE SOMETHING COOL?
SURE.
HEY, MY PHONE!
WHAT THE WHAT?
LET'S SEE THEM UPLOAD FROM THOSE.

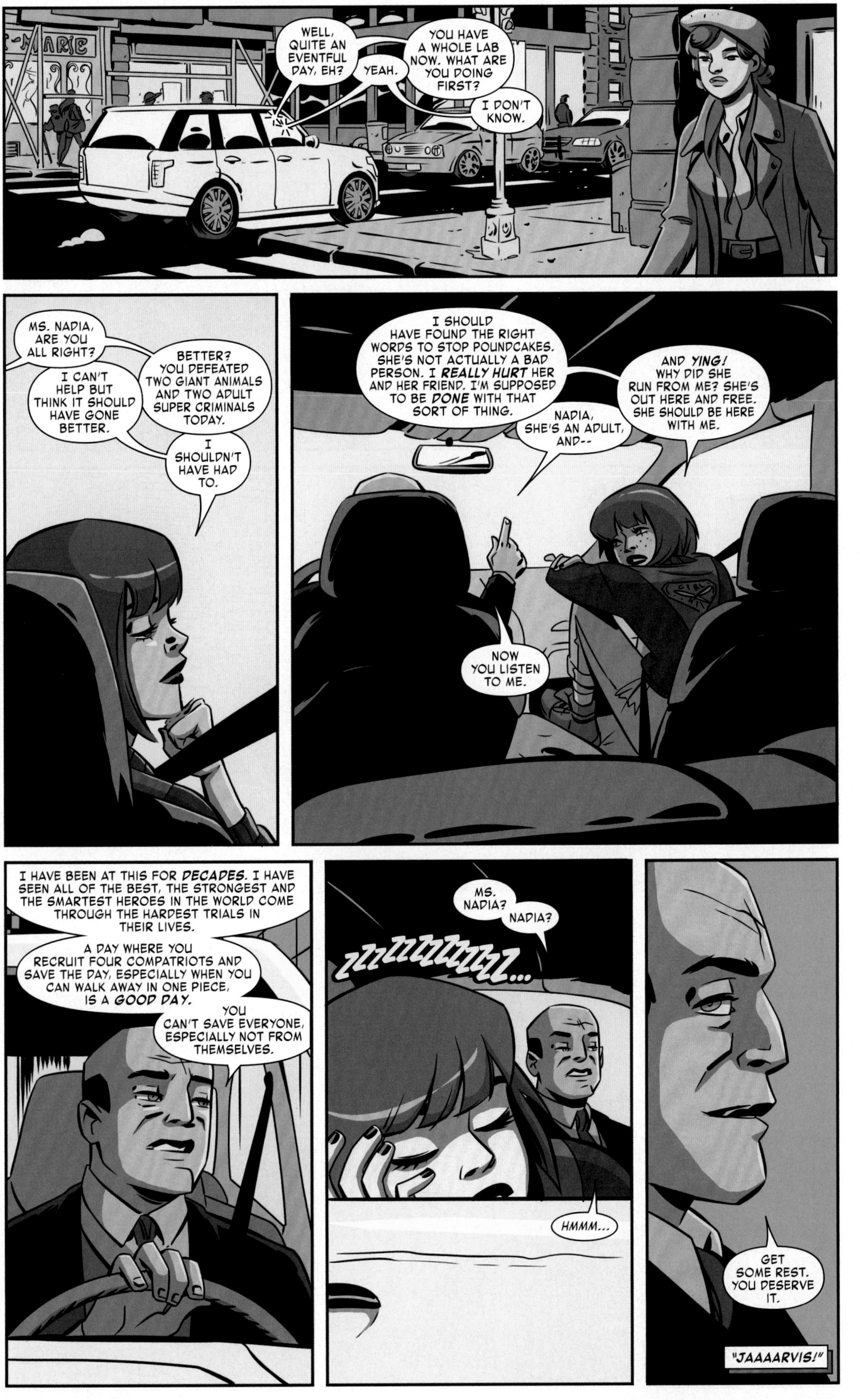
WELL, QUITE AN EVENTFUL DAY, EH?
YEAH.
YOU HAVE A WHOLE LAB NOW. WHAT ARE YOU DOING FIRST?
I DON'T KNOW.
MS. NADIA, ARE YOU ALL RIGHT?
I CAN'T HELP BUT THINK IT SHOULD HAVE GONE BETTER.
BETTER? YOU DEFEATED TWO GIANT ANIMALS AND TWO ADULT SUPER CRIMINALS TODAY.
I SHOULDN'T HAVE HAD TO.
I SHOULD HAVE FOUND THE RIGHT WORDS TO STOP POUNDCAKES. SHE'S NOT ACTUALLY A BAD PERSON. I REALLY HURT HER AND HER FRIEND. I'M SUPPOSED TO BE DONE WITH THAT SORT OF THING.
AND YING! WHY DID SHE RUN FROM ME? SHE'S OUT HERE AND FREE. SHE SHOULD BE HERE WITH ME.
NADIA, SHE'S AN ADULT, AND--
NOW YOU LISTEN TO ME.
I HAVE BEEN AT THIS FOR DECADES. I HAVE SEEN ALL OF THE BEST, THE STRONGEST AND THE SMARTEST HEROES IN THE WORLD COME THROUGH THE HARDEST TRIALS IN THEIR LIVES.
A DAY WHERE YOU RECRUIT FOUR COMPATRIOTS AND SAVE THE DAY, ESPECIALLY WHEN YOU CAN WALK AWAY IN ONE PIECE, IS A GOOD DAY.
YOU CAN'T SAVE EVERYONE, ESPECIALLY NOT FROM THEMSELVES.
MS. NADIA?
NADIA?
ZZZZZZZZZZZZZ...
HMMM...
GET SOME REST. YOU DESERVE IT.
"JAAAARVIS!"

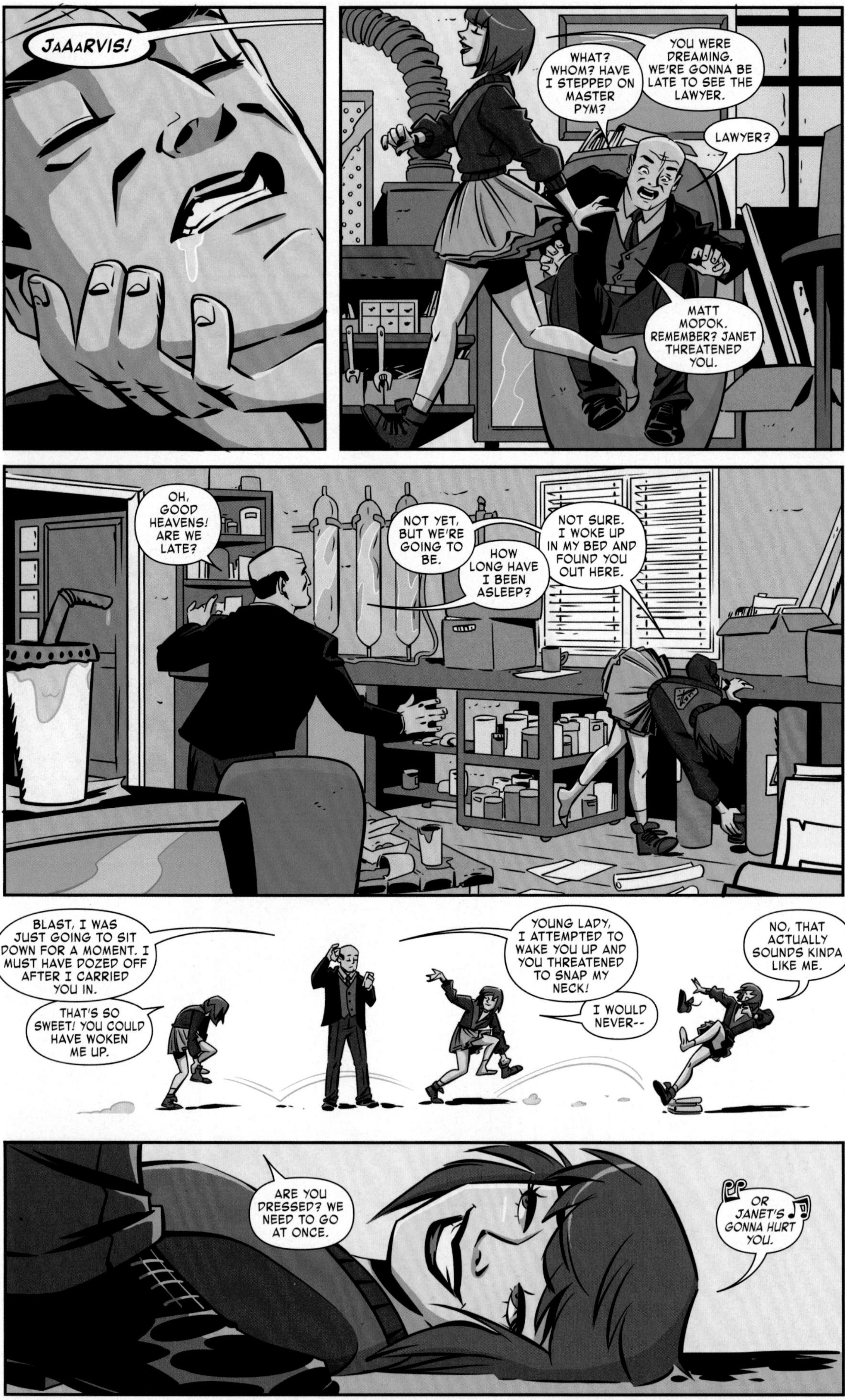
JaAaRVIS!
WHAT? WHOM? HAVE I STEPPED ON MASTER PYM?
YOU WERE DREAMING. WE'RE GONNA BE LATE TO SEE THE LAWYER.
LAWYER?
MATT MODOK. REMEMBER? JANET THREATENED YOU.
OH, GOOD HEAVENS! ARE WE LATE?
NOT YET, BUT WE'RE GOING TO BE.
HOW LONG HAVE I BEEN ASLEEP?
NOT SURE. I WOKE UP IN MY BED AND FOUND YOU OUT HERE.
BLAST, I WAS JUST GOING TO SIT DOWN FOR A MOMENT. I MUST HAVE DOZED OFF AFTER I CARRIED YOU IN.
THAT'S SO SWEET! YOU COULD HAVE WOKEN ME UP.
YOUNG LADY, I ATTEMPTED TO WAKE YOU UP AND YOU THREATENED TO SNAP MY NECK!
I WOULD NEVER--
NO, THAT ACTUALLY SOUNDS KINDA LIKE ME.
ARE YOU DRESSED? WE NEED TO GO AT ONCE.
OR JANET'S GONNA HURT YOU.

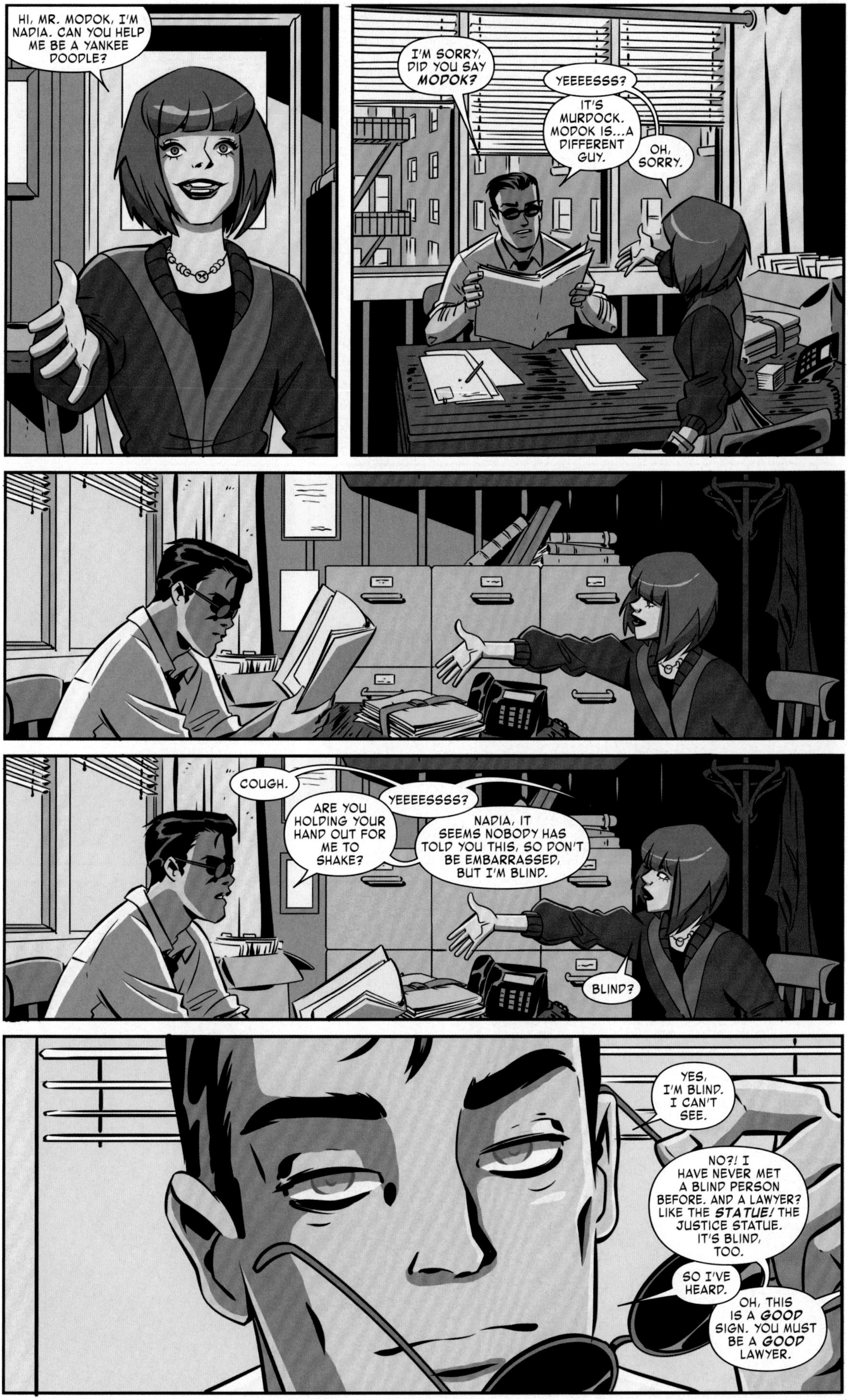
HI, MR. MODOK, I'M NADIA. CAN YOU HELP ME BE A YANKEE DOODLE?
I'M SORRY, DID YOU SAY *MODOK?*
YEEEESSS?
IT'S MURDOCK. MODOK IS...A DIFFERENT GUY.
OH, SORRY.
COUGH.
YEEEESSSS?
ARE YOU HOLDING YOUR HAND OUT FOR ME TO SHAKE?
NADIA, IT SEEMS NOBODY HAS TOLD YOU THIS, SO DON'T BE EMBARRASSED, BUT I'M BLIND.
BLIND?
YES, I'M BLIND. I CAN'T SEE.
NO?! I HAVE NEVER MET A BLIND PERSON BEFORE. AND A LAWYER? LIKE THE *STATUE!* THE JUSTICE STATUE. IT'S BLIND, TOO.
SO I'VE HEARD.
OH, THIS IS A *GOOD* SIGN. YOU MUST BE A *GOOD* LAWYER.

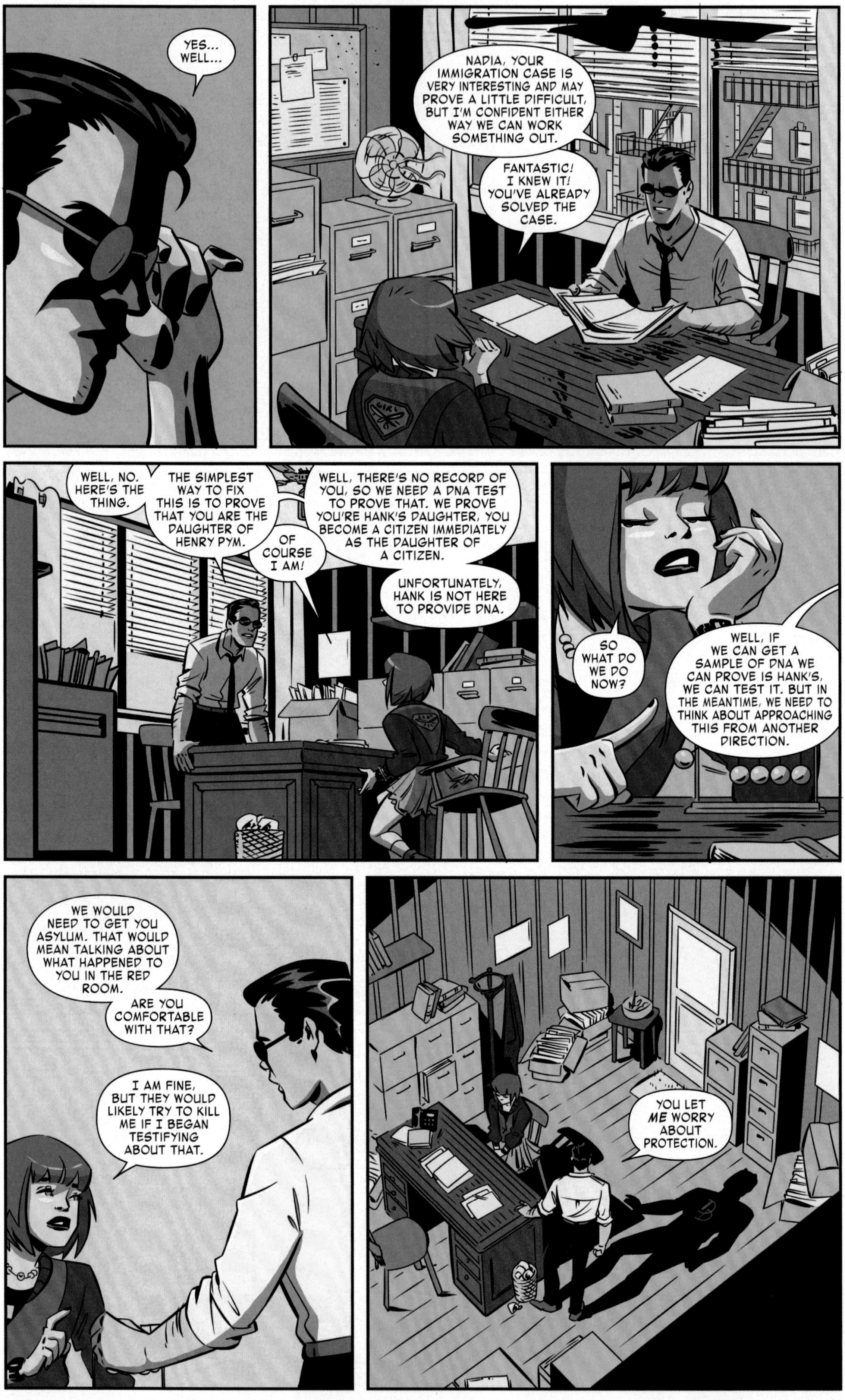
YES... WELL...
NADIA, YOUR IMMIGRATION CASE IS VERY INTERESTING AND MAY PROVE A LITTLE DIFFICULT, BUT I'M CONFIDENT EITHER WAY WE CAN WORK SOMETHING OUT.
FANTASTIC! I KNEW IT! YOU'VE ALREADY SOLVED THE CASE.
WELL, NO. HERE'S THE THING.
THE SIMPLEST WAY TO FIX THIS IS TO PROVE THAT YOU ARE THE DAUGHTER OF HENRY PYM.
OF COURSE I AM!
WELL, THERE'S NO RECORD OF YOU, SO WE NEED A DNA TEST TO PROVE THAT. WE PROVE YOU'RE HANK'S DAUGHTER, YOU BECOME A CITIZEN IMMEDIATELY AS THE DAUGHTER OF A CITIZEN.
UNFORTUNATELY, HANK IS NOT HERE TO PROVIDE DNA.
SO WHAT DO WE DO NOW?
WELL, IF WE CAN GET A SAMPLE OF DNA WE CAN PROVE IS HANK'S, WE CAN TEST IT. BUT IN THE MEANTIME, WE NEED TO THINK ABOUT APPROACHING THIS FROM ANOTHER DIRECTION.
WE WOULD NEED TO GET YOU ASYLUM. THAT WOULD MEAN TALKING ABOUT WHAT HAPPENED TO YOU IN THE RED ROOM.
ARE YOU COMFORTABLE WITH THAT?
I AM FINE, BUT THEY WOULD LIKELY TRY TO KILL ME IF I BEGAN TESTIFYING ABOUT THAT.
YOU LET *ME* WORRY ABOUT PROTECTION.

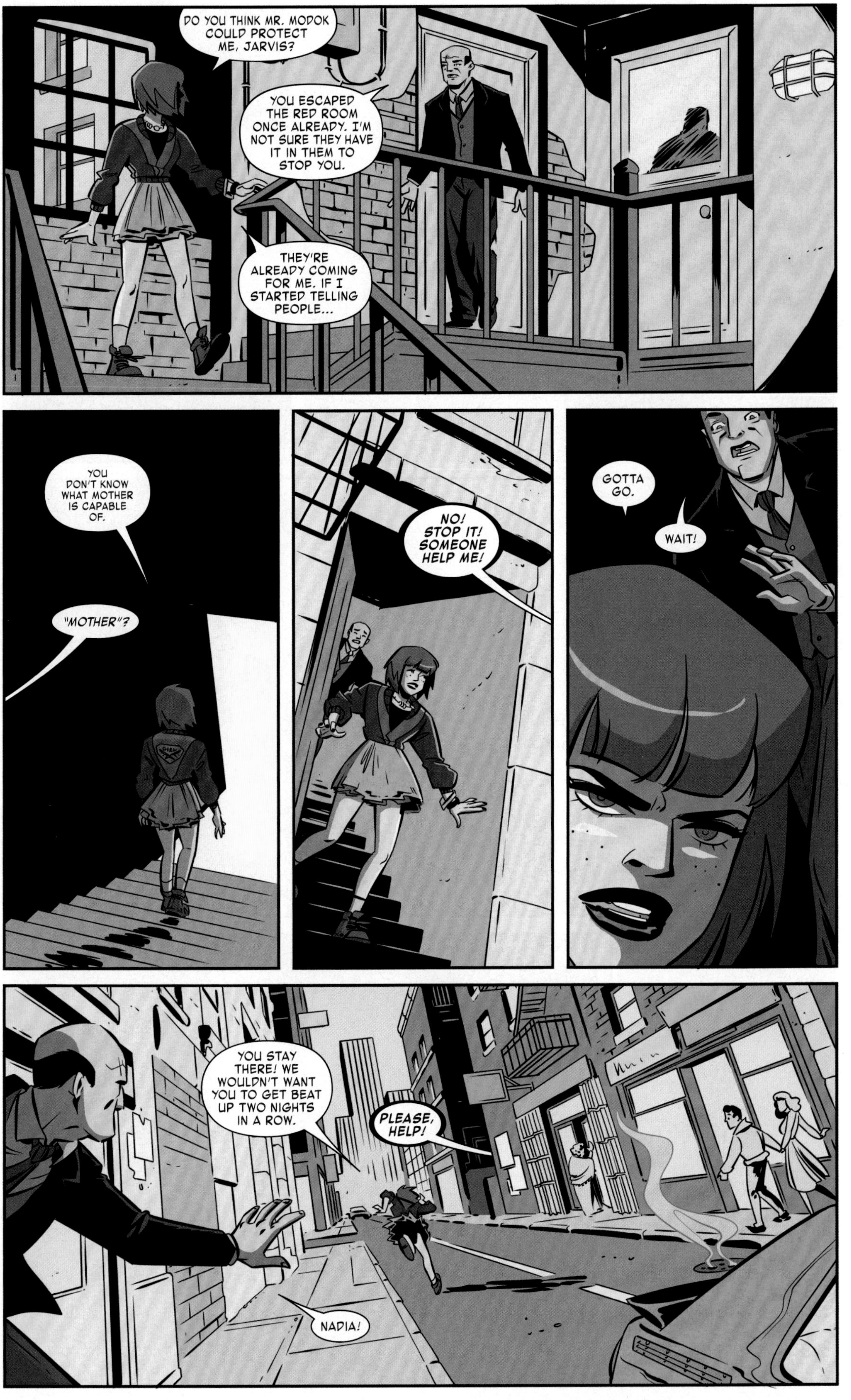
DO YOU THINK MR. MODOK COULD PROTECT ME, JARVIS?
YOU ESCAPED THE RED ROOM ONCE ALREADY. I'M NOT SURE THEY HAVE IT IN THEM TO STOP YOU.
THEY'RE ALREADY COMING FOR ME. IF I STARTED TELLING PEOPLE...
YOU DON'T KNOW WHAT MOTHER IS CAPABLE OF.
"MOTHER"?
NO! STOP IT! SOMEONE HELP ME!
GOTTA GO.
WAIT!
YOU STAY THERE! WE WOULDN'T WANT YOU TO GET BEAT UP TWO NIGHTS IN A ROW.
PLEASE, HELP!
NADIA!

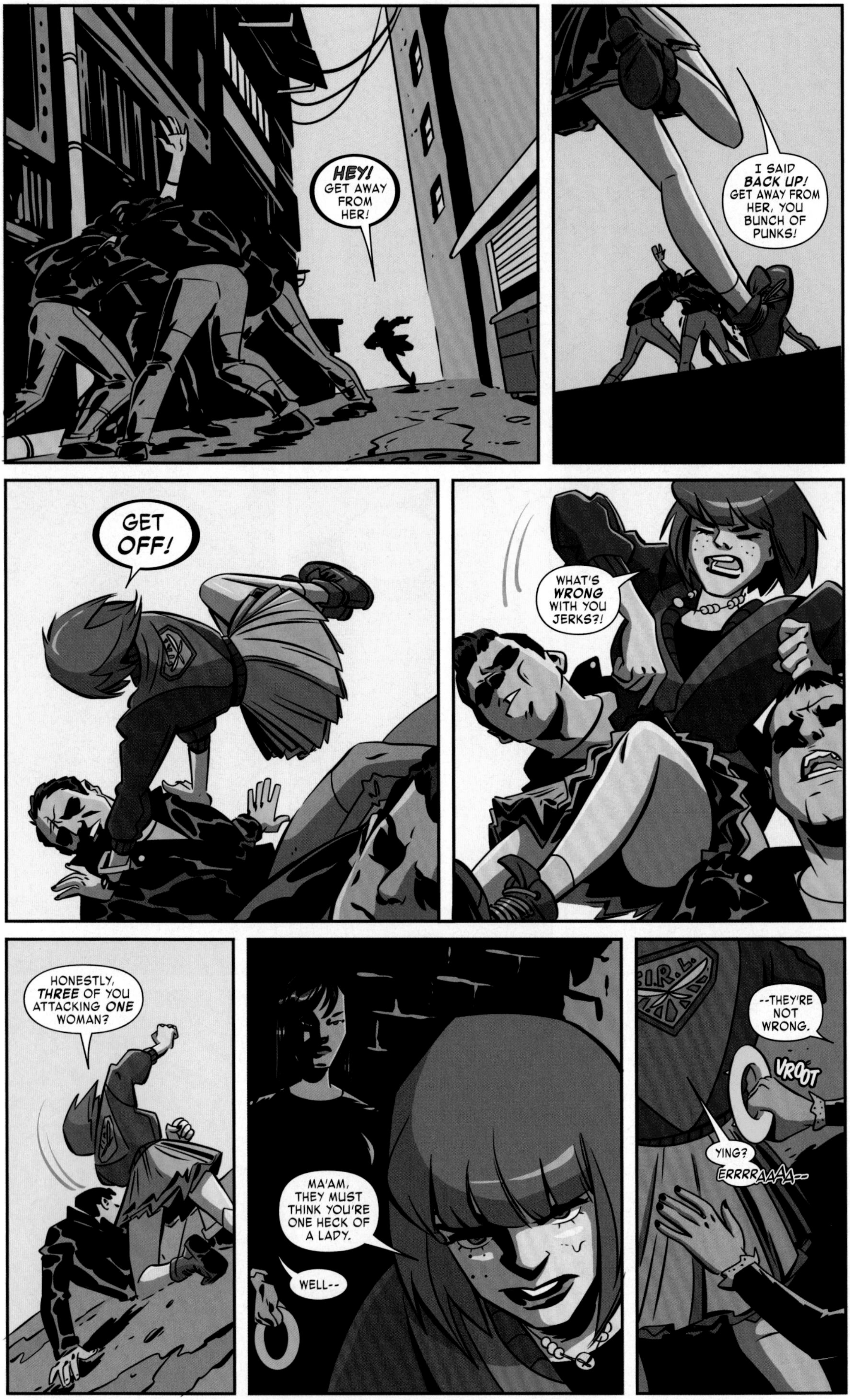
HEY! GET AWAY FROM HER!
I SAID BACK UP! GET AWAY FROM HER, YOU BUNCH OF PUNKS!
GET OFF!
WHAT'S WRONG WITH YOU JERKS?!
HONESTLY, THREE OF YOU ATTACKING ONE WOMAN?
MA'AM, THEY MUST THINK YOU'RE ONE HECK OF A LADY.
WELL--
--THEY'RE NOT WRONG.
VROOT
YING?
ERRRRAAAA--

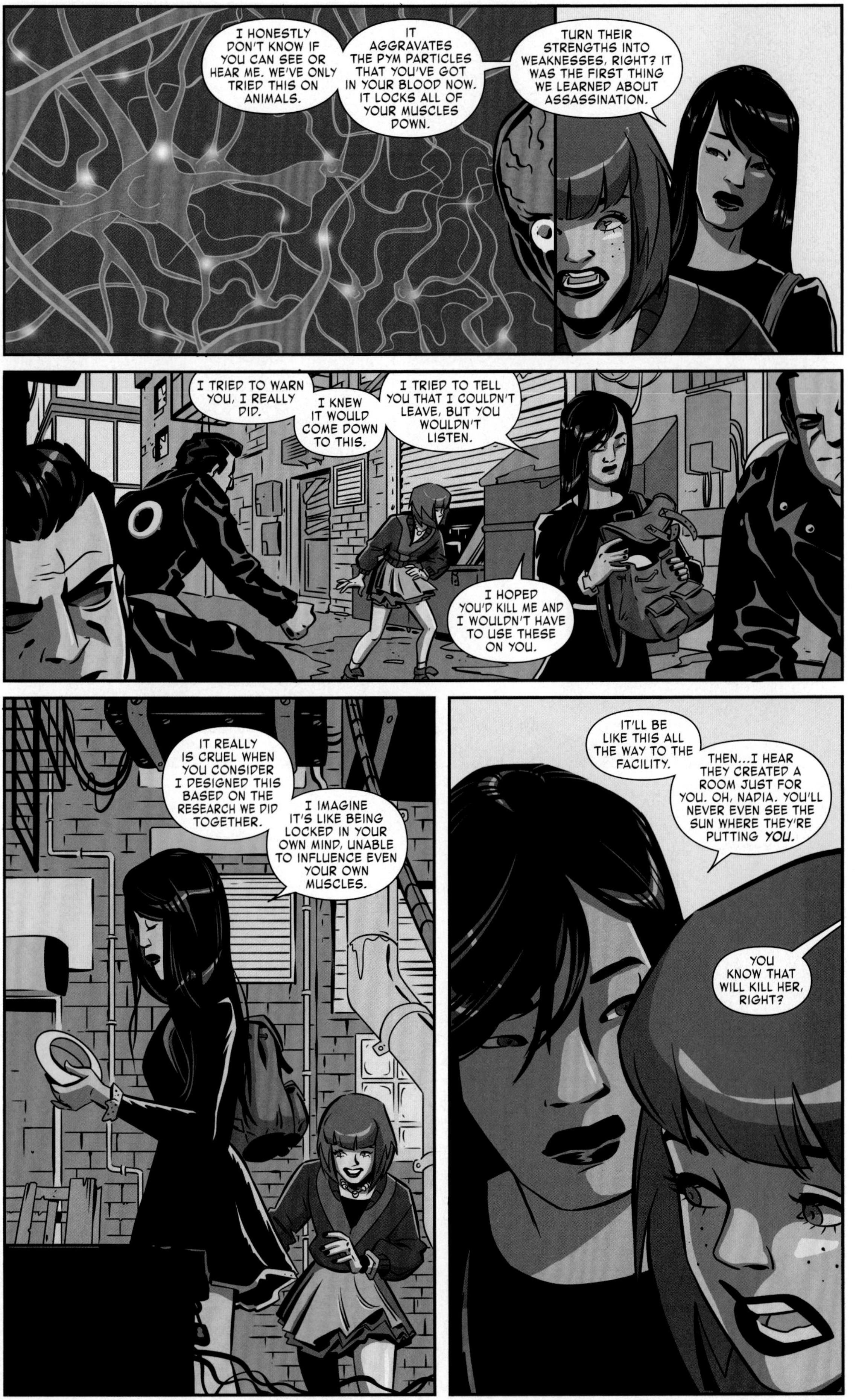
I HONESTLY DON'T KNOW IF YOU CAN SEE OR HEAR ME. WE'VE ONLY TRIED THIS ON ANIMALS.
IT AGGRAVATES THE PYM PARTICLES THAT YOU'VE GOT IN YOUR BLOOD NOW. IT LOCKS ALL OF YOUR MUSCLES DOWN.
TURN THEIR STRENGTHS INTO WEAKNESSES, RIGHT? IT WAS THE FIRST THING WE LEARNED ABOUT ASSASSINATION.
I TRIED TO WARN YOU, I REALLY DID.
I KNEW IT WOULD COME DOWN TO THIS.
I TRIED TO TELL YOU THAT I COULDN'T LEAVE, BUT YOU WOULDN'T LISTEN.
I HOPED YOU'D KILL ME AND I WOULDN'T HAVE TO USE THESE ON YOU.
IT REALLY IS CRUEL WHEN YOU CONSIDER I DESIGNED THIS BASED ON THE RESEARCH WE DID TOGETHER.
I IMAGINE IT'S LIKE BEING LOCKED IN YOUR OWN MIND, UNABLE TO INFLUENCE EVEN YOUR OWN MUSCLES.
IT'LL BE LIKE THIS ALL THE WAY TO THE FACILITY.
THEN...I HEAR THEY CREATED A ROOM JUST FOR YOU. OH, NADIA. YOU'LL NEVER EVEN SEE THE SUN WHERE THEY'RE PUTTING *YOU.*
YOU KNOW THAT WILL KILL HER, RIGHT?

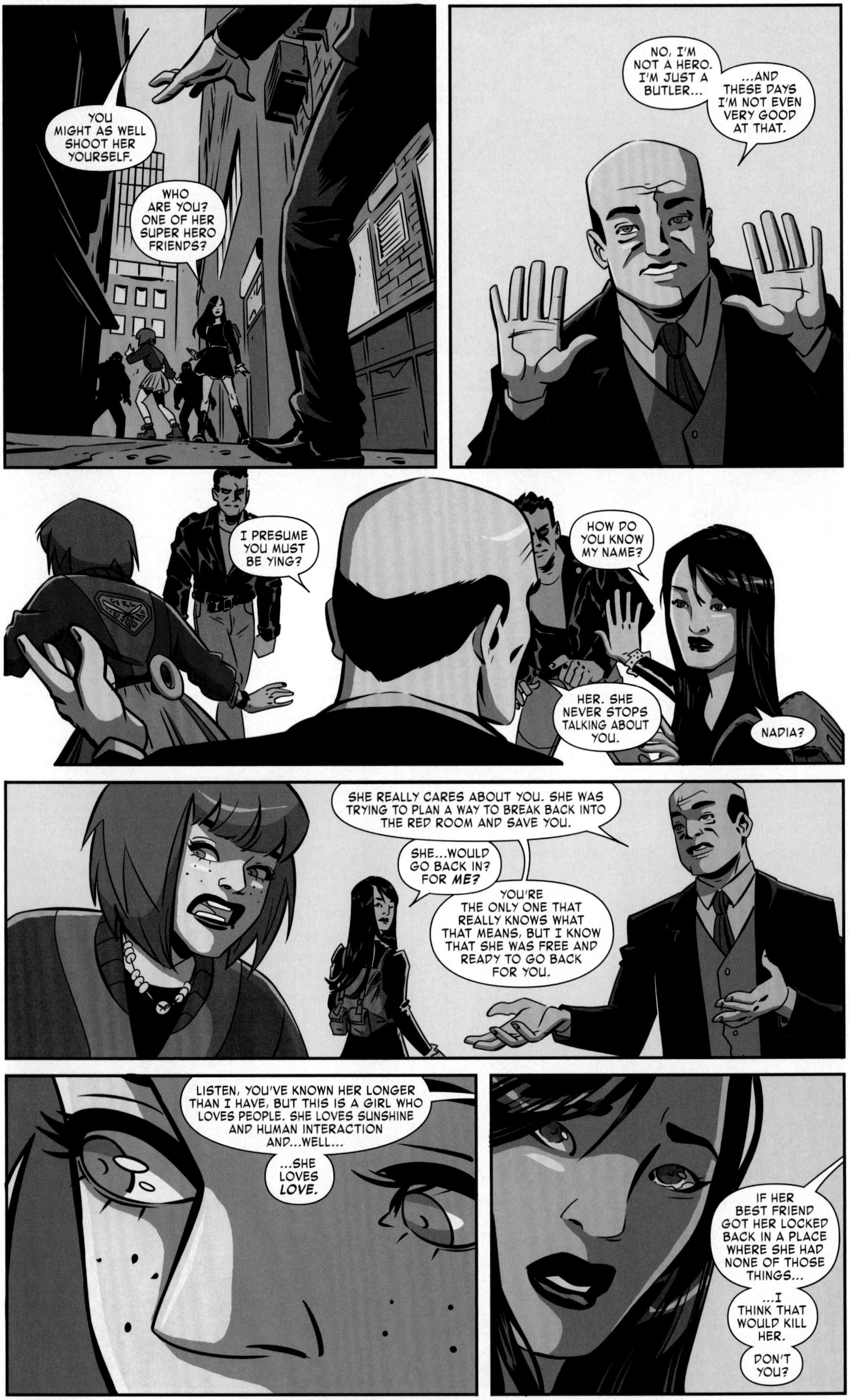
YOU MIGHT AS WELL SHOOT HER YOURSELF.
WHO ARE YOU? ONE OF HER SUPER HERO FRIENDS?
NO, I'M NOT A HERO. I'M JUST A BUTLER...
...AND THESE DAYS I'M NOT EVEN VERY GOOD AT THAT.
I PRESUME YOU MUST BE YING?
HOW DO YOU KNOW MY NAME?
HER. SHE NEVER STOPS TALKING ABOUT YOU.
NADIA?
SHE REALLY CARES ABOUT YOU. SHE WAS TRYING TO PLAN A WAY TO BREAK BACK INTO THE RED ROOM AND SAVE YOU.
SHE...WOULD GO BACK IN? FOR ME?
YOU'RE THE ONLY ONE THAT REALLY KNOWS WHAT THAT MEANS, BUT I KNOW THAT SHE WAS FREE AND READY TO GO BACK FOR YOU.
LISTEN, YOU'VE KNOWN HER LONGER THAN I HAVE, BUT THIS IS A GIRL WHO LOVES PEOPLE. SHE LOVES SUNSHINE AND HUMAN INTERACTION AND...WELL...
...SHE LOVES LOVE.
IF HER BEST FRIEND GOT HER LOCKED BACK IN A PLACE WHERE SHE HAD NONE OF THOSE THINGS...
...I THINK THAT WOULD KILL HER.
DON'T YOU?

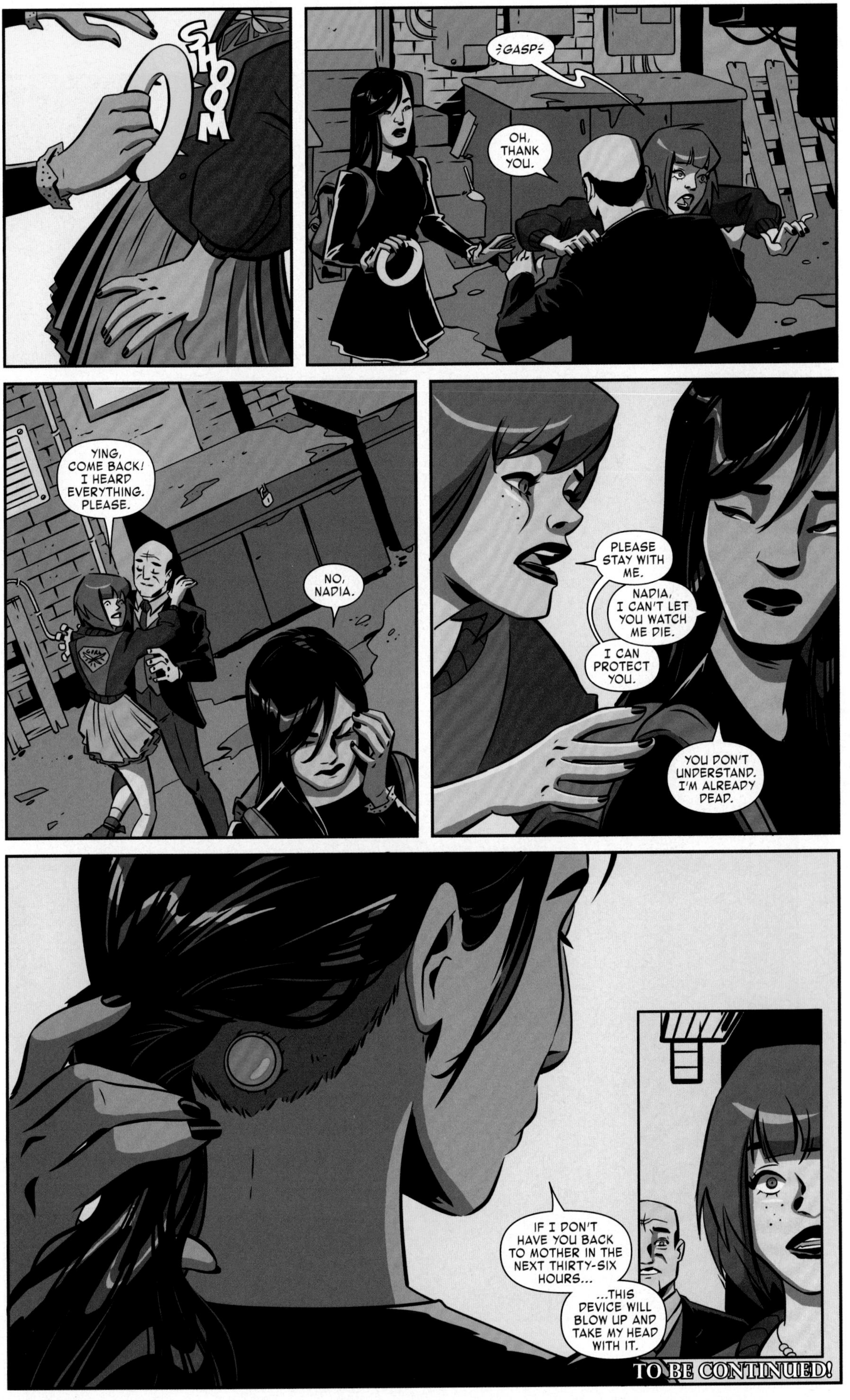
SHOOM
GASP
OH, THANK YOU.
YING, COME BACK! I HEARD EVERYTHING. PLEASE.
NO, NADIA.
PLEASE STAY WITH ME.
NADIA, I CAN'T LET YOU WATCH ME DIE.
I CAN PROTECT YOU.
YOU DON'T UNDERSTAND. I'M ALREADY DEAD.
IF I DON'T HAVE YOU BACK TO MOTHER IN THE NEXT THIRTY-SIX HOURS...
...THIS DEVICE WILL BLOW UP AND TAKE MY HEAD WITH IT.
TO BE CONTINUED!

ALL-NEW, ALL-DIFFERENT AVENGERS #14

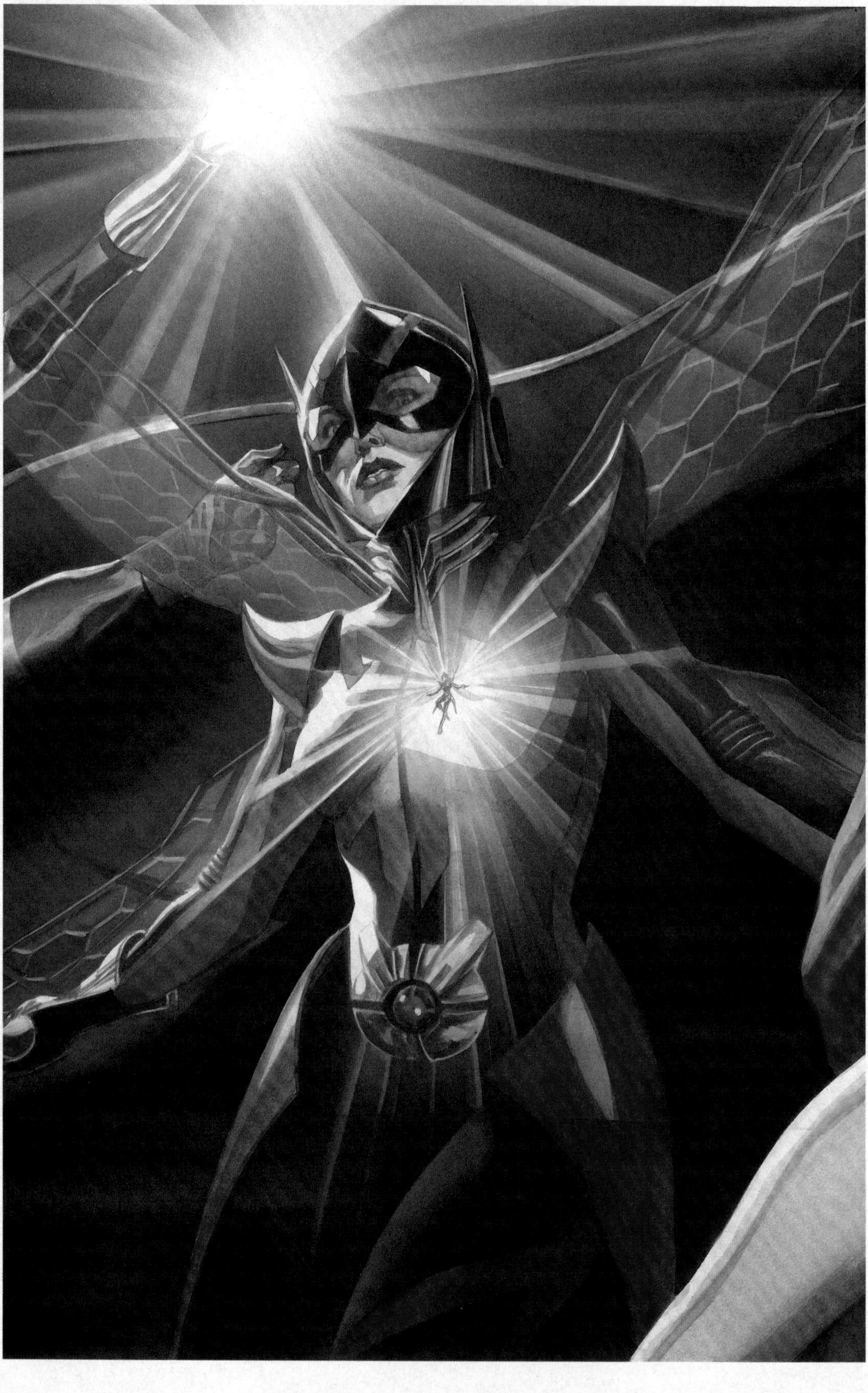

AND THERE CAME A DAY, A DAY UNLIKE ANY OTHER, WHEN EARTH'S MIGHTIEST HEROES (OR THE ONES THAT WERE AROUND THAT DAY, ANYWAY) FOUND THEMSELVES UNITED AGAINST A COMMON THREAT. ON THAT DAY, THE AVENGERS WERE BORN--TO FIGHT THE FOES NO SINGLE SUPER HERO COULD WITHSTAND!

NOW CAPTAIN AMERICA, IRON MAN, THOR, VISION, SPIDER-MAN, MS. MARVEL, NOVA AND WASP ARE THE...

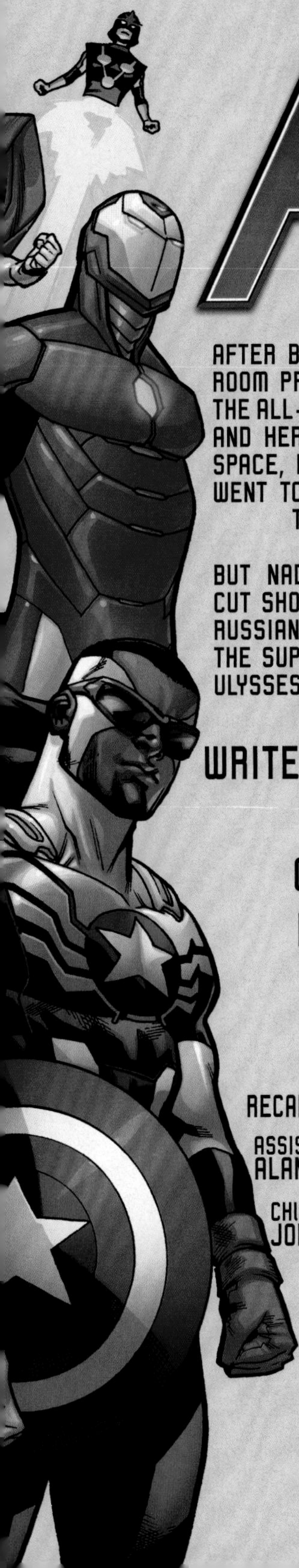

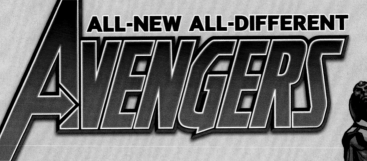

ALL-NEW ALL-DIFFERENT AVENGERS

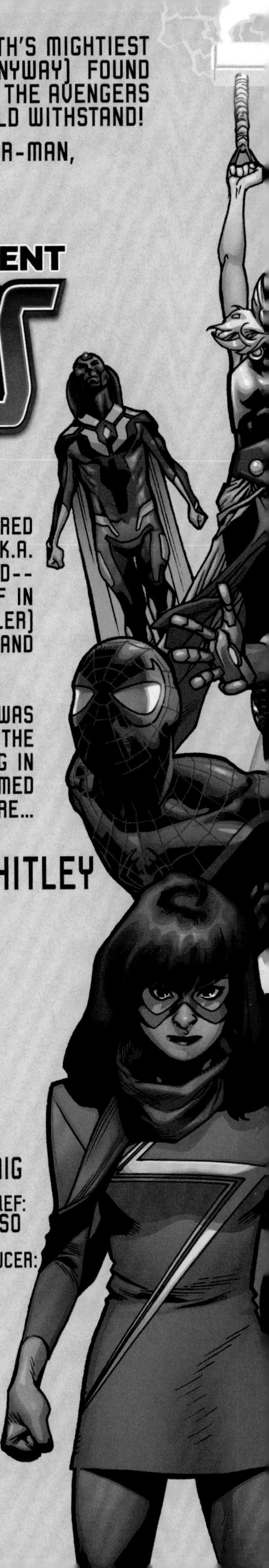

AFTER BEING HIDDEN AWAY BY THE SINISTER RUSSIAN RED ROOM PROGRAM FOR MOST OF HER LIFE, NADIA PYM, A.K.A. THE ALL-NEW WASP, HAS A LOT TO LEARN ABOUT THE WORLD--AND HER OWN FAMILY. WHILE THE AVENGERS WERE OFF IN SPACE, NADIA AND JARVIS (THE AVENGERS' LOYAL BUTLER) WENT TO VISIT JANET VAN DYNE, THE ORIGINAL WASP AND THE EX-WIFE OF NADIA'S FATHER, HANK PYM.

BUT NADIA'S BONDING TIME WITH HER STEPMOTHER WAS CUT SHORT BY THE ARRIVAL OF A GROUP OF MEN FROM THE RUSSIAN CONSULATE. MEANWHILE, TENSIONS ARE RISING IN THE SUPER HERO COMMUNITY OVER A NEW INHUMAN NAMED ULYSSES, WHO CLAIMS TO BE ABLE TO PREDICT THE FUTURE...

WRITERS: MARK WAID & JEREMY WHITLEY

ARTIST: ADAM KUBERT

COLOR ARTIST: SONIA OBACK

LETTERER: VC'S CORY PETIT

COVER ARTIST: ALEX ROSS

VARIANT COVER ARTISTS:
MIKE McKONE; PAUL RENAUD

RECAP PAGE ART BY: MAHMUD ASRAR & DAVE McCAIG

ASSISTANT EDITOR: ALANNA SMITH
EDITOR: TOM BREVOORT
EDITOR IN CHIEF: AXEL ALONSO

CHIEF CREATIVE OFFICER: JOE QUESADA
PUBLISHER: DAN BUCKLEY
EXEC. PRODUCER: ALAN FINE

THE AVENGERS CREATED BY
STAN LEE and JACK KIRBY

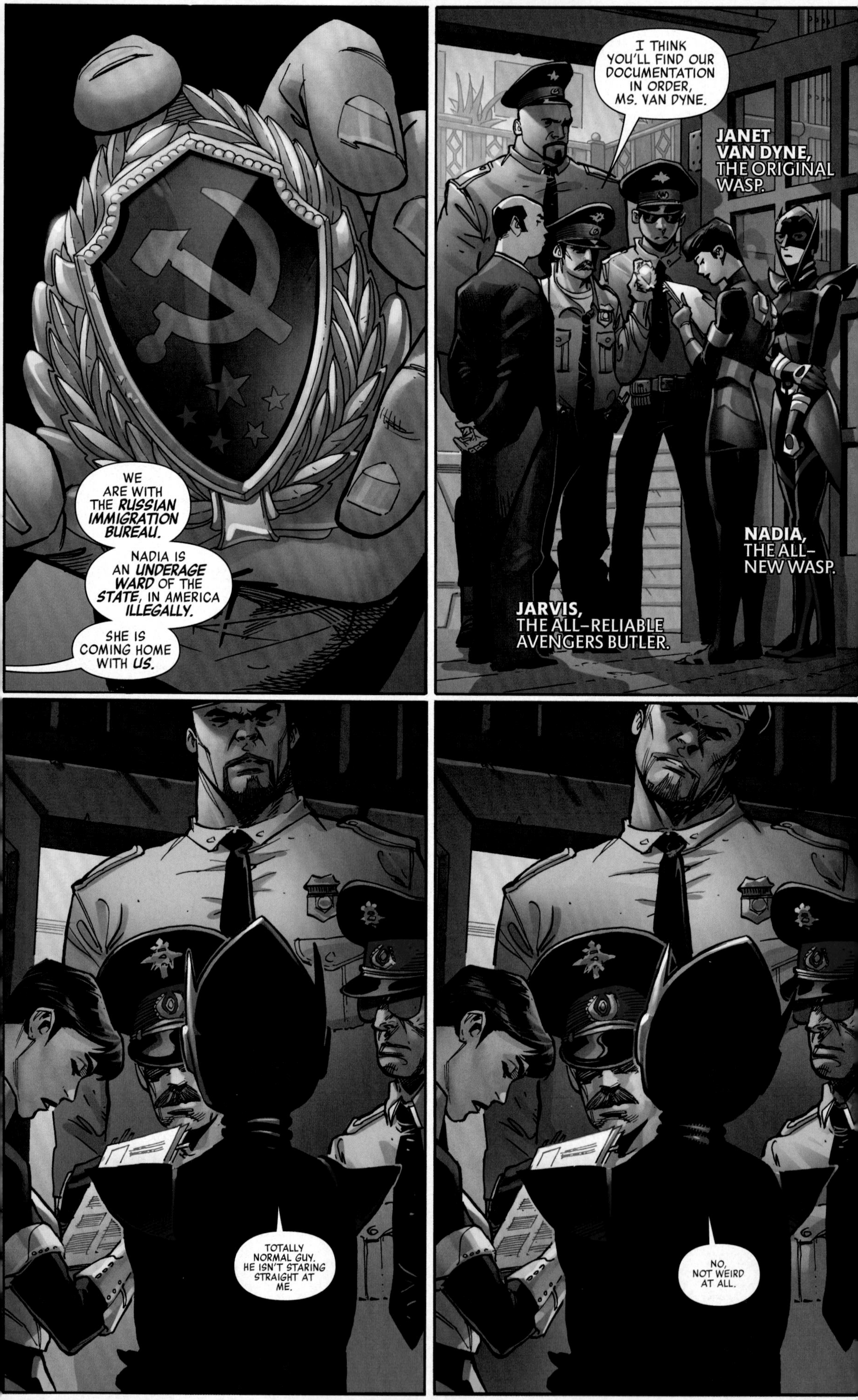
WE ARE WITH THE RUSSIAN IMMIGRATION BUREAU.
NADIA IS AN UNDERAGE WARD OF THE STATE, IN AMERICA ILLEGALLY.
SHE IS COMING HOME WITH US.
I THINK YOU'LL FIND OUR DOCUMENTATION IN ORDER, MS. VAN DYNE.
JANET VAN DYNE, THE ORIGINAL WASP.
NADIA, THE ALL-NEW WASP.
JARVIS, THE ALL-RELIABLE AVENGERS BUTLER.
TOTALLY NORMAL GUY. HE ISN'T STARING STRAIGHT AT ME.
NO, NOT WEIRD AT ALL.

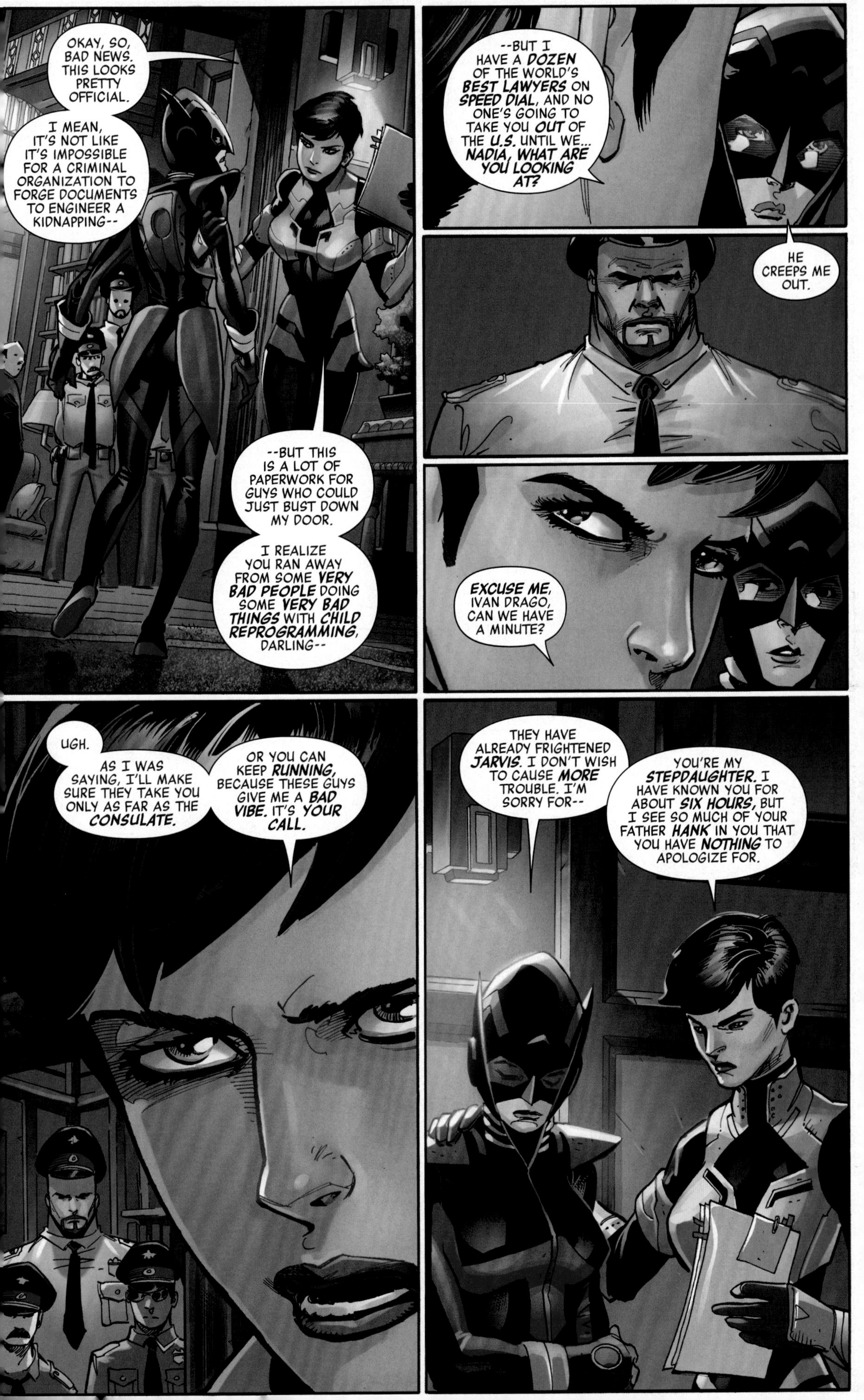

OKAY, SO, BAD NEWS. THIS LOOKS PRETTY OFFICIAL.
I MEAN, IT'S NOT LIKE IT'S IMPOSSIBLE FOR A CRIMINAL ORGANIZATION TO FORGE DOCUMENTS TO ENGINEER A KIDNAPPING--
--BUT THIS IS A LOT OF PAPERWORK FOR GUYS WHO COULD JUST BUST DOWN MY DOOR.
I REALIZE YOU RAN AWAY FROM SOME VERY BAD PEOPLE DOING SOME VERY BAD THINGS WITH CHILD REPROGRAMMING, DARLING--
--BUT I HAVE A DOZEN OF THE WORLD'S BEST LAWYERS ON SPEED DIAL, AND NO ONE'S GOING TO TAKE YOU OUT OF THE U.S. UNTIL WE... NADIA, WHAT ARE YOU LOOKING AT?
HE CREEPS ME OUT.
EXCUSE ME, IVAN DRAGO, CAN WE HAVE A MINUTE?
UGH.
AS I WAS SAYING, I'LL MAKE SURE THEY TAKE YOU ONLY AS FAR AS THE CONSULATE.
OR YOU CAN KEEP RUNNING, BECAUSE THESE GUYS GIVE ME A BAD VIBE. IT'S YOUR CALL.
THEY HAVE ALREADY FRIGHTENED JARVIS. I DON'T WISH TO CAUSE MORE TROUBLE. I'M SORRY FOR--
YOU'RE MY STEPDAUGHTER. I HAVE KNOWN YOU FOR ABOUT SIX HOURS, BUT I SEE SO MUCH OF YOUR FATHER HANK IN YOU THAT YOU HAVE NOTHING TO APOLOGIZE FOR.

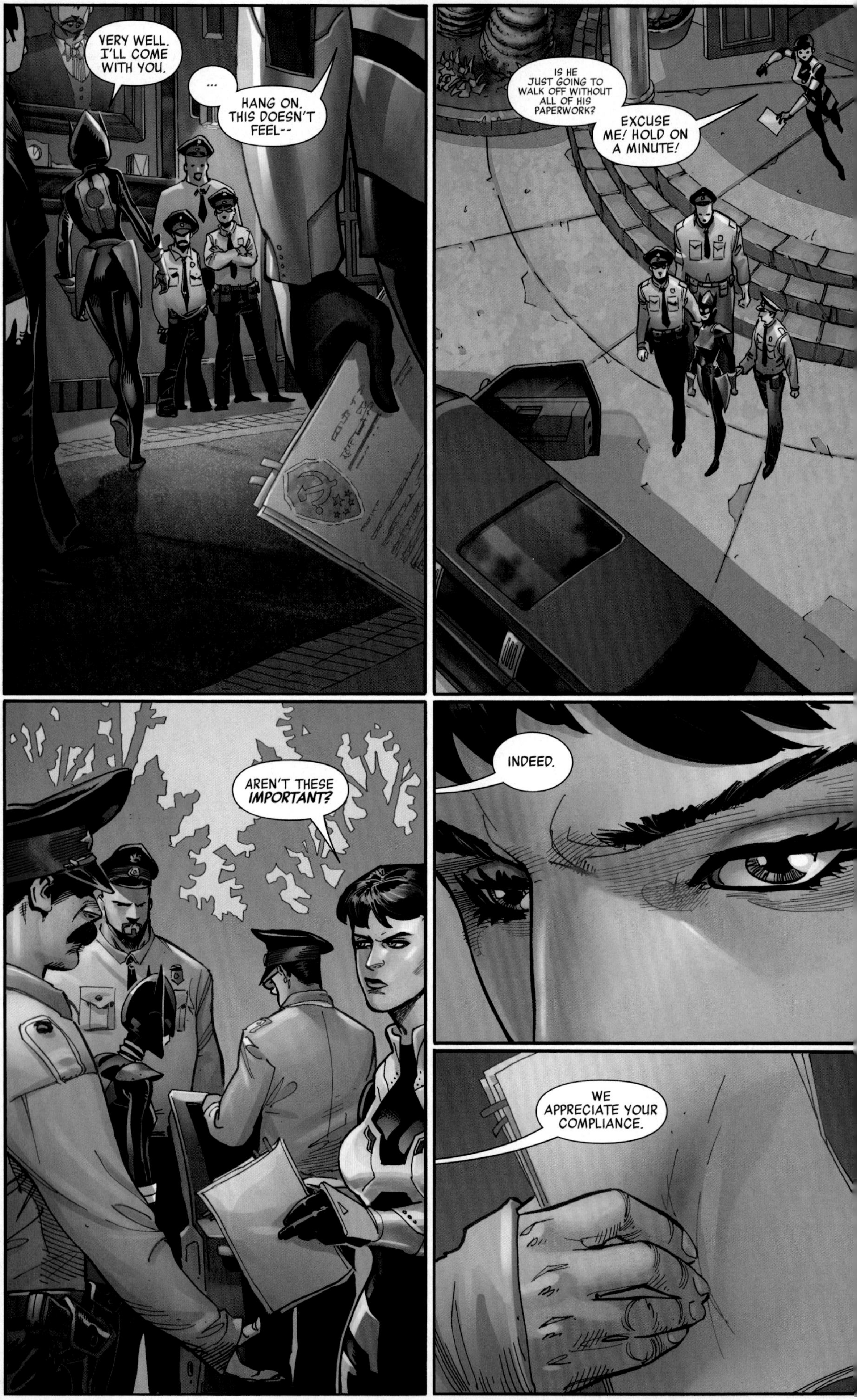
VERY WELL. I'LL COME WITH YOU.
...
HANG ON. THIS DOESN'T FEEL--
IS HE JUST GOING TO WALK OFF WITHOUT ALL OF HIS PAPERWORK?
EXCUSE ME! HOLD ON A MINUTE!
AREN'T THESE IMPORTANT?
INDEED.
WE APPRECIATE YOUR COMPLIANCE.

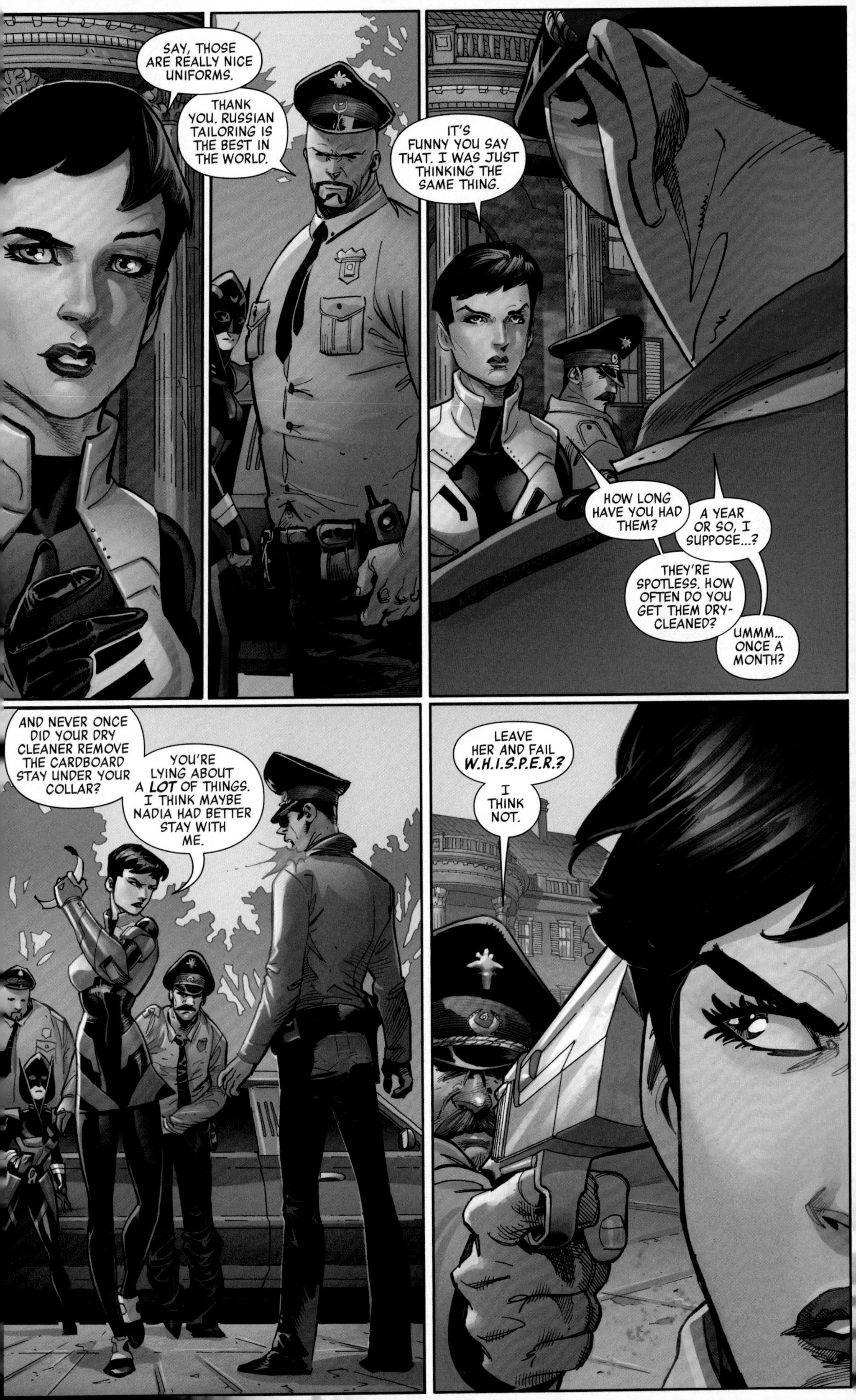
SAY, THOSE ARE REALLY NICE UNIFORMS.
THANK YOU. RUSSIAN TAILORING IS THE BEST IN THE WORLD.
IT'S FUNNY YOU SAY THAT. I WAS JUST THINKING THE SAME THING.
HOW LONG HAVE YOU HAD THEM?
A YEAR OR SO, I SUPPOSE...?
THEY'RE SPOTLESS. HOW OFTEN DO YOU GET THEM DRY-CLEANED?
UMMM... ONCE A MONTH?
AND NEVER ONCE DID YOUR DRY CLEANER REMOVE THE CARDBOARD STAY UNDER YOUR COLLAR?
YOU'RE LYING ABOUT A LOT OF THINGS. I THINK MAYBE NADIA HAD BETTER STAY WITH ME.
LEAVE HER AND FAIL W.H.I.S.P.E.R.?
I THINK NOT.

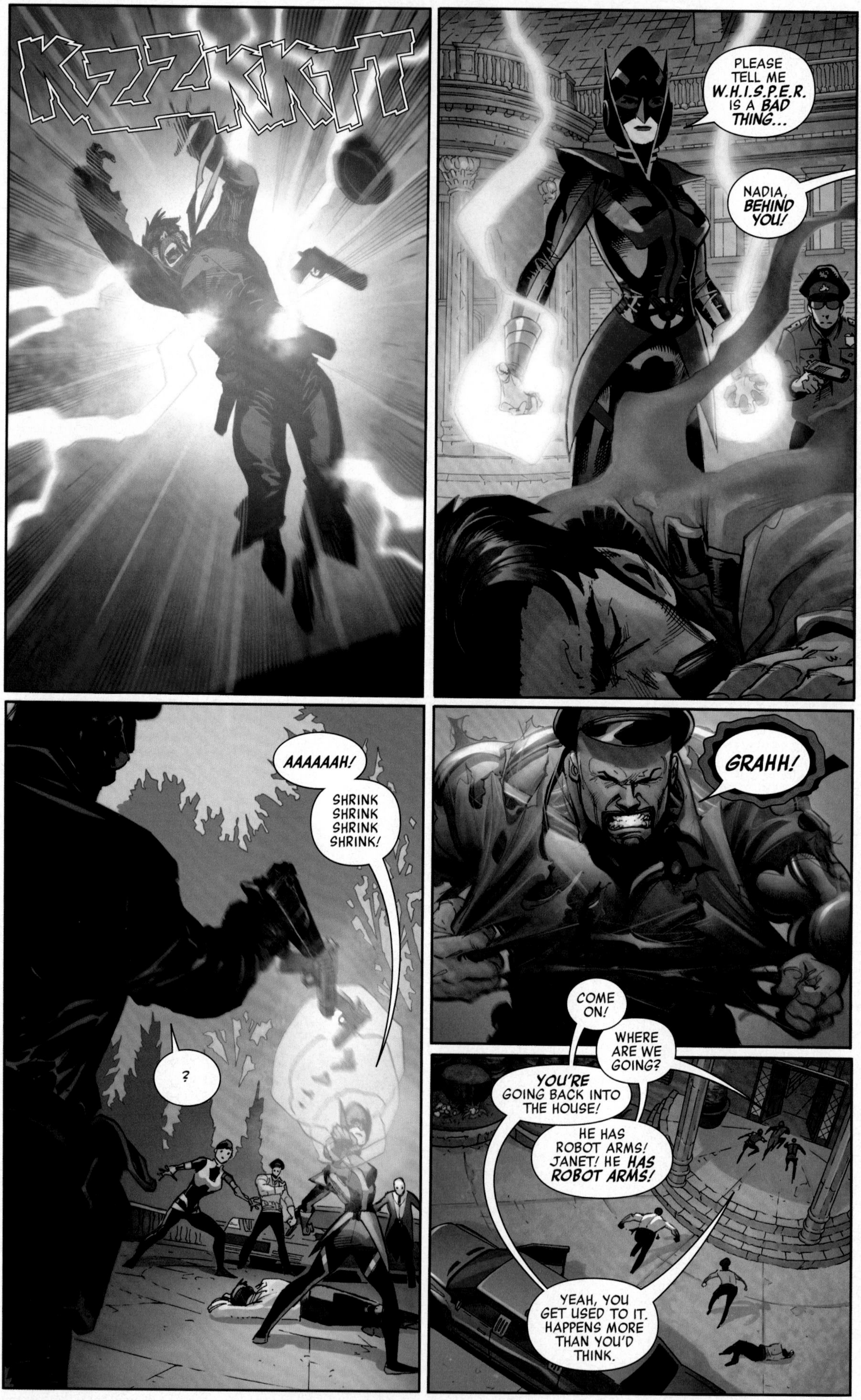
KZZZKKKTT
PLEASE TELL ME W.H.I.S.P.E.R. IS A BAD THING...
NADIA, BEHIND YOU!
AAAAAAH!
SHRINK SHRINK SHRINK SHRINK!
?
GRAHH!
COME ON!
WHERE ARE WE GOING?
YOU'RE GOING BACK INTO THE HOUSE!
HE HAS ROBOT ARMS! JANET! HE HAS ROBOT ARMS!
YEAH, YOU GET USED TO IT. HAPPENS MORE THAN YOU'D THINK.

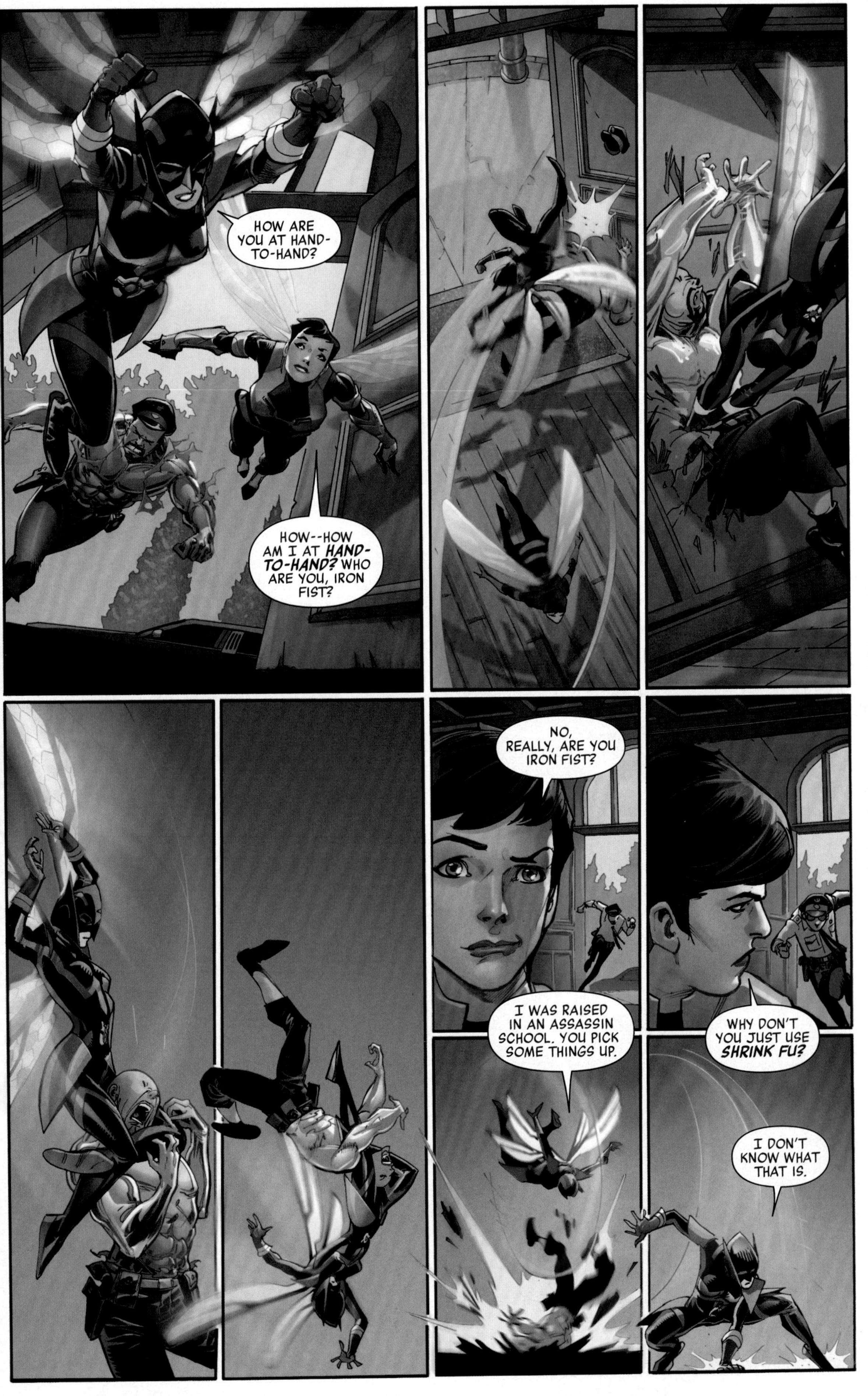
HOW ARE YOU AT HAND-TO-HAND?
HOW--HOW AM I AT HAND-TO-HAND? WHO ARE YOU, IRON FIST?
NO, REALLY, ARE YOU IRON FIST?
I WAS RAISED IN AN ASSASSIN SCHOOL. YOU PICK SOME THINGS UP.
WHY DON'T YOU JUST USE SHRINK FU?
I DON'T KNOW WHAT THAT IS.

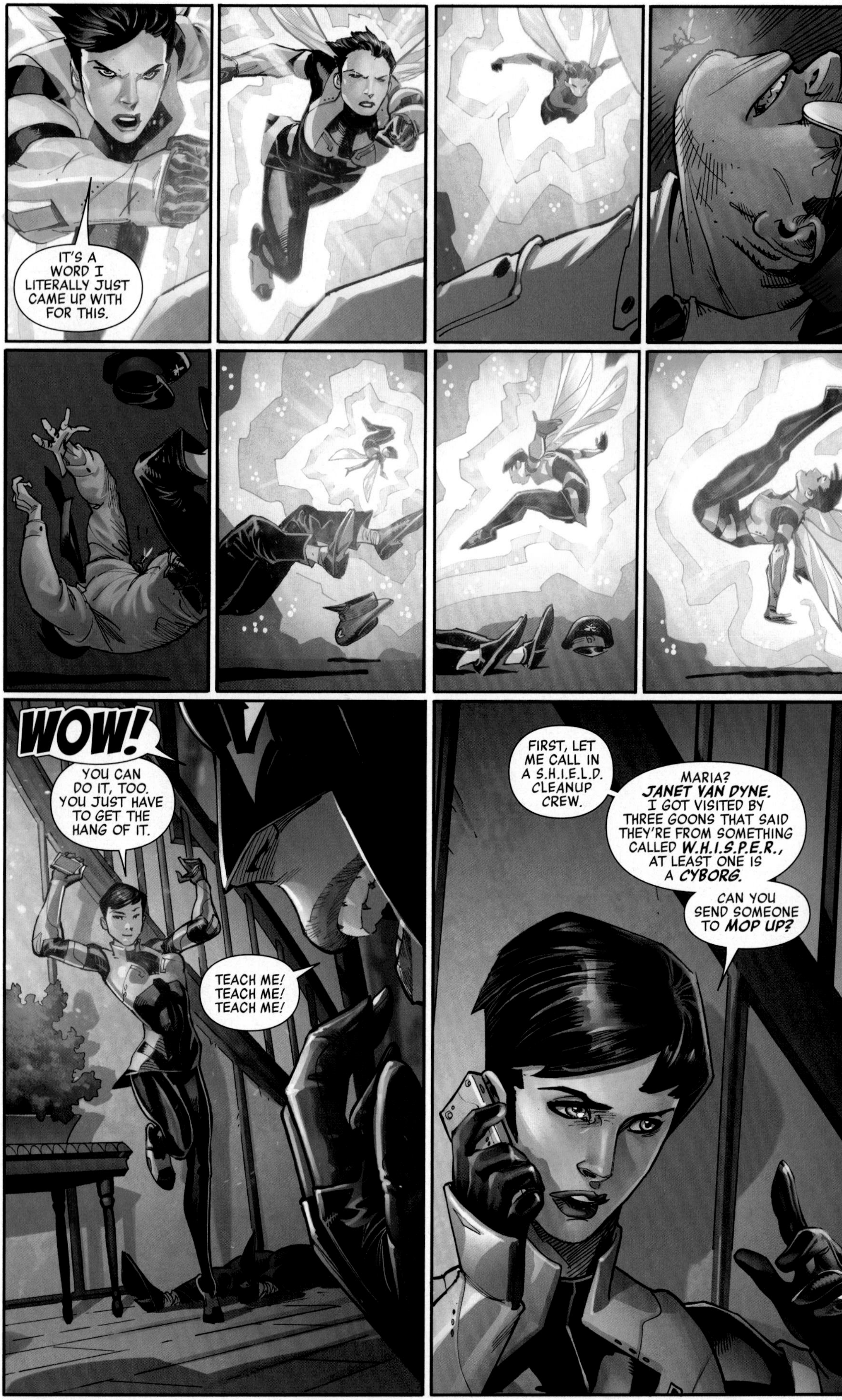
IT'S A WORD I LITERALLY JUST CAME UP WITH FOR THIS.
WOW!
YOU CAN DO IT, TOO. YOU JUST HAVE TO GET THE HANG OF IT.
TEACH ME! TEACH ME! TEACH ME!
FIRST, LET ME CALL IN A S.H.I.E.L.D. CLEANUP CREW.
MARIA? JANET VAN DYNE. I GOT VISITED BY THREE GOONS THAT SAID THEY'RE FROM SOMETHING CALLED W.H.I.S.P.E.R., AT LEAST ONE IS A CYBORG.
CAN YOU SEND SOMEONE TO MOP UP?

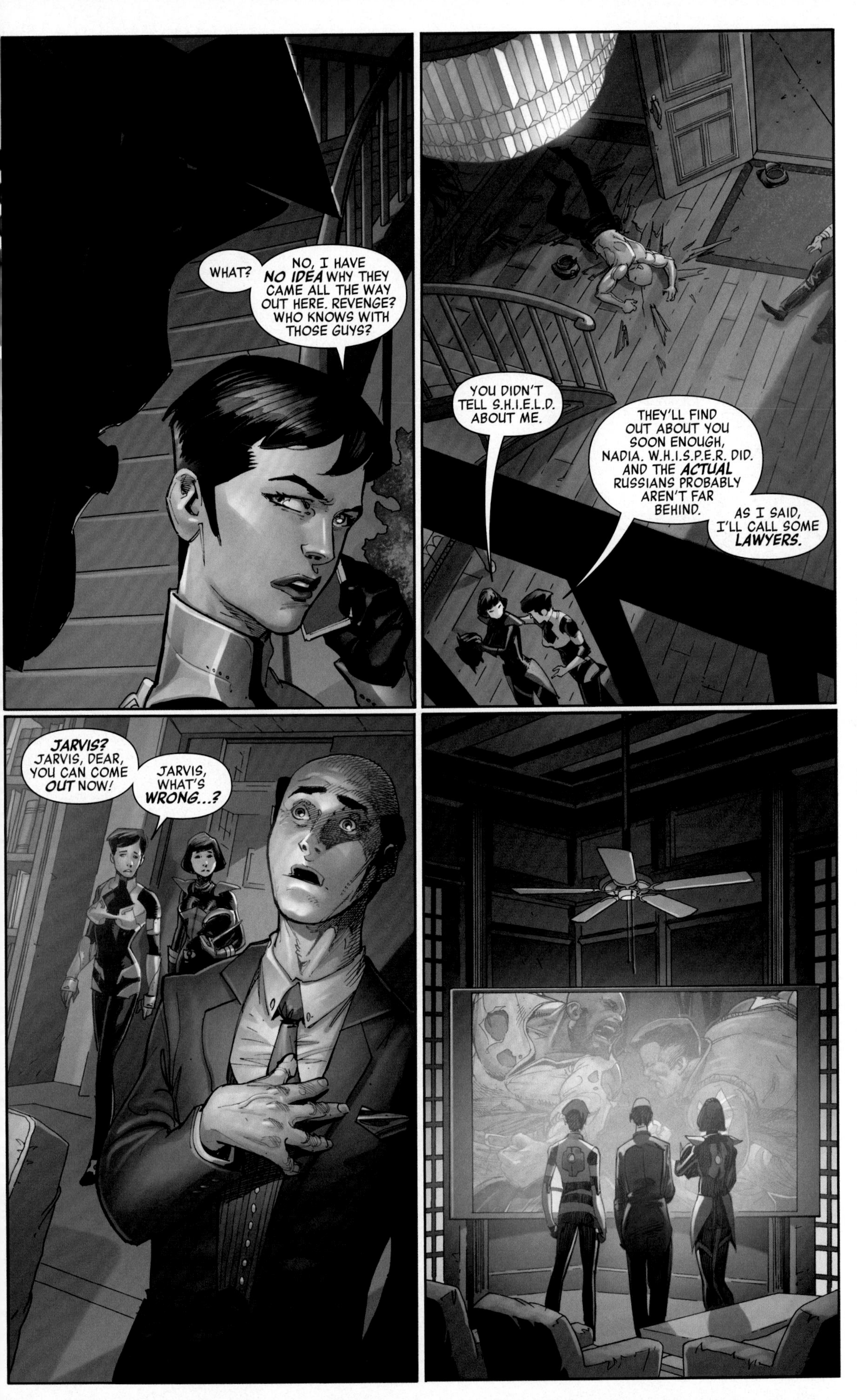

WHAT?
NO, I HAVE NO IDEA WHY THEY CAME ALL THE WAY OUT HERE. REVENGE? WHO KNOWS WITH THOSE GUYS?
YOU DIDN'T TELL S.H.I.E.L.D. ABOUT ME.
THEY'LL FIND OUT ABOUT YOU SOON ENOUGH, NADIA. W.H.I.S.P.E.R. DID. AND THE ACTUAL RUSSIANS PROBABLY AREN'T FAR BEHIND.
AS I SAID, I'LL CALL SOME LAWYERS.
JARVIS? JARVIS, DEAR, YOU CAN COME OUT NOW!
JARVIS, WHAT'S WRONG...?

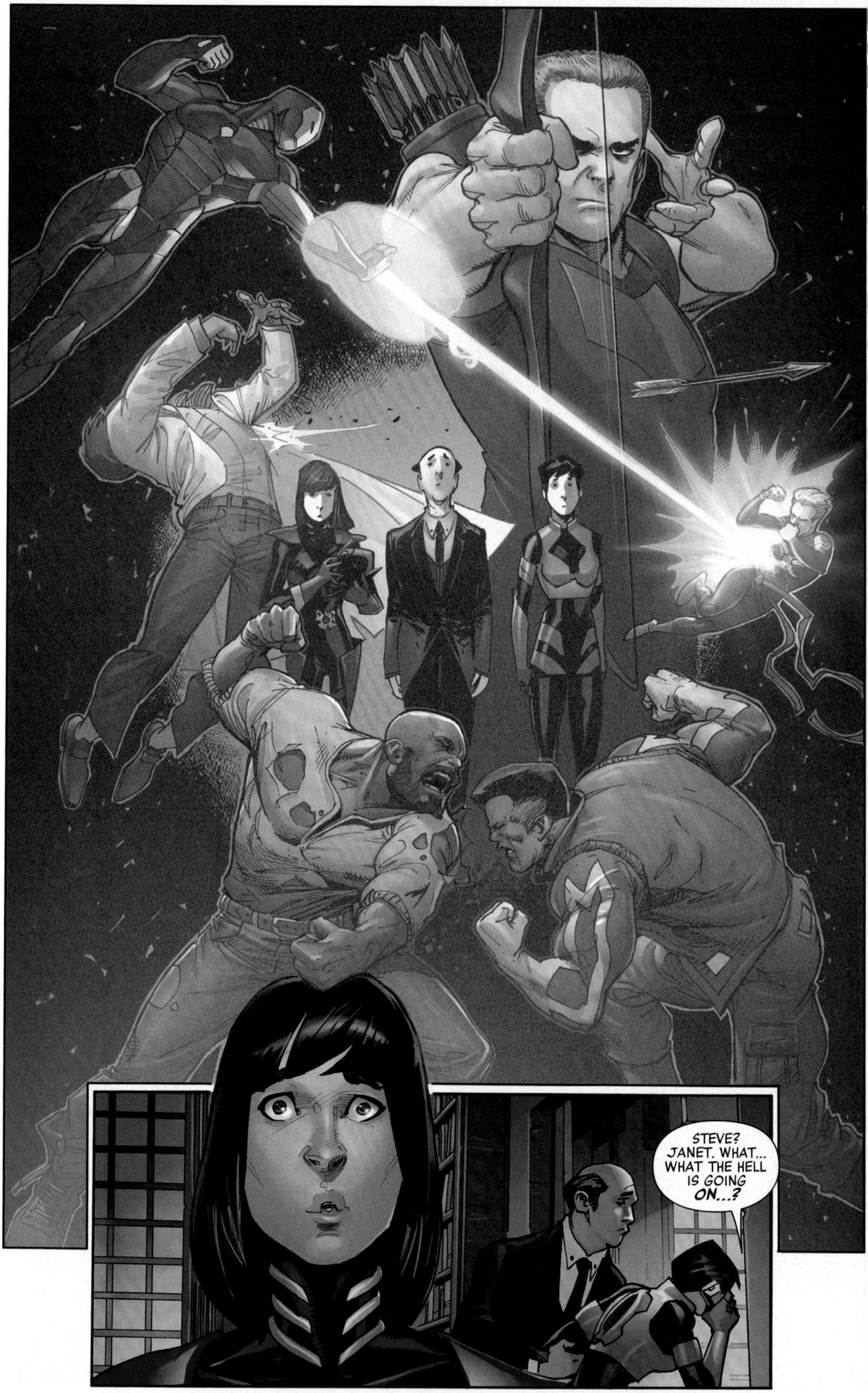
STEVE? JANET. WHAT... WHAT THE HELL IS GOING ON...?

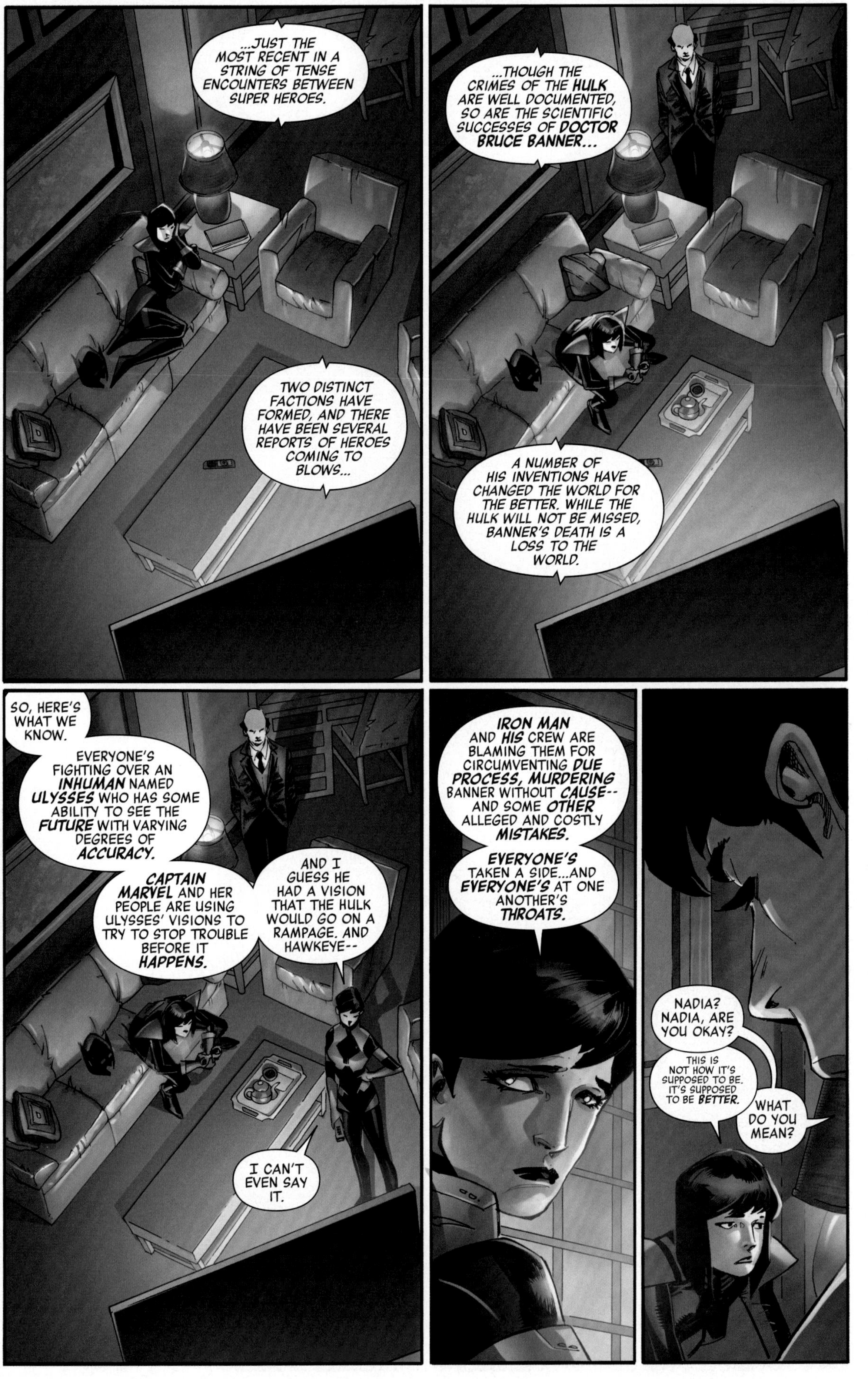
...JUST THE MOST RECENT IN A STRING OF TENSE ENCOUNTERS BETWEEN SUPER HEROES.
TWO DISTINCT FACTIONS HAVE FORMED, AND THERE HAVE BEEN SEVERAL REPORTS OF HEROES COMING TO BLOWS...
...THOUGH THE CRIMES OF THE HULK ARE WELL DOCUMENTED, SO ARE THE SCIENTIFIC SUCCESSES OF DOCTOR BRUCE BANNER...
A NUMBER OF HIS INVENTIONS HAVE CHANGED THE WORLD FOR THE BETTER. WHILE THE HULK WILL NOT BE MISSED, BANNER'S DEATH IS A LOSS TO THE WORLD.
SO, HERE'S WHAT WE KNOW.
EVERYONE'S FIGHTING OVER AN INHUMAN NAMED ULYSSES WHO HAS SOME ABILITY TO SEE THE FUTURE WITH VARYING DEGREES OF ACCURACY.
CAPTAIN MARVEL AND HER PEOPLE ARE USING ULYSSES' VISIONS TO TRY TO STOP TROUBLE BEFORE IT HAPPENS.
AND I GUESS HE HAD A VISION THAT THE HULK WOULD GO ON A RAMPAGE. AND HAWKEYE--
I CAN'T EVEN SAY IT.
IRON MAN AND HIS CREW ARE BLAMING THEM FOR CIRCUMVENTING DUE PROCESS, MURDERING BANNER WITHOUT CAUSE-- AND SOME OTHER ALLEGED AND COSTLY MISTAKES.
EVERYONE'S TAKEN A SIDE...AND EVERYONE'S AT ONE ANOTHER'S THROATS.
NADIA? NADIA, ARE YOU OKAY?
THIS IS NOT HOW IT'S SUPPOSED TO BE. IT'S SUPPOSED TO BE BETTER.
WHAT DO YOU MEAN?

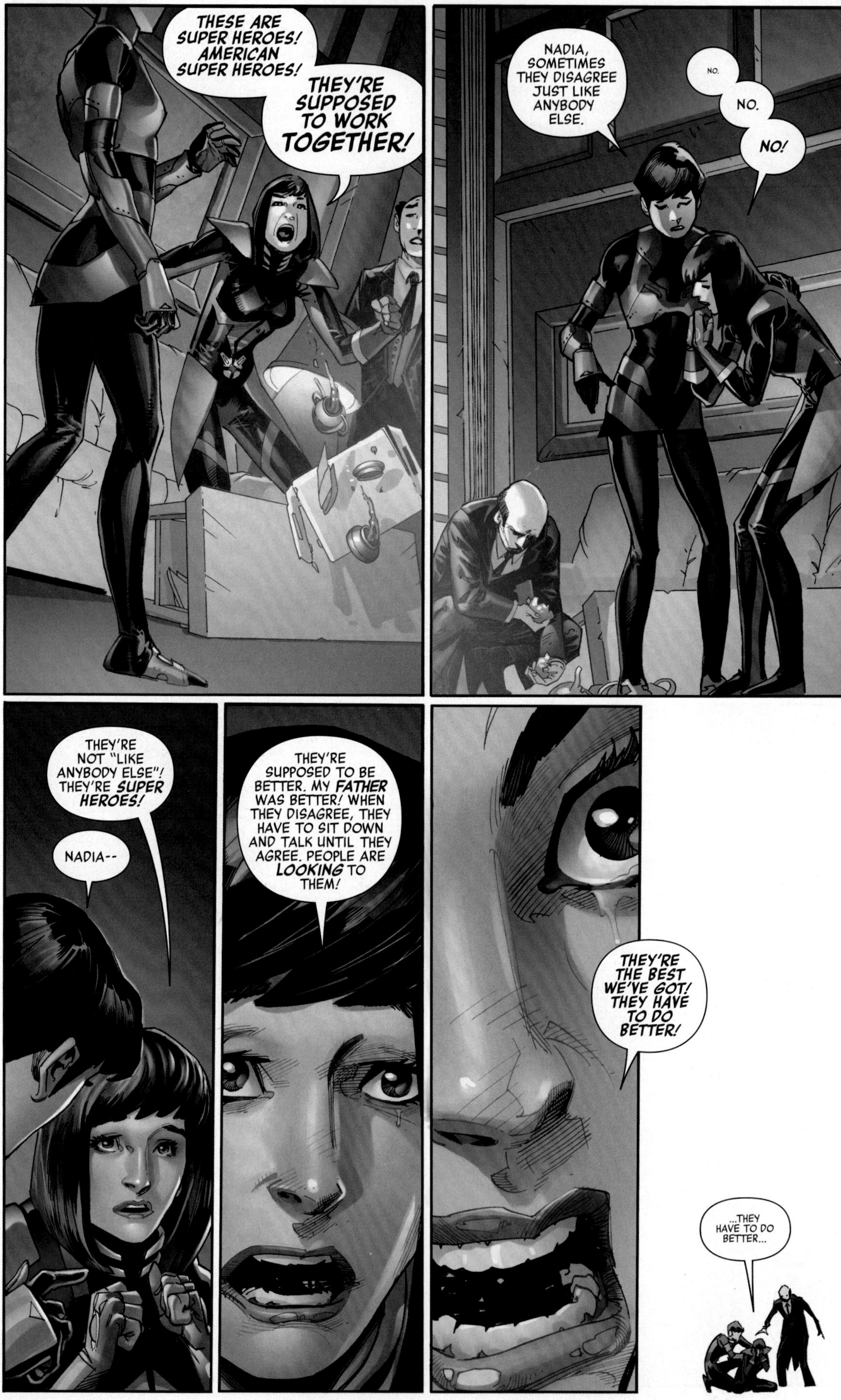
THESE ARE SUPER HEROES! AMERICAN SUPER HEROES!
THEY'RE SUPPOSED TO WORK TOGETHER!
NADIA, SOMETIMES THEY DISAGREE JUST LIKE ANYBODY ELSE.
NO.
NO.
NO!
THEY'RE NOT "LIKE ANYBODY ELSE"! THEY'RE SUPER HEROES!
NADIA--
THEY'RE SUPPOSED TO BE BETTER. MY FATHER WAS BETTER! WHEN THEY DISAGREE, THEY HAVE TO SIT DOWN AND TALK UNTIL THEY AGREE. PEOPLE ARE LOOKING TO THEM!
THEY'RE THE BEST WE'VE GOT! THEY HAVE TO DO BETTER!
...THEY HAVE TO DO BETTER...

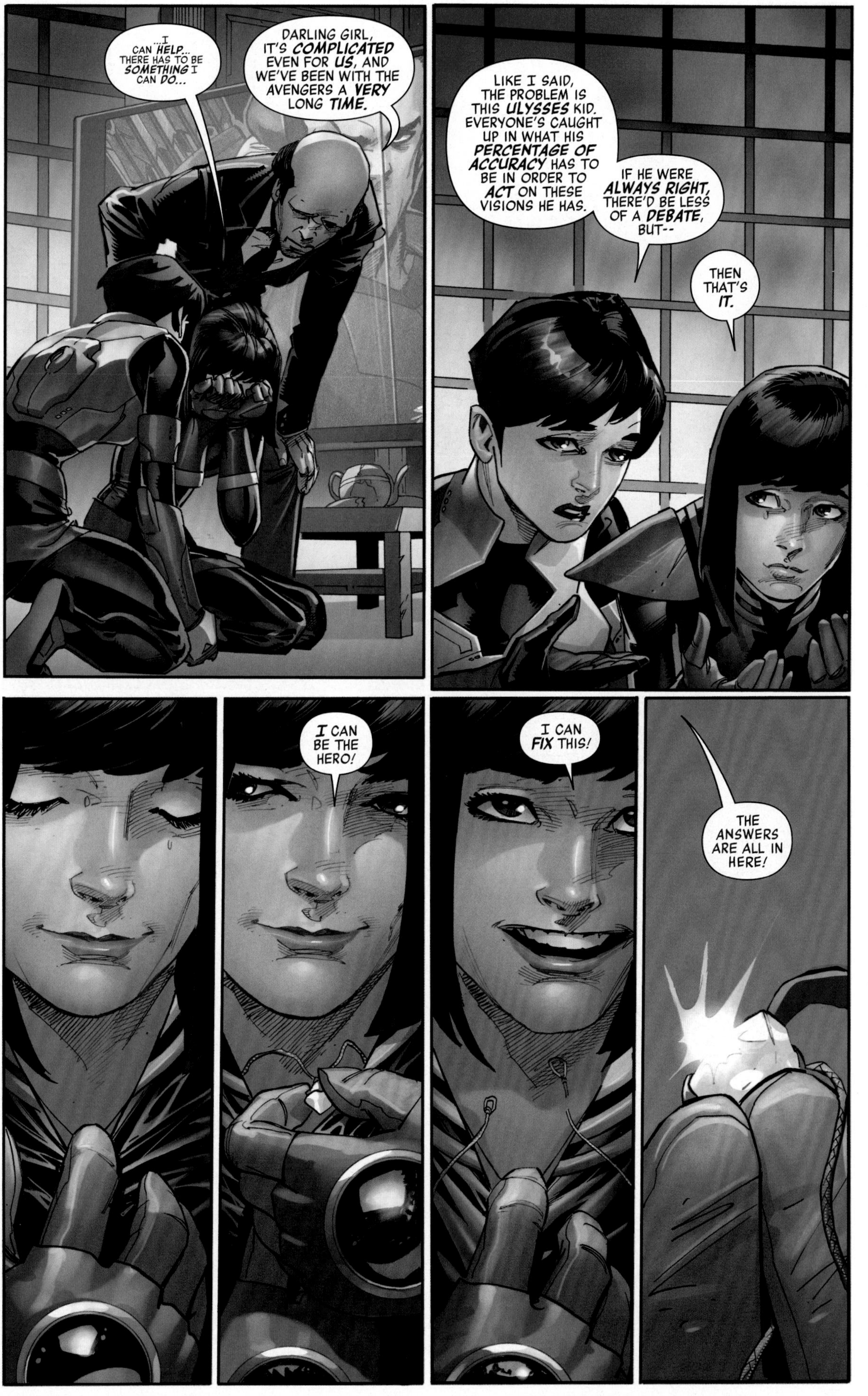
...I CAN HELP... THERE HAS TO BE SOMETHING I CAN DO...
DARLING GIRL, IT'S COMPLICATED EVEN FOR US, AND WE'VE BEEN WITH THE AVENGERS A VERY LONG TIME.
LIKE I SAID, THE PROBLEM IS THIS ULYSSES KID. EVERYONE'S CAUGHT UP IN WHAT HIS PERCENTAGE OF ACCURACY HAS TO BE IN ORDER TO ACT ON THESE VISIONS HE HAS.
IF HE WERE ALWAYS RIGHT, THERE'D BE LESS OF A DEBATE, BUT--
THEN THAT'S IT.
I CAN BE THE HERO!
I CAN FIX THIS!
THE ANSWERS ARE ALL IN HERE!

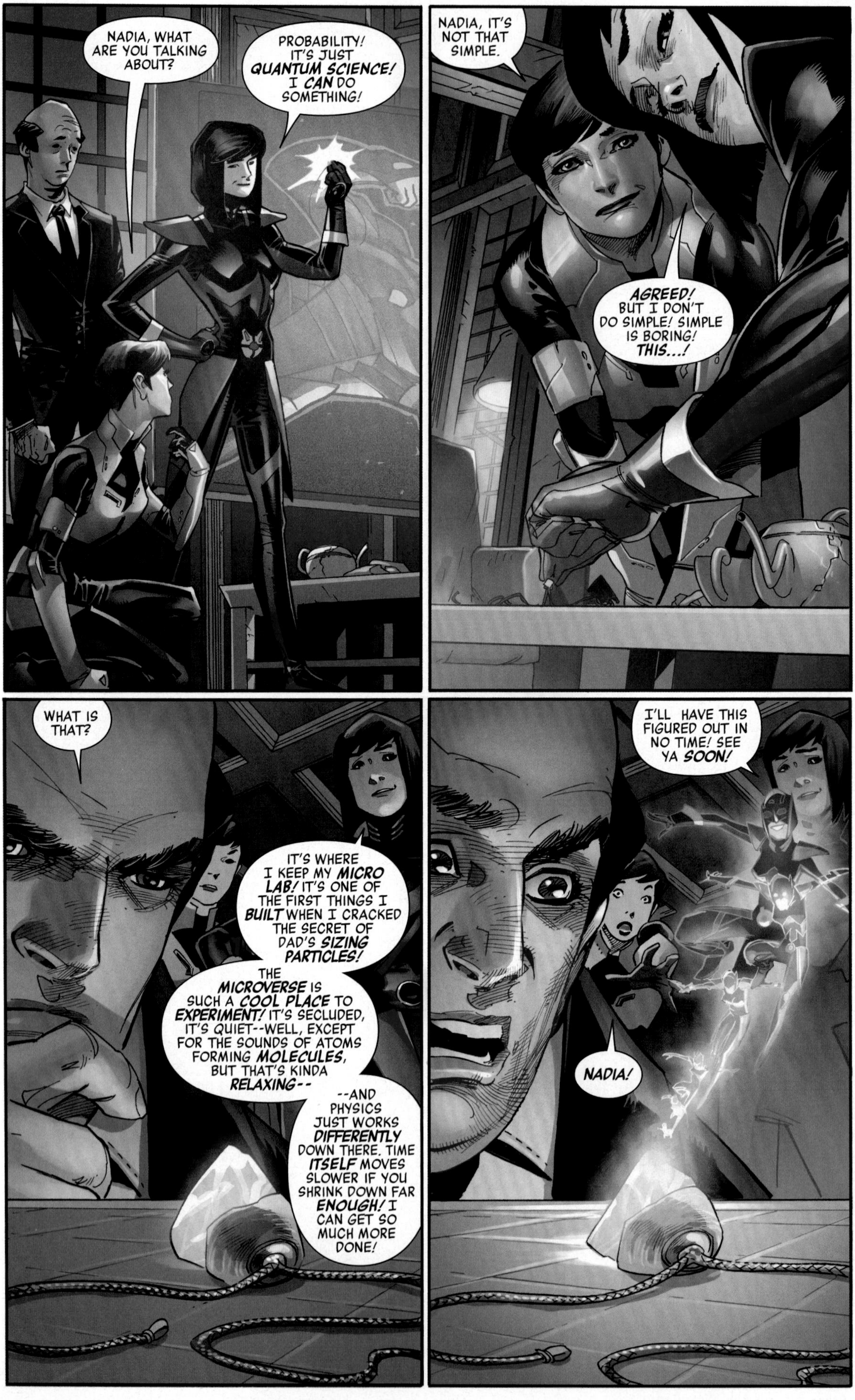
NADIA, WHAT ARE YOU TALKING ABOUT?
PROBABILITY! IT'S JUST QUANTUM SCIENCE! I CAN DO SOMETHING!
NADIA, IT'S NOT THAT SIMPLE.
AGREED! BUT I DON'T DO SIMPLE! SIMPLE IS BORING! THIS...!
WHAT IS THAT?
IT'S WHERE I KEEP MY MICRO LAB! IT'S ONE OF THE FIRST THINGS I BUILT WHEN I CRACKED THE SECRET OF DAD'S SIZING PARTICLES!
THE MICROVERSE IS SUCH A COOL PLACE TO EXPERIMENT! IT'S SECLUDED, IT'S QUIET--WELL, EXCEPT FOR THE SOUNDS OF ATOMS FORMING MOLECULES, BUT THAT'S KINDA RELAXING--
--AND PHYSICS JUST WORKS DIFFERENTLY DOWN THERE. TIME ITSELF MOVES SLOWER IF YOU SHRINK DOWN FAR ENOUGH! I CAN GET SO MUCH MORE DONE!
I'LL HAVE THIS FIGURED OUT IN NO TIME! SEE YA SOON!
NADIA!

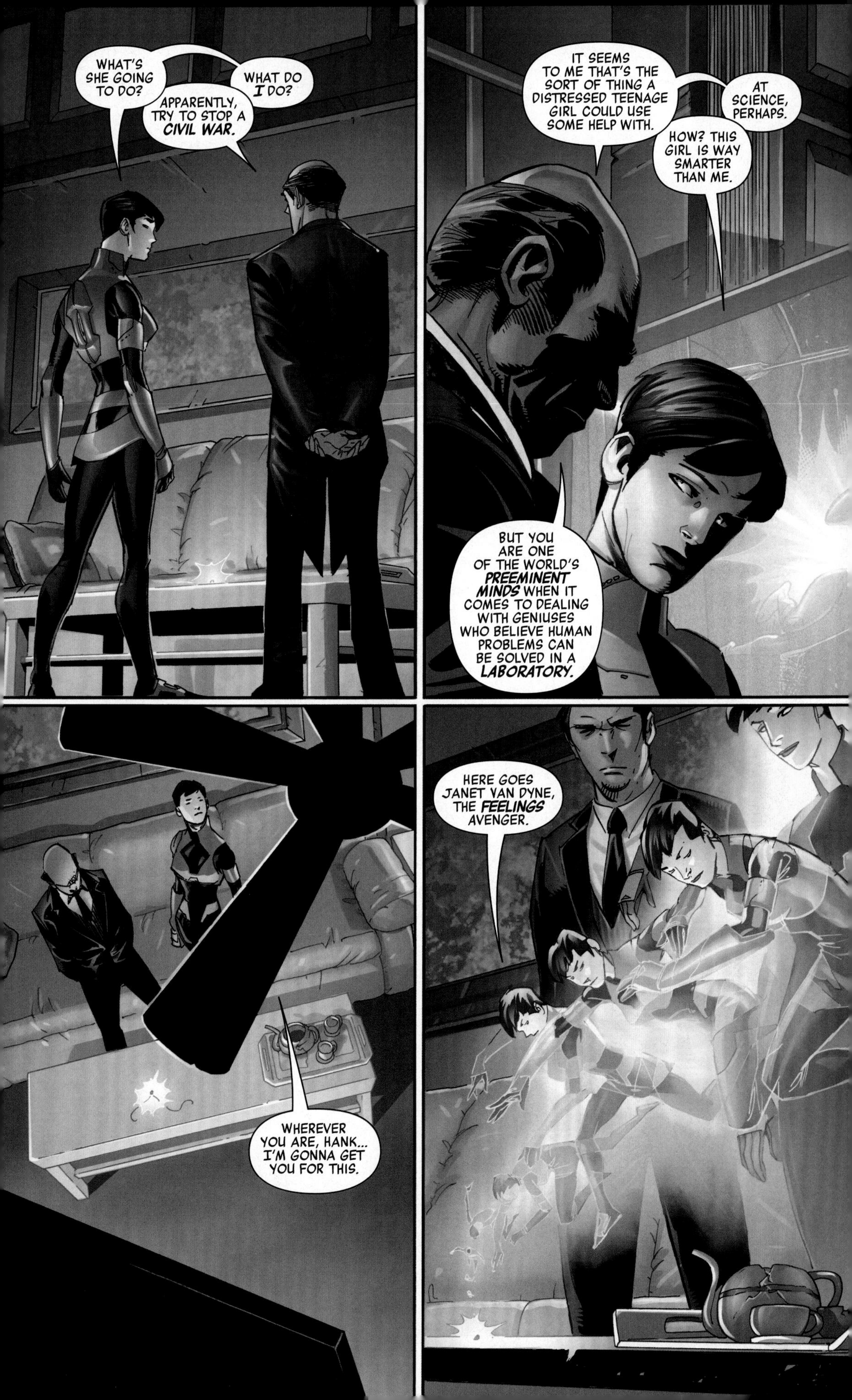
WHAT'S SHE GOING TO DO?
APPARENTLY, TRY TO STOP A CIVIL WAR.
WHAT DO I DO?
IT SEEMS TO ME THAT'S THE SORT OF THING A DISTRESSED TEENAGE GIRL COULD USE SOME HELP WITH.
HOW? THIS GIRL IS WAY SMARTER THAN ME.
AT SCIENCE, PERHAPS.
BUT YOU ARE ONE OF THE WORLD'S PREEMINENT MINDS WHEN IT COMES TO DEALING WITH GENIUSES WHO BELIEVE HUMAN PROBLEMS CAN BE SOLVED IN A LABORATORY.
WHEREVER YOU ARE, HANK... I'M GONNA GET YOU FOR THIS.
HERE GOES JANET VAN DYNE, THE FEELINGS AVENGER.

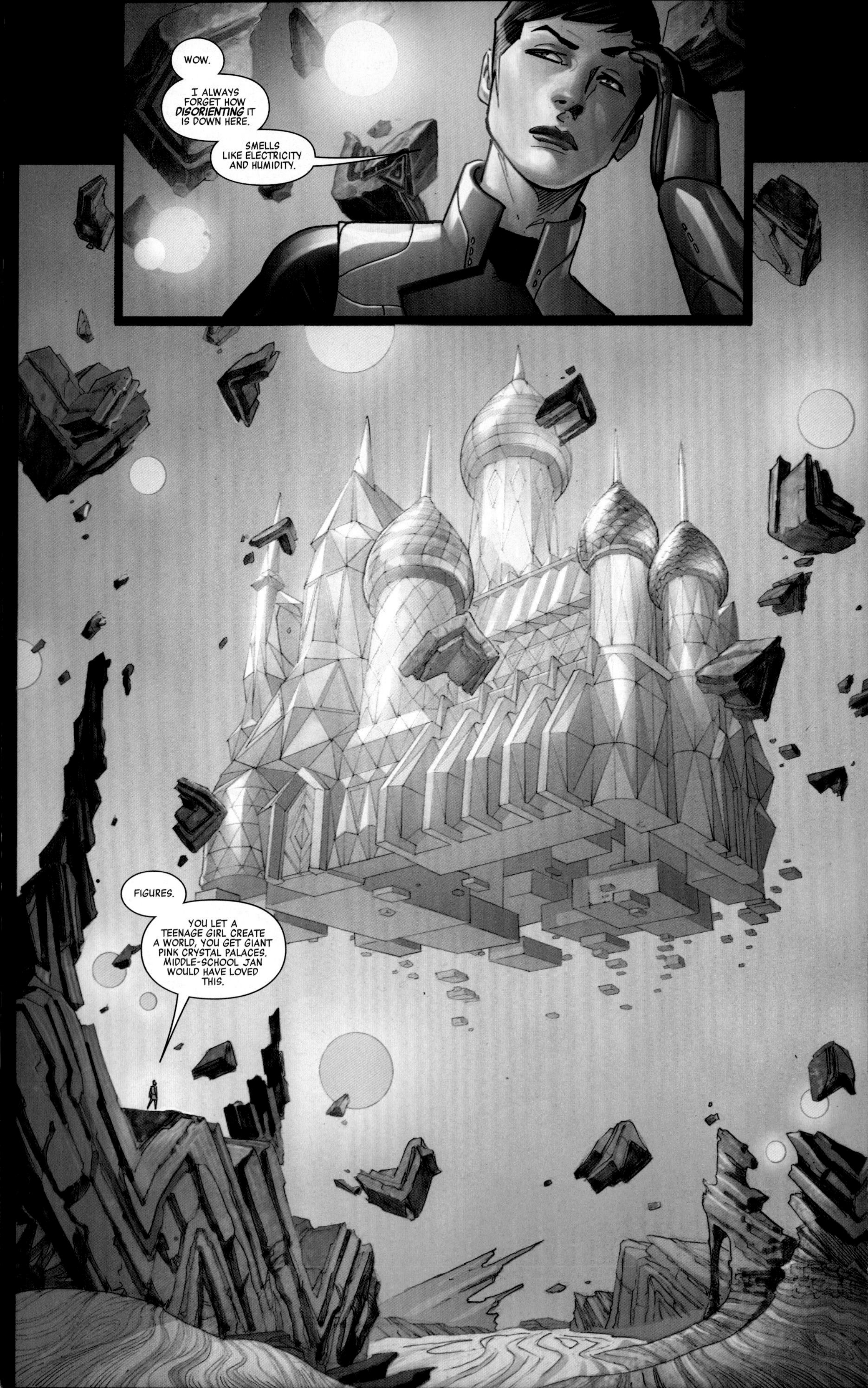
WOW.
I ALWAYS FORGET HOW DISORIENTING IT IS DOWN HERE.
SMELLS LIKE ELECTRICITY AND HUMIDITY.
FIGURES.
YOU LET A TEENAGE GIRL CREATE A WORLD, YOU GET GIANT PINK CRYSTAL PALACES. MIDDLE-SCHOOL JAN WOULD HAVE LOVED THIS.

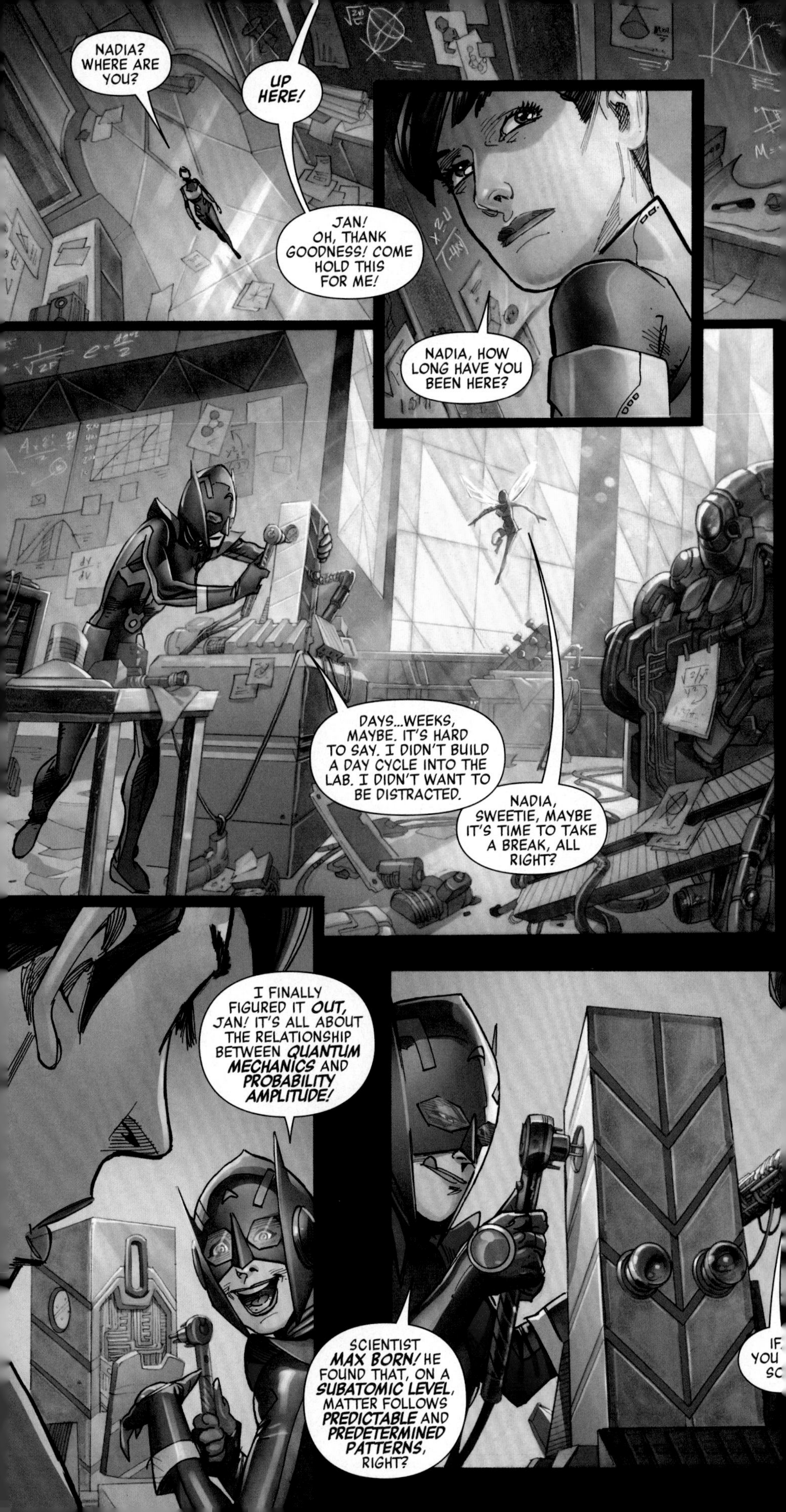
NADIA? WHERE ARE YOU?
UP HERE!
JAN! OH, THANK GOODNESS! COME HOLD THIS FOR ME!
NADIA, HOW LONG HAVE YOU BEEN HERE?
DAYS...WEEKS, MAYBE. IT'S HARD TO SAY. I DIDN'T BUILD A DAY CYCLE INTO THE LAB. I DIDN'T WANT TO BE DISTRACTED.
NADIA, SWEETIE, MAYBE IT'S TIME TO TAKE A BREAK, ALL RIGHT?
I FINALLY FIGURED IT OUT, JAN! IT'S ALL ABOUT THE RELATIONSHIP BETWEEN QUANTUM MECHANICS AND PROBABILITY AMPLITUDE!
SCIENTIST MAX BORN! HE FOUND THAT, ON A SUBATOMIC LEVEL, MATTER FOLLOWS PREDICTABLE AND PREDETERMINED PATTERNS, RIGHT?

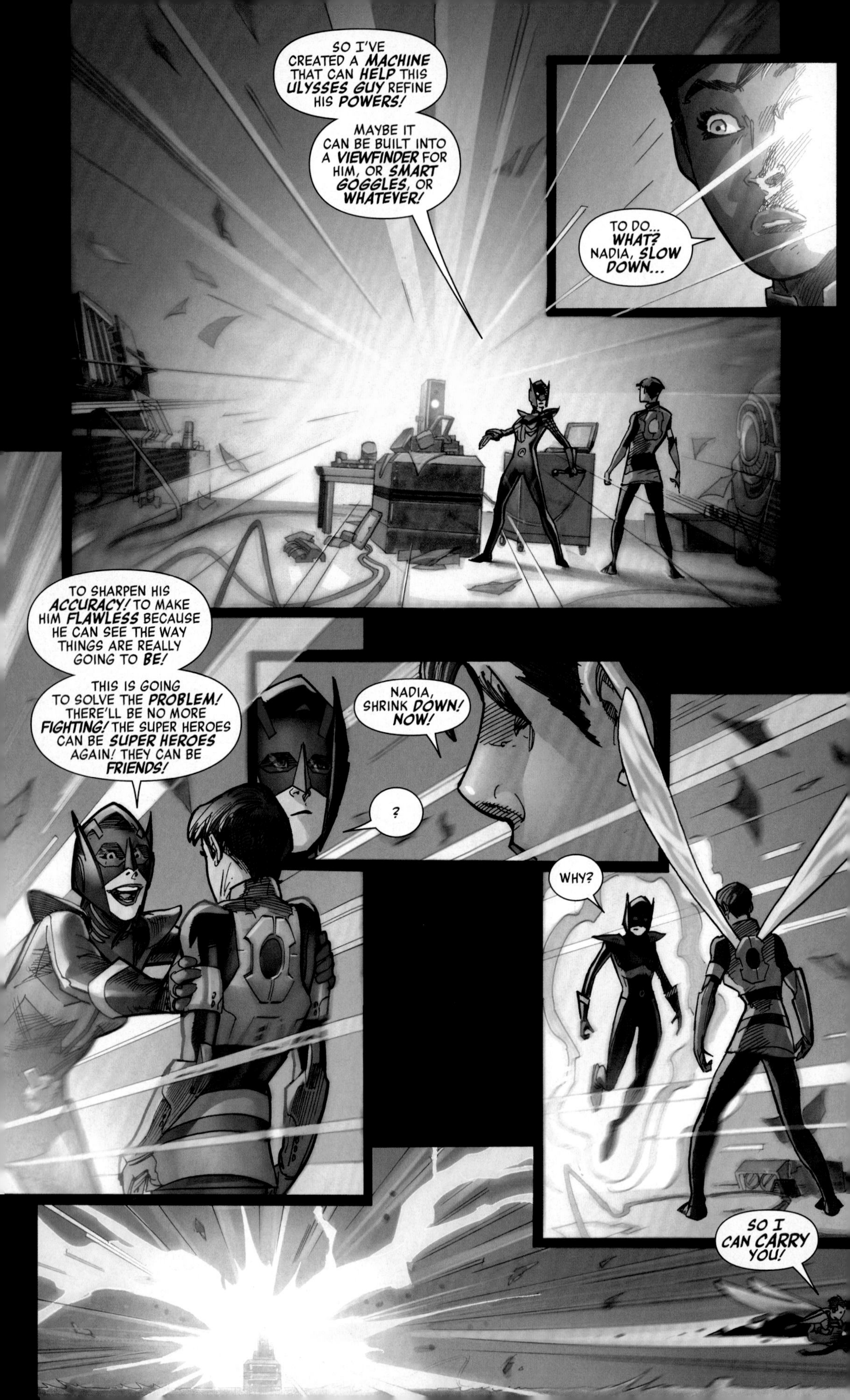

SO I'VE CREATED A MACHINE THAT CAN HELP THIS ULYSSES GUY REFINE HIS POWERS!
MAYBE IT CAN BE BUILT INTO A VIEWFINDER FOR HIM, OR SMART GOGGLES, OR WHATEVER!
TO DO... WHAT? NADIA, SLOW DOWN...
TO SHARPEN HIS ACCURACY! TO MAKE HIM FLAWLESS BECAUSE HE CAN SEE THE WAY THINGS ARE REALLY GOING TO BE!
THIS IS GOING TO SOLVE THE PROBLEM! THERE'LL BE NO MORE FIGHTING! THE SUPER HEROES CAN BE SUPER HEROES AGAIN! THEY CAN BE FRIENDS!
NADIA, SHRINK DOWN! NOW!
?
WHY?
SO I CAN CARRY YOU!

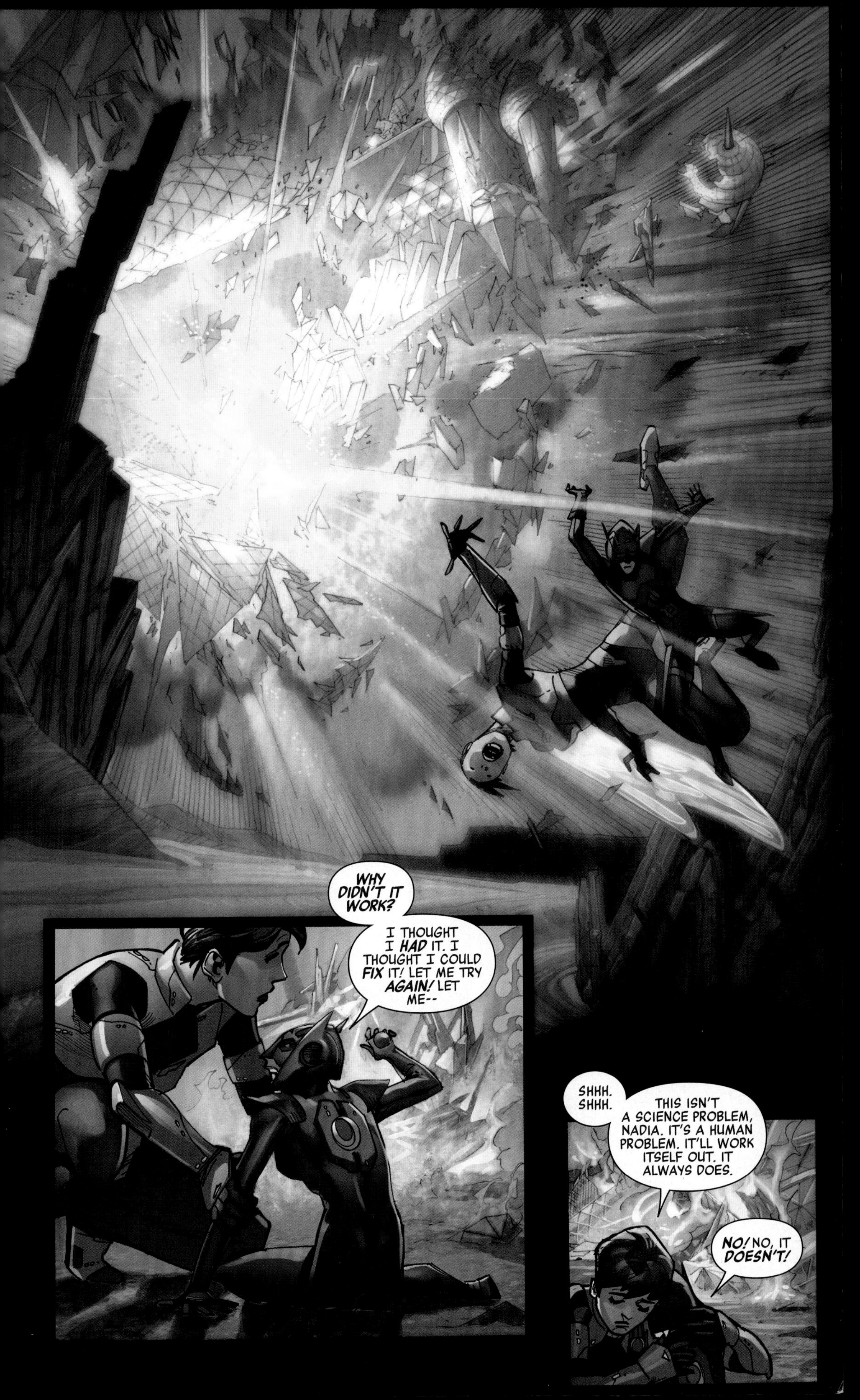
WHY DIDN'T IT WORK?
I THOUGHT I HAD IT. I THOUGHT I COULD FIX IT! LET ME TRY AGAIN! LET ME--
SHHH. SHHH.
THIS ISN'T A SCIENCE PROBLEM, NADIA. IT'S A HUMAN PROBLEM. IT'LL WORK ITSELF OUT. IT ALWAYS DOES.
NO! NO, IT DOESN'T!

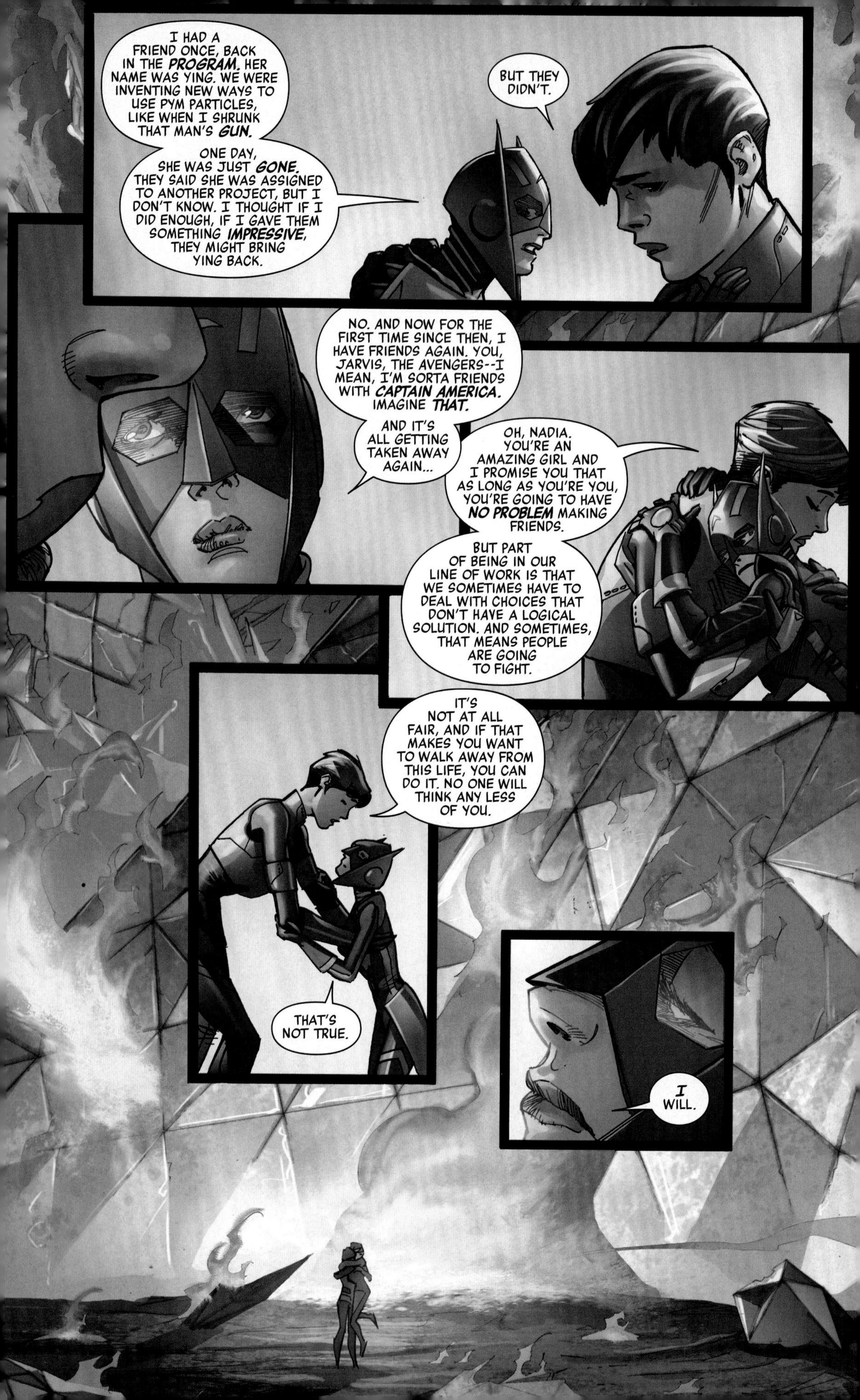
I HAD A FRIEND ONCE, BACK IN THE PROGRAM. HER NAME WAS YING. WE WERE INVENTING NEW WAYS TO USE PYM PARTICLES, LIKE WHEN I SHRUNK THAT MAN'S GUN.
ONE DAY, SHE WAS JUST GONE. THEY SAID SHE WAS ASSIGNED TO ANOTHER PROJECT, BUT I DON'T KNOW. I THOUGHT IF I DID ENOUGH, IF I GAVE THEM SOMETHING IMPRESSIVE, THEY MIGHT BRING YING BACK.
BUT THEY DIDN'T.
NO. AND NOW FOR THE FIRST TIME SINCE THEN, I HAVE FRIENDS AGAIN. YOU, JARVIS, THE AVENGERS--I MEAN, I'M SORTA FRIENDS WITH CAPTAIN AMERICA. IMAGINE THAT.
AND IT'S ALL GETTING TAKEN AWAY AGAIN...
OH, NADIA. YOU'RE AN AMAZING GIRL AND I PROMISE YOU THAT AS LONG AS YOU'RE YOU, YOU'RE GOING TO HAVE NO PROBLEM MAKING FRIENDS.
BUT PART OF BEING IN OUR LINE OF WORK IS THAT WE SOMETIMES HAVE TO DEAL WITH CHOICES THAT DON'T HAVE A LOGICAL SOLUTION. AND SOMETIMES, THAT MEANS PEOPLE ARE GOING TO FIGHT.
IT'S NOT AT ALL FAIR, AND IF THAT MAKES YOU WANT TO WALK AWAY FROM THIS LIFE, YOU CAN DO IT. NO ONE WILL THINK ANY LESS OF YOU.
THAT'S NOT TRUE.
I WILL.

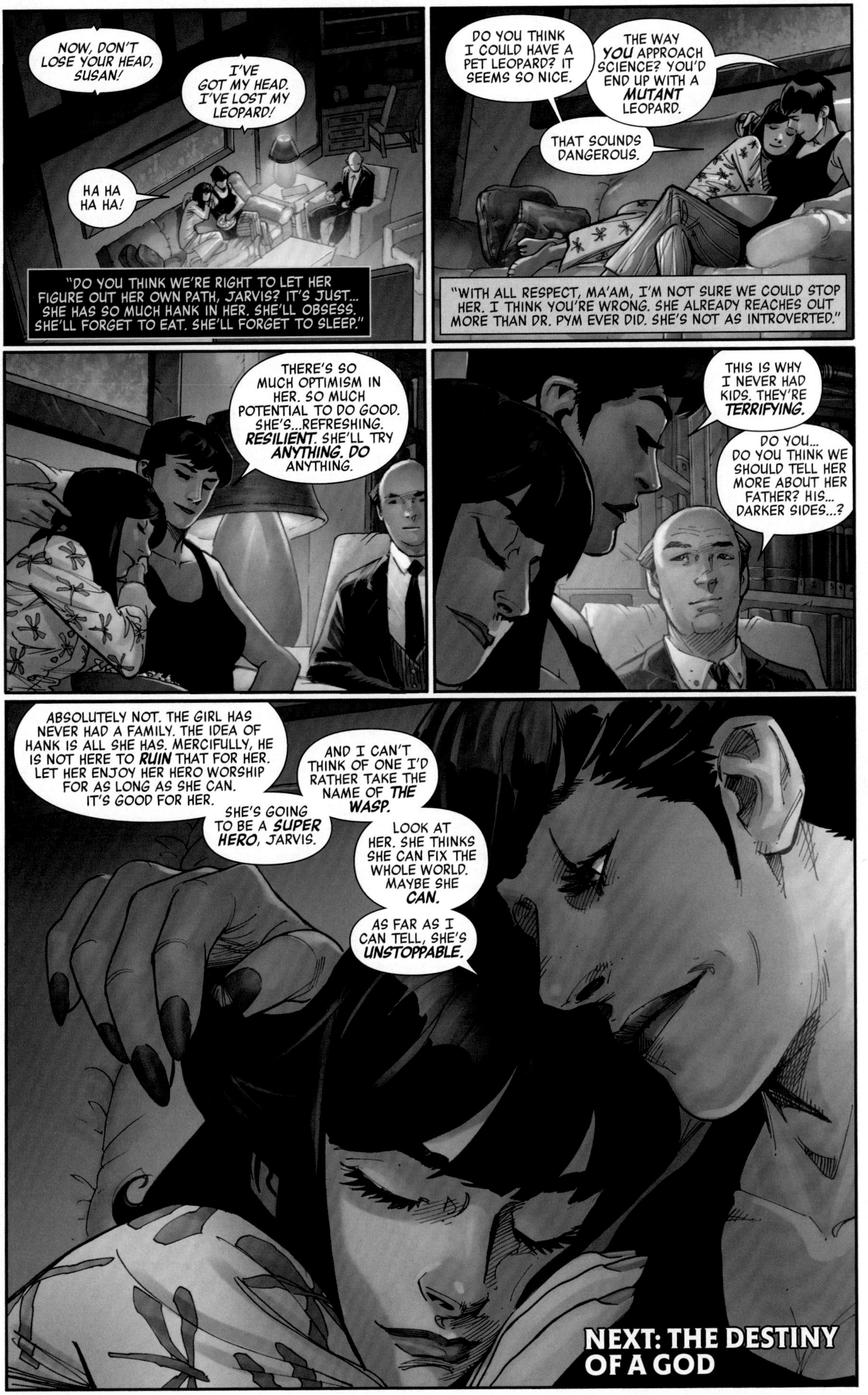
NOW, DON'T LOSE YOUR HEAD, SUSAN!
I'VE GOT MY HEAD. I'VE LOST MY LEOPARD!
HA HA HA HA!
"DO YOU THINK WE'RE RIGHT TO LET HER FIGURE OUT HER OWN PATH, JARVIS? IT'S JUST... SHE HAS SO MUCH HANK IN HER. SHE'LL OBSESS. SHE'LL FORGET TO EAT. SHE'LL FORGET TO SLEEP."
DO YOU THINK I COULD HAVE A PET LEOPARD? IT SEEMS SO NICE.
THE WAY **YOU** APPROACH SCIENCE? YOU'D END UP WITH A **MUTANT** LEOPARD.
THAT SOUNDS DANGEROUS.
"WITH ALL RESPECT, MA'AM, I'M NOT SURE WE COULD STOP HER. I THINK YOU'RE WRONG. SHE ALREADY REACHES OUT MORE THAN DR. PYM EVER DID. SHE'S NOT AS INTROVERTED."
THERE'S SO MUCH OPTIMISM IN HER. SO MUCH POTENTIAL TO DO GOOD. SHE'S...REFRESHING. **RESILIENT.** SHE'LL TRY **ANYTHING. DO** ANYTHING.
THIS IS WHY I NEVER HAD KIDS. THEY'RE **TERRIFYING.**
DO YOU... DO YOU THINK WE SHOULD TELL HER MORE ABOUT HER FATHER? HIS... DARKER SIDES...?
ABSOLUTELY NOT. THE GIRL HAS NEVER HAD A FAMILY. THE IDEA OF HANK IS ALL SHE HAS. MERCIFULLY, HE IS NOT HERE TO **RUIN** THAT FOR HER. LET HER ENJOY HER HERO WORSHIP FOR AS LONG AS SHE CAN. IT'S GOOD FOR HER.
SHE'S GOING TO BE A **SUPER HERO**, JARVIS.
AND I CAN'T THINK OF ONE I'D RATHER TAKE THE NAME OF **THE WASP.**
LOOK AT HER. SHE THINKS SHE CAN FIX THE WHOLE WORLD. MAYBE SHE **CAN.**
AS FAR AS I CAN TELL, SHE'S **UNSTOPPABLE.**
NEXT: THE DESTINY OF A GOD

AGENTS OF G.I.R.L.

Hello, you magnificent people! Nadia here to welcome you to our letters page, "Agents of G.I.R.L."

Why do we call our letters page that, you ask? Well, that's a really good question! You're so on top of things! While we love getting letters about how much you love the book (of course you love the book, I'm delightful!), we are also hard at work recruiting lady adventure scientists for G.I.R.L. (Genius In action Research Labs). And I may be able to fly, but even I can't get to every lady genius in the world.

So send us your suggestions for comic-reading, nerdy-birdy science adventure ladies, and we'll use this space to profile our new members. Elsa even agreed to draw their pictures! Can you believe that? She's so nice and I love her accent!

But now I'm rambling, so here are our first new recruits: Rachel Silverstein (@irrelephantidae on Twitter) and Marina Chanidou (@MarinaLovesChem)!

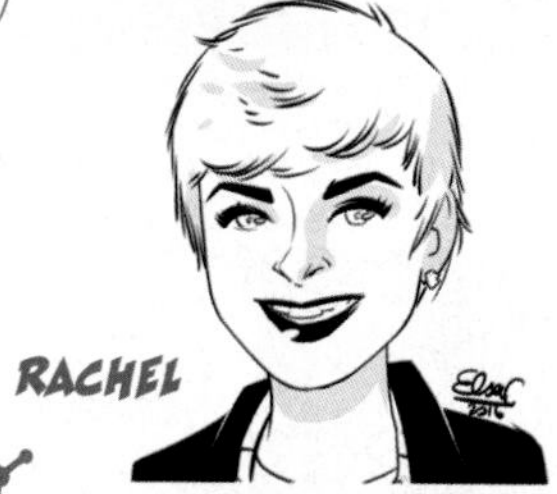
RACHEL

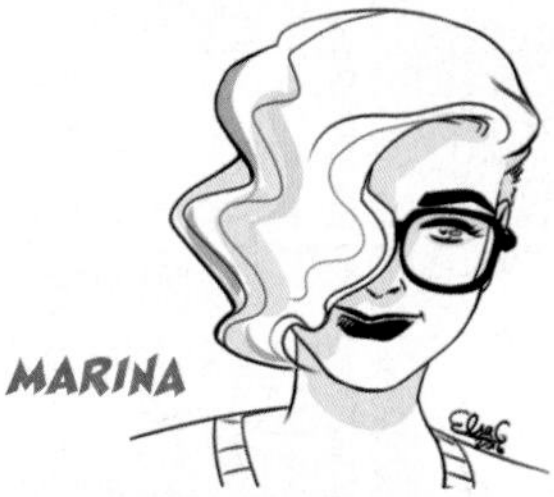
MARINA

WHAT KIND OF WORK DO YOU DO?

Rachel: I'm a proboscidean paleontologist, meaning I study extinct elephant fossils. If you were wondering, not all paleontologists study dinosaurs! Of course, they're cool and all, but Ice Age megafauna (large mammals) are what do it for me.

Marina: I am a PhD student at a UK university studying chemistry, specifically analytical chemistry. I like to describe this as CSI but it takes longer and you usually don't get any clear answers! Right now I analyze food samples, but my goal is to apply my method to archaeological remains and test them for residues of different foodstuffs.

WHAT EXCITES YOU ABOUT YOUR WORK?

Rachel: I think most people, professional paleontologists or not, would agree the field of paleontology is inherently exciting. I personally look forward to the collaboration aspect of it. Not all scientists like to work with others, but I prefer to share ideas and findings with my colleagues. Nothing excites me more than getting messages about new fossil elephant findings and the work being done on them.

Marina: This leads to the exciting bit. What I'm trying to do is more accurately identify what people in the past ate! Well, it's exciting for me, okay? In modern samples I can identify even small adulteration of one type of food to another (for example, traces of pork fat somewhere where there shouldn't be any pork, or cheaper vegetable oils in what is supposed to be virgin olive oil). It would be very cool to do that for archaeological samples as well. (For example, did Ancient Britons use olive oil, and if they did, was it imported from Greece or Spain or Italy?) The exciting part is that there is a problem and I'm working out the solution. There is no ready path, I am the one who will choose how I will go about answering this question and I will decide what to do every step of the way. It's like a puzzle, but you don't get a picture to tell you what it's supposed to look like. You don't even know if the picture is square, rectangular or circular!

WHY WOULD YOU ENCOURAGE YOUNG WOMEN TO GET INTO SCIENCE?

Rachel: Young women should get into science because they want to! Don't let anyone tell you you can't be a scientist, regardless of what science you want to pursue. This is your reminder you can do it. Really. I've found female scientists to be the most supportive human beings on the planet. Even if what you do is a hobby, that doesn't make you less of a scientist. Remember that, ladies!

Marina: Same reason I would encourage them to do anything: if they like it, it seems interesting to them or they are good at it, they should go ahead and do it! I would encourage all young women to take science courses at school anyway for a number of reasons. First of all, it's really cool and you might like it! But even if you don't like it, science teaches you a way of thinking. It teaches you that there are problems and there are solutions. And even if you can't find the solutions now, you're laying the groundwork for others eventually solving a problem. We are indeed standing on the shoulders of giants, but even a small change puts us higher than we were before. Science teaches you to work, evaluate, adapt and never accept something without evidence--and when the evidence changes, to accept it and change with it.

WHAT FEMALE SCIENTISTS (REAL OR FICTIONAL) HAVE INSPIRED YOU IN YOUR WORK?

Rachel: I have to give a shout-out to Dr. Katy Smith, a fellow female proboscidean paleontologist (who also reads comics!), as my inspiration. Dr. Smith has always been there to encourage me to continue my studies to my full potential and give help whenever she can with my work.

Marina: I can't remember many fictional female scientists from the books I was reading when I was younger. But I did have a female physics teacher in high school and she was brilliant--a brilliant physicist and a brilliant educator. She asked us in class how many of us had taken something apart to see what it looks like and the people who raised their hands were mostly boys and me. She said it is okay for girls to experiment, to mess with things, to fix things and find out how things work. One day she was telling some of us a story about how she was running an experiment in the lab and it took more than 24 hours and she had to stay there and make sure everything was going well. Her boyfriend at the time was not impressed. She said "Sometimes men don't understand that I will forget about a date if I'm in the lab." That's when I thought, "What's not to understand? Of course the experiment was more important than the date! You can have a date any time, science is more important." I was hooked!

DO YOU HAVE A FAVORITE EXAMPLE OF CLEVER/UNUSUAL/NONSENSICAL USE OF SCIENCE IN COMICS?

Rachel: As a paleontologist, I always thought the concept of the villain Dinosaur Man was hilarious. He reminds me of everything that went wrong in *Jurassic Park*, but in comic book-form!

Marina: Most science reads like magic in comics and I need to really suspend disbelief to follow it. That is one thing that I would love to be improved. One that I do enjoy very much and is surprisingly quite a realistic depiction of a scientist's life is *Blood Stain* by Linda Sejic.

HOW LONG HAVE YOU BEEN READING COMICS? WHAT WAS YOUR FIRST EVER COMIC BOOK?

Rachel: I've been reading comics since I was 12. I remember bringing them with me to class in middle school and trying to hide while reading them. I would read Marvel, DC, indie--anything, really. My first Marvel comic I got into at a young age was SPIDER-MAN.

Marina: I started reading comics when I was around six. My first books were *Asterix the Gaul* and *Lucky Luke*. Then I read a lot of Disney Comics--Carl Barks was a favorite creator. Finally, when I was 17, I went to an actual comic book shop. And picked up *Medieval Lady Death!* Sure, she was semi-naked, but she was a woman kicking ass in a world that wanted her gone!

Please send all of your suggestions for girl, lady or lady-identifying geniuses to us at MHEROES@MARVEL.COM and mark your letters "Okay to Print"! You can also tweet at us using the hashtag #AgentsOfGIRL! Come back next month to meet more amazing science ladies!

AGENTS of G.I.R.L.

Oh my gosh, what a cliffhanger! Hey, new friends, it's Nadia! I'm so glad to see you again. You look great! Winter must really agree with you! Don't worry, Team Wasp will be back next month to bring you another chapter of our story, but in the meantime, I have some more really special lady scientists to share with you. These new Agents of G.I.R.L. are extra amazing, so please check out what new recruits Jin Kim Montclare (@jkmontclare) and Raychelle Burks, Ph.D. (@DrRubidium) had to say!

JIN

RAYCHELLE

WHAT KIND OF WORK DO YOU DO?

Jin: I am a professor of chemical and biomolecular engineering, and I work on engineering new types of proteins. Proteins are important biomolecules that exist in foods such as eggs, milk and meat as well as in all living organisms--including humans. My research focuses on creating a protein that can detoxify toxic nerve agents such as pesticides as well as creating new protein biomaterials that can deliver important therapies to treat human disorders.

Raychelle: I'm a chemistry professor and spend my time teaching and doing research. My area of focus is analytical chemistry, specifically designing detection techniques for compounds of forensic interest (drugs, explosives, chemical or biological weapons, etc.). My research group is currently focused on using color image analysis as a stand-in for colorimetry--and we're using cell phones to do it!

WHAT EXCITES YOU ABOUT YOUR WORK?

Jin: Two things really excite me: that I get to 1) work on research that can ultimately help people (by removing toxins or treating diseases) and 2) interact with a wonderful group of young aspiring engineers and scientists making exciting advances in research.

Raychelle: I love the challenge of coming up with low-tech, affordable, reliable and portable detection schemes. It gives me and my students an opportunity to play super-science MacGyver!

WHY ARE YOU PASSIONATE ABOUT YOUNG WOMEN GETTING INTO SCIENCE?

Jin: Being a woman in STEM, I feel fortunate to be doing what I love to do as an educator and researcher! My path was made possible through the support of my mentors from K-12 to now, so I do my part by encouraging other young women to pursue STEM. More than half the students I mentor directly at NYU are women, and I am quite proud of it! I have also actively engaged in mentoring programs including STEM Women on Fire as part of the Ultimate Mentor Adventure

Contest! I work with science teachers at local K-12 schools to help effectively convey scienctific ideas and make them exciting. In fact, in collaboration with InSchoolApps, we made an app called LewisDots for kids to make chemical structures and learn about bonding!

Raychelle: As a black female scientist, I am familiar with the historical and current barriers to our access and advancement in STEM career fields. Margot Lee Shetterly's great book *Hidden Figures* (now a feature film) speaks to such struggles. While gains have been made in accessibility, we have a long way to go in making STEM careers equally within reach for woman of color and other under-represented minorities.

WHAT FEMALE SCIENTISTS (REAL OR FICTIONAL) HAVE INSPIRED YOU IN YOUR WORK?

Jin: When I was little, my hero was Marie Curie. She not only won a Nobel Prize in Physics, but years later, she was awarded the prize in Chemistry, too! Very few individuals are awarded the Nobel Prize, so to earn two in two different fields is AMAZING! In terms of inspiration for my work, my graduate advisor Alanna Schepartz has mentored me through my own dissertation work on miniature proteins at Yale while serving as an incredible role model. Finally, the Nobel Laureate Ada Yonath, who was responsible for determining a high-resolution structure of the ribosome (a gigantic complex that helps decode DNA into protein), is an amazing source of inspiration because my group employs the insights from such structures to make cool proteins in the lab.

Raychelle: When I was little, I didn't know of any female scientists--talk about hidden figures! It wasn't until I was a senior in high school that I discovered Dr. Mae Jemison, medical doctor and NASA astronaut. Before that, I looked to my favorite fictional super-brain, Agatha Christie's Miss Marple, for inspiration. She is one hell of a quantitative thinker! When I'm in need of inspiration, I look to Jeannette Brown's *African American Woman Chemists*. I am also inspired by

my science friends: Dr. Danielle Lee, Dr. Stephanie Page, Dr. Kate Clancy and Dr. Malika Jeffries-El.

DO YOU HAVE A FAVORITE EXAMPLE OF CLEVER/UNUSUAL/OR NONSENSICAL USE OF SCIENCE IN COMICS?

Jin: I thought it was clever that the characters from X-Men had super-powers due to mutations. It made absolute sense to me since mutations in DNA can cause changes in living things in order to adapt (like a giraffe's neck to allow them to reach the treetops for food).

Raychelle: I'm a sucker for super-hero-by-vampirism. Okay, that sounds splashier than super-hero-by-blood transfusion. She-Hulk fits the bill! Hulking out is a bit like a blood-borne disease? It almost makes sense, except...it totally doesn't! I love these sci-fi stretches!

HOW LONG HAVE YOU BEEN READING COMICS AND WAT WAS YOUR FIRST COMIC BOOK?

Jin: I started reading comics when I was in elementary school with *Archie Comics*, but my favorites have been *Sandman* and *Lucifer*…and of course *Rocket Girl* and most recently MOON GIRL & DEVIL DINOSAUR! For MG & DD, I love that the protagonist is a girl STEM genius and I even get consulted on it for inspirational scientist/engineer quotes (because my husband, Brandon Montclare, is writing it)!

Raychelle: I started reading comic books in high school, jumping into the Wonder Woman reboot by George Pérez when I stumbled across in my local public library. It caught my eye because I grew up watching reruns of Linda Carter's *Woman Woman*!

Please send all of your suggestions for girl, lady or lady-identifying geniuses in science and technology to us at MHEROES@MARVEL.COM and mark your letters "Okay to Print"! You can also tweet at us using the hashtag #AgentsOfGIRL.

Until next month, *do svidaniya!*

Nadia

AGENTS of G.I.R.L.

WHAT?! A super villain who is also a lady pro wrestler! I'm so excited to see what happens next! (Just kidding, I already know how it ends :)

Hi again, Nadia here! Can you believe we've already been together for three months? You wouldn't believe the recommendations we've gotten for Agents of G.I.R.L.! Today's agents are pretty special though. Not only are they an optical engineer and an aerospace engineer, but they're also COSPLAYERS! Check out Sadie Geerligs (@sadiebydesign) and Nia Jetter (@thinqueaboutit)!

SADIE

NIA

WHAT KIND OF WORK DO YOU DO?

Sadie: I am an applications engineer in connectivity for a fiber-optic company, AFL. In my current role I focus on developing products for card edge connectivity and embedded optics. I was lucky to find AFL after earning my bachelor's degree in Optical Engineering from Rose-Hulman Institute of Technology in 2012.

Nia: I am an aerospace engineer specializing in spacecraft autonomy, I have been working in my field for just over 16 years. There's a delay in communication between the Earth and space vehicles, so it is important that the vehicle be able to perform many functions autonomously, including controlling different subsystems and being able to fix or save itself if something is going wrong. I perform analyses and write algorithms that allow the space vehicle to operate without human intervention.

WHAT EXCITES YOU ABOUT YOUR WORK?

Sadie: I love that my job presents different challenges for me each day. My current position requires in-depth customer interaction to help develop products for their unique applications. When I was going through school, I was extremely nervous that a job in engineering would require me to sit at a desk all day and be super antisocial. It is extremely exciting to be able to see a product through the development stages to commercialization.

Nia: I love what I do! I feel like it is what I was made to do! I love math and I love solving problems. I love coming up with a vision of what technology we are going to need in the future and then determining a roadmap that we need to follow to get there. One of the greatest things about my job is that after we build the satellite or space-based vehicle, we are responsible for working the early portion of the mission before we hand the satellite over to the customer. I've had the opportunity to work thirteen missions in our mission control center. You get to see something that you worked so hard on actually performing its function up in space. It can be an incredible problem-solving experience!

WHY ARE YOU PASSIONATE ABOUT YOUNG WOMEN GETTING INTO ENGINEERING?

Sadie: At graduation, we all donned pins in memory of the former president of Rose-Hulman, Matt Branam, with his quote "Make it happen. Make it fun." He taught the students of Rose that you should make your dreams become reality, and have fun while you do it. It is really important to me to see women in fields that make them happy. I encourage anyone who has a passion for engineering, science or really anything to exploit that passion because it will lead you to greater things. Engineering has not only been a career that sustains my life, but a path to finding who I was meant to be. I wish nothing more than for other women to find the path that leads them to that same sort of belonging and happiness.

Nia: The greatest advancement is made when it is based in a foundation of diversity of thought. If a group of people with a similar backgrounds and trains of thought get together to solve a problem, they may miss an even better solution that would have been introduced by someone with a different background. Having a large portion of our society underrepresented in science and technology fields inhibits our society as a whole. It is important that, from a very young age, we make sure that no one is made to feel like science or math is too hard, or a "boy" thing. Having seen consistent resistance wear people down and make them choose to apply their brilliance to another, non-technical field, I try to be the opposite of that. I love mentoring and volunteering in schools, doing activities and explaining things simply to make sure that kids know that anyone can do anything that they put their mind to. It's important for boys to know--and see--that girls can do anything too, so that they have no reason to expect anything less than that from women in the future.

WHICH FEMALE ENGINEERS (REAL OR FICTIONAL) HAVE INSPIRED YOU IN YOUR WORK?

Sadie: My inspiration comes all of from the fantastic ladies that have surrounded me since I started down the path of my engineering career. The thing I find the most inspiring about all of these amazing women is that, like me, they all have passions outside of their careers that they are equally talented at. My friend Katherine runs a successful blog, *Engineering in Style*, that showcases that women in engineering can also be super stylish. And I remember enjoying *Sailor Moon* because all of her friends have different talents. As a super awkward bookworm through my younger years, I always had a great appreciation for Mercury because she was a nerd and a badass! Some other really cool fictional ladies that have surfaced as women in science fields become more and more common--like Asami Sato, Winry Rockbell and Honey Lemon.

Nia: I had a female math teacher in the sixth grade who was very encouraging and really helped me realize that I was strong in math. The fact that she pulled me aside and encouraged me really made a difference. Uhura was also a great inspiration. My mother is a huge *Star Trek* fan, particularly of Nichelle Nichols. I was fortunate enough to meet Nichelle Nichols while I was cosplaying as Uhura!

DO YOU HAVE A FAVORITE EXAMPLE OF CLEVER/UNUSUAL/NONSENSICAL USE OF SCIENCE IN COMICS?

Sadie: Since science fiction has often been a precursor to scientific discovery, there aren't a lot of things that I find too out there. In fact, I find that most of the things in comics make people dream big enough to achieve goals that people would scoff at. If I had to pick a commonly used concept that irks me, though, it would probably be time travel. It's a very large concept to wrap a brain around, and I just don't really think it's been thought through properly yet. Don't get me wrong, I thoroughly enjoy *Back to the Future* and *The Flash*, but I just feel like aliens are more within our grasp than time travel. To the person that proves me wrong, I can't wait for you to tell all of the skeptics, "I told you so!"

Nia: I'm a sucker for super-hero-by-vampirism. Okay, that sounds splashier than super-hero-by-blood transfusion. She-Hulk fits the bill! Hulking out is a bit like a blood-borne disease? It almost makes sense, except...it totally doesn't! I love these sci-fi stretches!

HOW LONG HAVE YOU BEEN READING COMICS AND WHAT WAS YOUR FIRST COMIC BOOK?

Sadie: Truthfully, I didn't grow up reading comics, but I watched a whole lot of *Batman* and *Superman: The Animated Series*. About two years ago, I decided I was going to get into comics for the sake of my cosplay and bought several comics to kickstart my love. My main objective was to obtain a *Supergirl* comic, but I left with multiple copies of the PRINCESS LEIA comic as well, which remains one of my favorite storylines. I have also fallen in love with SPIDER-GWEN, CAPTAIN MARVEL and GWENPOOL. It will be really exciting to add UNSTOPPABLE WASP to my lineup of super-awesome ladies in my comic collection, and maybe someday in cosplay. After all, how could I not when her character is basically my tagline brought to life? Engineer by day, super hero by night.

Nia: My first comic book was a John Stewart *Green Lantern* book. I don't remember how old I was. I remember there being so many comics around me that I felt like I was surrounded--my dad was going through his old comics. I remember my dad explaining the Green Lantern to me and how John Stewart was his favorite. I remember being fascinated for the first time by how the pictures were just as important as the words in telling the stories. And cosplaying gives me the opportunity to represent and pay homage to some of my favorite characters. :)

See you next month for wrestling AND a special appearance from my new lawyer, Matt! You know, if comic books about lawyers are your thing.

Do svidaniya,

Nadia

AGENTS OF G.I.R.L.

Oh, hi there! It's Nadia. I'm so glad to see you again. You've been sending some really amazing recommendations for Agents of G.I.R.L. using the hashtag #AgentsofGIRL and by emailing us at mheroes@marvel.com, and we can't wait to share them. So without further ado, welcome Stephanie (@plasmagrrl), our experimental plasma physicist, and Claudia Astorino (@claudistics), our biological anthropologist. Science Ladies, take it away!

STEPHANIE

CLAUDIA

WHAT KIND OF WORK DO YOU DO AND WHY?

Stephanie: I work in experimental plasma physics (plasma is the fourth state of matter). The work that I do is focused on understanding plasma stability conditions so we can build fusion reactors to meet the growing energy needs of our society. Fusion energy is what powers stars like our sun; my work contributes to building a similar reliable, clean-energy source here on Earth. Working to meet the energy needs of the future, in a responsible and thoughtful way, is very important to me, and that's why I do the work that I do.

Claudia: I'm a biological anthropologist studying morphological variation--or differences in the shape and size of physical traits--in the skulls and teeth of humans and our fossilized hominin ancestors. I seek to characterize how much difference exists in skulls and teeth from members of the same species due to population affinity, sex, environmental factors, age and other variables of interest. This work will help us figure out how to interpret trait variation and answer questions like, "Is this the same species/different species/sex difference/a subadult or old adult?" so that we can interpret the fossil record more accurately! Whole species have been identified based only on a single tooth!

WHAT EXCITES YOU ABOUT YOUR WORK?

Stephanie: There's very rarely a boring day, and there are lots of moving parts that go into plasma science research on this scale. Lasers need to be tuned and aligned, particle injectors need to be fired at precise times, dozens of computers have to talk to each other to record and save data every time we run an experiment, a four-story capacitor bank has to be discharged every time we make a plasma, vacuum pumps and valves all have to be inspected and maintained on a regular basis, and there's always analytical work to do, new algorithms to write and new computer programs to create and refine as we study our experimental results.

Claudia: I really love going to work knowing that I'm helping answer questions no one has addressed before, or at least not in the same way, and that my work is adding a little bit more to what we already know (or think we know) about the past. I was OBSESSED with paleontology as a kid--my mind was blown that there were all these cool animals and plants that lived long ago in a world we wouldn't recognize, that didn't look like and behave like anything alive today. THAT IS SO COOL. Like many kids, dinosaurs were my gateway into paleo awesomeness, but during college,

I became fascinated by human evolution, too.

WHY ARE YOU PASSIONATE ABOUT YOUNG WOMEN GETTING INTO SCIENCE?

Stephanie: First, because science is really cool and anyone interested in it should be able to pursue it. Second, because science is only as good as the people practicing it. If you exclude people because of gender or race, you are limiting the field from the beginning; you're excluding talented, brilliant people with novel points of view for no good reason other than prejudice. Only by including and supporting people with as many backgrounds as possible can we actually push science to be the best it can possibly be.

Claudia: Women--and other minority groups--face a number of barriers that prevent us from becoming interested in science, staying in science and reaching senior positions in science. This is even more the case for women of color, native women, disabled women, poor women, queer women, trans women and intersex women. There are all these women out there who have the potential to be badass scientists, but lack the support both societally and within scientific culture to make that a reality. I want to help change the culture of science and academia to encourage, support and celebrate diverse scientists. Then we could concentrate on the cool stuff we study instead of spending our energies justifying why we should have seats at the table (or the lab bench). But supporting women in science is also about reminding girls and women that it's important and cool to have competency in scientific concepts in order to vote responsibly and be an ethical consumer, etc. Science should be accessible to everyone, whether you wear a lab coat to work or not!

WHAT FEMALE SCIENTISTS (REAL AND/OR FICTIONAL) HAVE INSPIRED YOU?

Stephanie: Valentina Tereshkova, the first woman in space, and Ms. Frizzle from *The Magic School Bus* books my mom read to me when I was little.

Claudia: I was obsessed with Rosalind Franklin as a kid. I couldn't believe how much she accomplished at such a young age, and was (and am) totally incensed that her peers Watson and Crick were rewarded for discovering the structure of DNA, when their discovery seemed to have heavily leaned on Franklin's meticulous prior work. I also loved that she was outspoken, didn't mince words, didn't take **** and didn't back down when she felt she was onto something. I've read Brenda Maddox's biography, *Rosalind Franklin: The Dark Lady of DNA* more times than I

can say. A few of my favs besides Queen Ros include Laura Bassi, Jane Goodall, Dorothy Crowfoot Hodgkin, Mae Jemison, Katherine Johnson, Lise Meitner and Barbara McClintock. Check 'em out!

DO YOU HAVE A FAVORITE EXAMPLE OF NONSENSICAL SCIENCE IN POPULAR CULTURE?

Stephanie: Almost every depiction of spaceships in movies and TV includes engine sounds; there's no air to carry sound waves in space, so there shouldn't be any sound, no matter how fast a spaceship is moving.

Claudia: "Favorite" isn't exactly the right word, but I do have a few pet peeves. Probably my "fave" is how we conceptualize what a theory is in popular culture. Popularly, we talk about a theory as an educated guess, something that's flimsy. But that's what scientists call a hypothesis--an educated guess that you then test. Scientifically, a theory is an explanation for a natural phenomenon that has been tested many, many times to achieve the same result. A theory is the closest you can get to finding out whether something is "true." I ask my students every semester to imagine what they'd think if someone declared, "I don't believe in gravity--I mean, it's JUST a theory." Most of my students laugh, but people think that this is a legitimate argument if you swap "gravity" for "evolution." Maybe we should all stop using the word "theory" so much, and start using its synonym, "law," instead!

HOW LONG HAVE YOU BEEN READING COMICS AND WHAT WAS YOUR FIRST COMIC BOOK?

Stephanie: The first comic book I read was *Superman: Red Son*, recommended by a friend around 2005; I'd watched cartoons as kid, but didn't start reading comics until graduate school. Once I started, I was hooked, though, and I've been reading them ever since.

Claudia: I've been reading comics for about three years. I never read comics before because I had the common misconception that comics were all super hero comics--but then, I started dating my girlfriend. She wanted me to read the *Sandman* series by Neil Gaiman because she loved it growing up. My girlfriend is the literal best, so I wanted to give them a try. I learned that comics AREN'T all super hero comics drawn in one of a few particular styles, and that there are as many ways to write and illustrate comics as you can imagine. I slowly started checking out other comics she owned, like *The Wicked and the Divine, Saga, Sex Criminals* and *Bitch Planet*, and even got into some fabulous super hero comics after all, like *MS. MARVEL, Batgirl, Black Canary* and *SuperCakes*.

That's all for this month! Tune in next month for your first look at the whole G.I.R.L. lab in action! Can we save Ying? Of course! We can do anything!

Nadia

#1 VARIANT BY SKOTTIE YOUNG

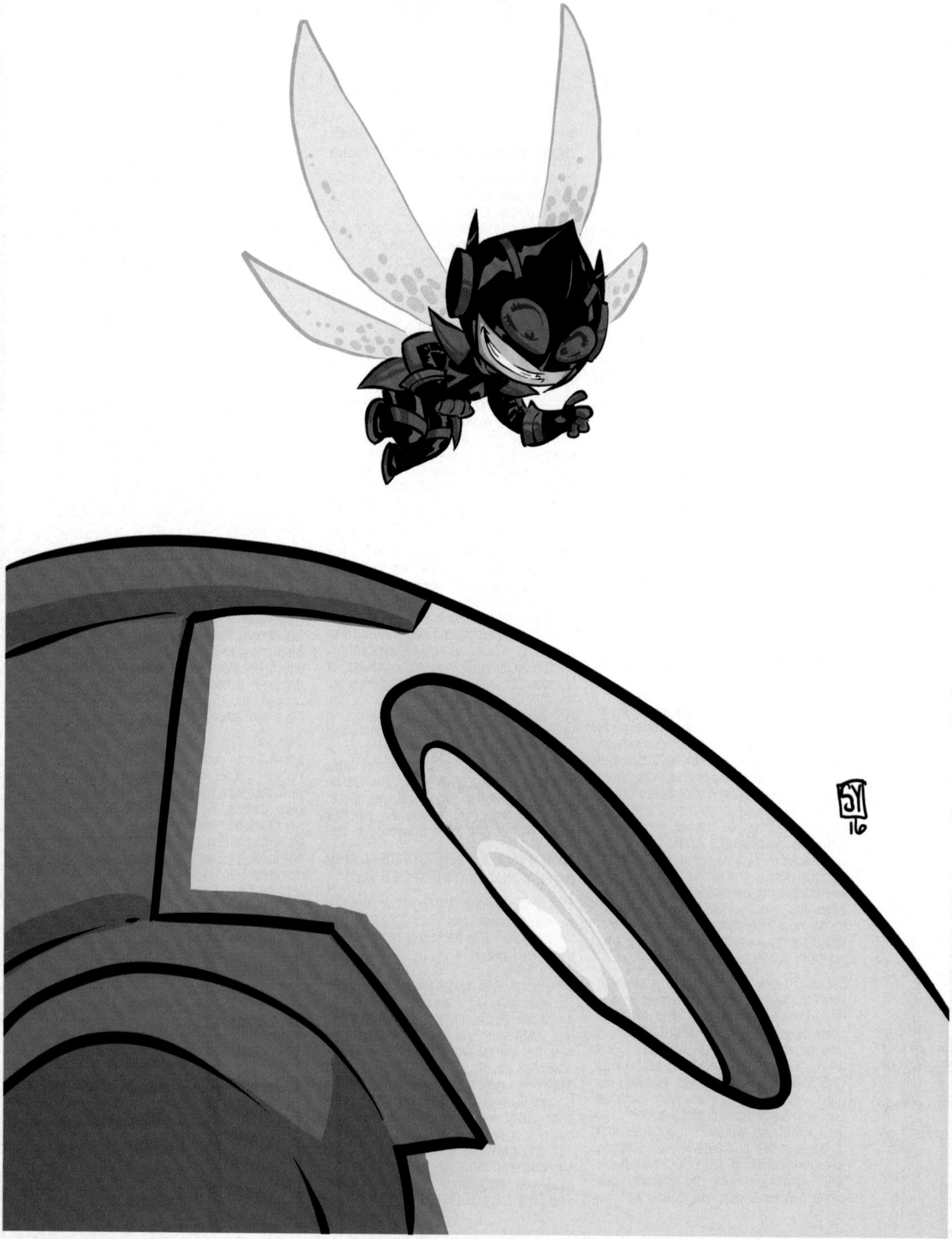

#1 VARIANT BY ELIZABETH TORQUE

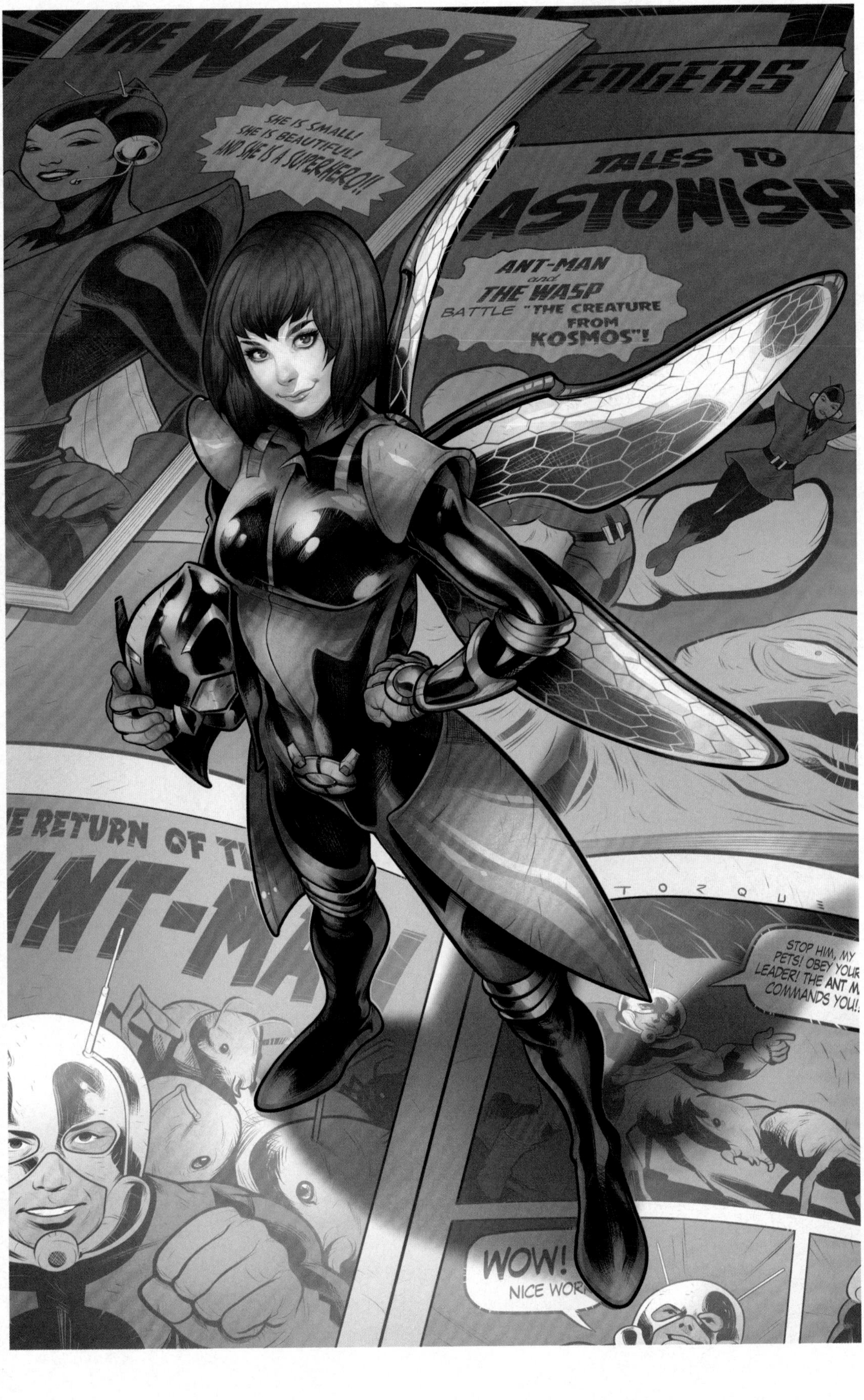
WASP
SHE IS SMALL! SHE IS BEAUTIFUL! AND SHE IS A SUPERHERO!!
TALES TO
ANT-MAN and THE WASP BATTLE "THE CREATURE FROM KOSMOS"!
TORQUE
WOW!

#1 MOVIE VARIANT BY ANDY PARK

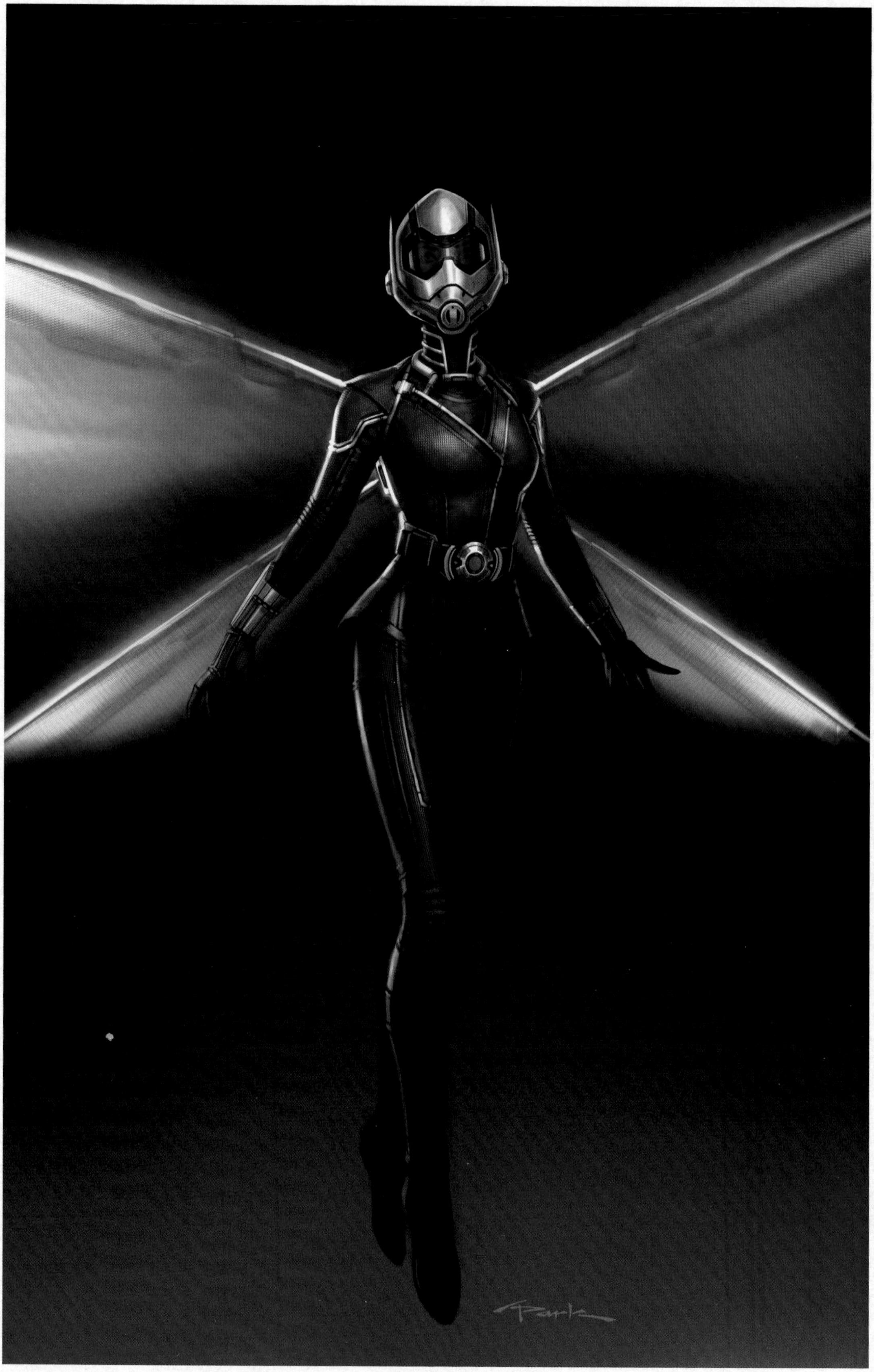

#1 ACTION FIGURE VARIANT BY JOHN TYLER CHRISTOPHER

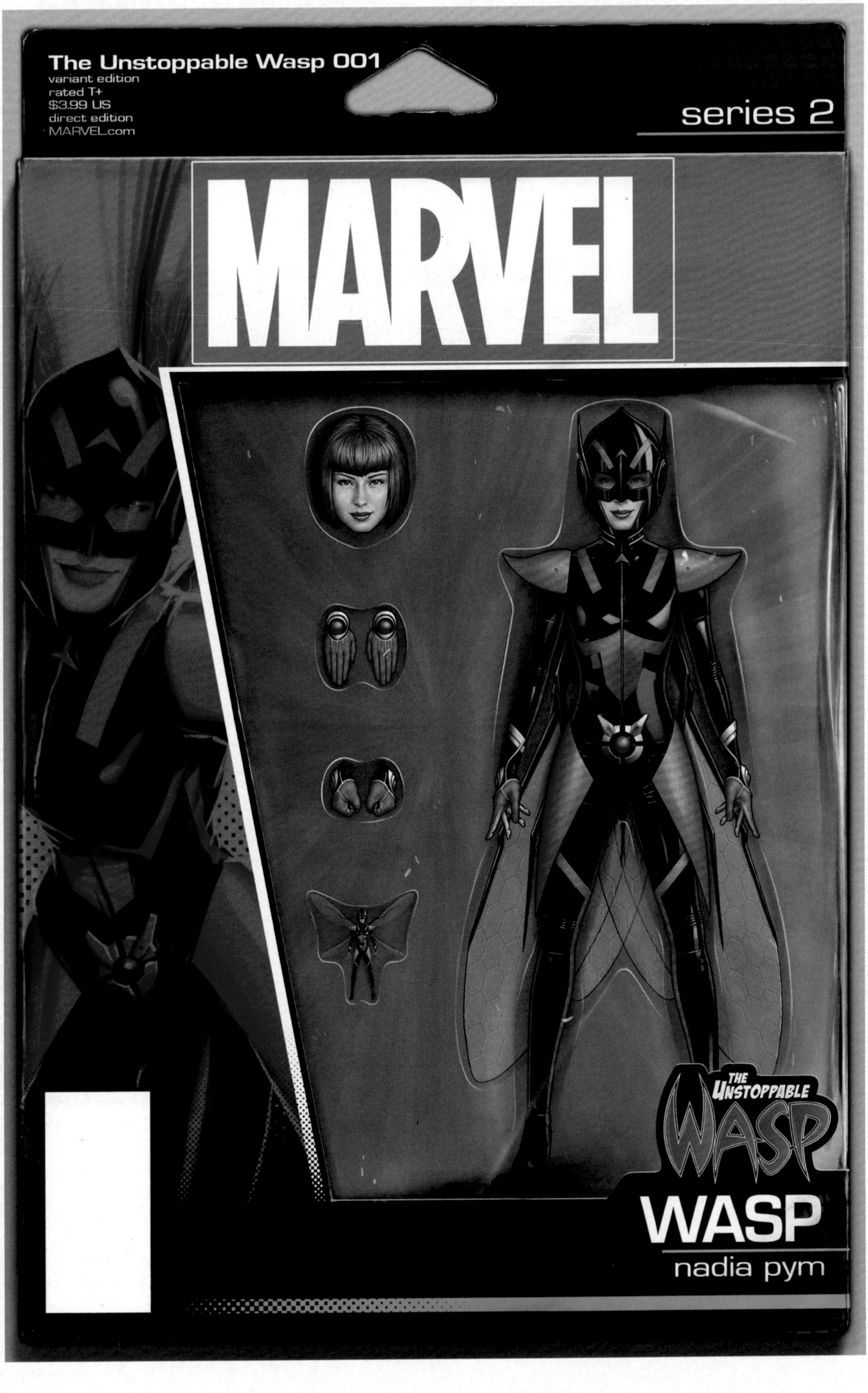
The Unstoppable Wasp 001
variant edition
rated T+
$3.99 US
direct edition
MARVEL.com
series 2
MARVEL
THE UNSTOPPABLE WASP
WASP
nadia pym

#1 HIP-HOP VARIANT BY NELSON BLAKE III & GURU-EFX

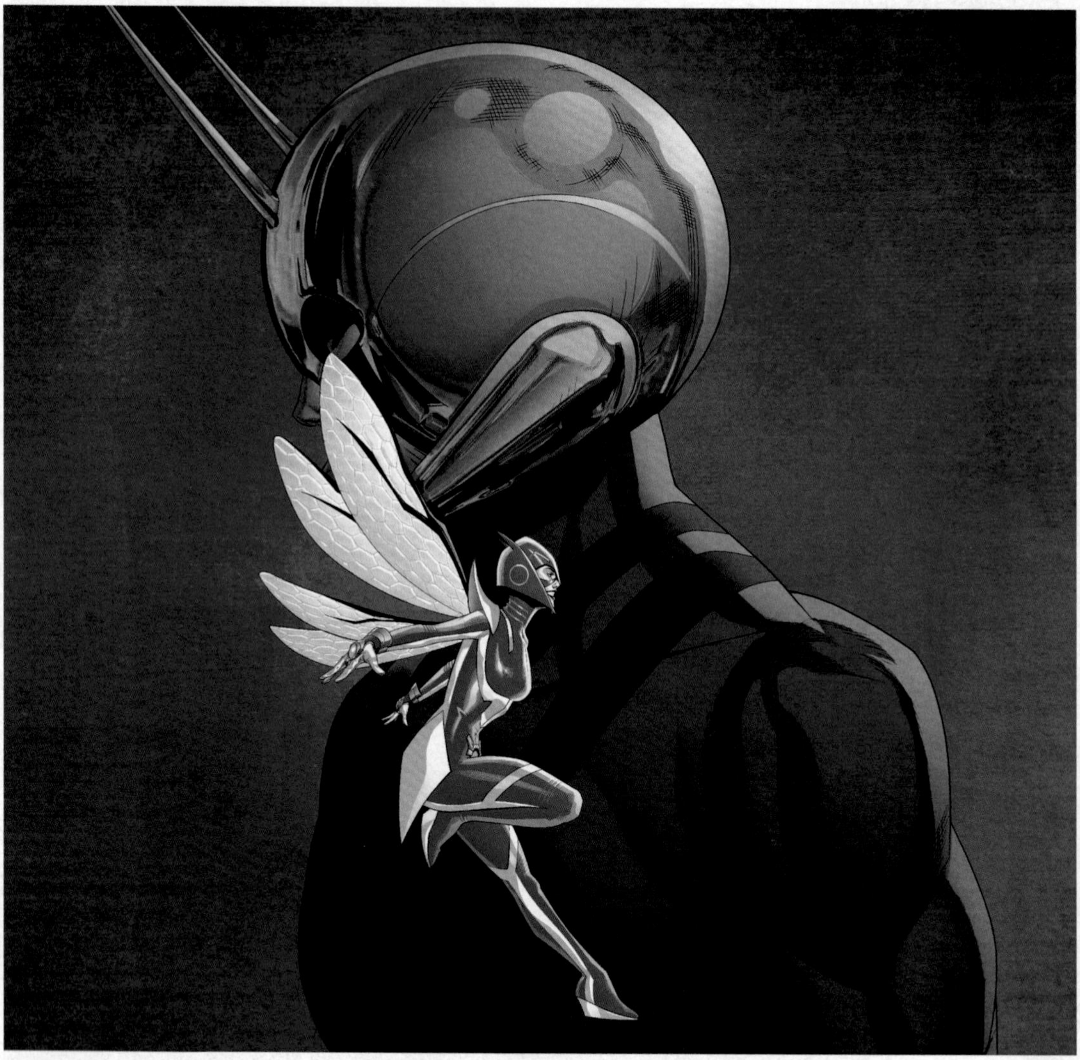